WRITING THE

RADICAL CENTER

D1086886

WRITING THE
RADICAL CENTER

---

*William Carlos Williams, John Dewey,
and American Cultural Politics*

JOHN BECK

STATE UNIVERSITY OF NEW YORK PRESS

Published by
STATE UNIVERSITY OF NEW YORK PRESS, ALBANY

©2001 State University of New York

All rights reserved

Printed in the United States of America

No part of this book may be used or reproduced in any manner whatsoever without written permission. No part of this book may be stored in a retrieval system or transmitted in any form or by any means including electronic, electrostatic, magnetic tape, mechanical, photocopying, recording, or otherwise without the prior permission in writing of the publisher.

For information, address State University of New York Press,
90 State Street, Suite 700, Albany, New York 12207

Production, Laurie Searl
Marketing, Jennifer Giovani-Giovani

Library of Congress Cataloging-in-Publication Data

Beck, John, 1963–
  Writing the radical center: William Carlos Williams, John Dewey, and American cultural politics/John Beck.
    p. cm.
  Includes bibliographical references (p.) and index.
  ISBN 0-7914-5119-4 (alk. paper)—ISBN 0-7914-5120-8 (pbk. : alk. paper)
  1. Williams, William Carlos, 1883–1963—Political and social views. 2. Culture—Political aspects—United States—History—20th century. 3. Politics and literature—United States—History—20th century. 4. Dewey, John, 1859–1952—Contributions in political science. 5. Political culture—United States—History—20th century. 6. United States—Political and government—20th century. 7. Radicalism—United States—History—20th century. 8. Political poetry, American—History and criticism. I. Title.

PS3545.I544 Z5745 2001
811'.52—dc2I

                                                                2001049041

          10   9   8   7   6   5   4   3   2   1

For P

CONTENTS

ACKNOWLEDGMENTS

I have gained from the generosity and advice of many people in the writing of this book. I am grateful to Darwin College, Cambridge, for awarding me an Adrian Research Fellowship, which gave me the time and support to complete the work I had begun as a doctorate under the inestimable supervision of the late Tony Tanner at King's. The American Literature and Twentieth Century Literature Graduate Seminars at Cambridge provided a valuable early forum for some of my ideas on Williams and Dewey. I am grateful to Jean Chothia, Maud Ellman, and Ian Bell for their suggestions, and in particular to Fiona Green and Kathleen Wheeler for their continued support and friendship. Thanks also to Linnie Blake, Matthew Cornford, Simon Perril, Nigel Tudman, and Sue Wragg for being such good friends, and to Michael Amos and Michael Tanner for their hospitality. At SUNY Press, I am grateful to Dale Cotton, Ron Helfrich, Laurie Searl, and the anonymous readers of the original manuscript for their criticisms and suggestions. Finally, thanks to Paula, for everything.

I gratefully acknowledge New Directions Publishing Corporation for permission to quote from the following copyrighted work by William Carlos Williams:

The Collected Poems of William Carlos Williams. Vol. 1: 1909–1939. Ed. A. Walton Litz and Christopher MacGowan (1986). Copyright © 1938 by New Directions Publishing Corporation.

The Embodiment of Knowledge. Copyright © 1974 by Florence H. Williams.

I Wanted to Write a Poem. Copyright © 1958 by William Carlos Williams.

Imaginations. Copyright © 1970 by Florence H. Williams.

In the American Grain. Copyright © 1933 by William Carlos Williams.

Paterson. Copyright © 1946, 1948, 1951 by William Carlos Williams.

Selected Essays of William Carlos Williams. Copyright © 1954 by William Carlos Williams.

Selected Letters of William Carlos Williams. Copyright © 1957 by William Carlos Williams.

I gratefully acknowledge Carcanet Press Limited for permission to quote from the following copyrighted work of William Carlos Williams:

The Collected Poems of William Carlos Williams. Vol. 1:1909–1939. Ed. A. Walton Litz and Christopher MacGowan (1986).

ABBREVIATIONS

William Carlos Williams:

A	*The Autobiography of William Carlos Williams*
CP1	*The Collected Poems of William Carlos Williams. Vol. 1: 1909–1939*
CP2	*The Collected Poems of William Carlos Williams. Vol. 2: 1939–1962*
EK	*The Embodiment of Knowledge*
GAN	*The Great American Novel* in *Imaginations*
IAG	*In the American Grain*
IWWP	*I Wanted to Write a Poem*
KH	*Kora in Hell* in *Imaginations*
N	*A Novelette* in *Imaginations*
P	*Paterson*
RI	*A Recognizable Image: William Carlos Williams on Art and Artists*
SA	*Spring and All* in *Imaginations*
SE	*Selected Essays of William Carlos Williams*
SL	*Selected Letters of William Carlos Williams*
VP	*A Voyage to Pagany*

John Dewey:

AE	*Art as Experience* (LW 10, 1934)
CC	*The Child and the Curriculum* (MW 2, 1902)
CF	*A Common Faith* (LW 9, 1934)
DE	*Democracy and Education* (MW 9, 1916)
EN	*Experience and Nature* (LW 1, 1925)
FC	*Freedom and Culture* (LW 13, 1939)
HNC	*Human Nature and Conduct* (MW 14, 1922)
LSA	*Liberalism and Social Action* (LW 11, 1935)
ION	*Individualism Old and New* (LW 5, 1929–1930)
PP	*The Public and its Problems* (LW 2, 1927)
QC	*The Quest for Certainty* (LW 4, 1929)

References to the works of John Dewey contained in the thirty-seven volumes of *The Early Works of John Dewey, 1882–1898, The Middle Works of John Dewey, 1899–1924,* and *The Later Works of John Dewey, 1925–54* editor, cite author and title followed by Southern Illinois University Press's short form, e.g., LW14, p 29 (Later Works, Volume 14, page 29), excluding the volumes abbreviated as above.

INTRODUCTION

What should the artist be today? What must he be? What can he do? To what purpose? What does he effect? How does he function? What enters into it? The economic, the sociological: how is he affected? How does his being a man or a woman, one of a certain race, an American enter into it?

—William Carlos Williams

Thus William Carlos Williams begins an essay of 1939 entitled "Against the Weather: A Study of the Artist," and an appropriate beginning for this study also, which will ask of Williams the questions he asks of himself. These questions are broad and demand a serious scrutiny of the artist's function in the contemporary world: what should, must an artist be, and what effect might he have? Situated as a precise historical moment—today—the contingencies of time and space are seen to both form the questions and to frame possible responses to them. These contingencies—the economic, the sociological, gender, race, and nationality— are identified as necessary conditions through which art is produced, unavoidably locating the artist within specific historical and cultural contexts, not as a disinterested observer but as a participating agent in the production of that history and culture. Williams insisted on the precise location of art as a concrete substance in the world, an object occupying so much space, so much time, displacing other objects by the measure of its own dimensions, shaped by and shaping the forces around it. Such a conception of art inevitably involves a consideration of art's responsibility, as Williams's questions indicate; responsibility in terms of being responsive to what is outside itself, and responsible for its effect on the world of which it is a part.

The kind of art Williams has in mind is clearly predicated upon the kind of environment it emerges from. Already, we have talked of art's cultural specificity, its concreteness, its responsiveness and responsibility, yet only under certain conditions can these qualities have the kind of meaning they have for Williams. We have spoken of an art that occupies its own space, assuming that this is an aspect

1

of its being, rather than a privilege enjoyed by virtue of politically sanctioned rights. Art is itself, can place itself, only if it is entitled, is free to announce itself. In conceiving of an art work as a concrete particular, we must remember that particularity is a notion informed by a belief in some kind of individual autonomy; in referring to responsibility, we are acknowledging the contractual nature of that autonomy. Already, in describing, or beginning to describe, the terms of Williams's notion of a contextualized art, we are using the language of liberal democracy. Williams's conception of art is embedded in this language, a language with particularly deep cultural resonance in America, a nation called into being by its lexicon of freedom and equality. This is also a language often uncertain of its provenance and its constituency, frequently contradicted by the objects it attempts to describe; a language yoked—as in the Declaration of Independence—to action, but abused by the distortion and violence of the actions it frequently provokes.

The questions Williams asks concerning art and the artist are, then, closely related to the conditions of American democracy, to the "economic, the sociological" forces that shape this democracy, and therefore impinge upon the consciousness of its citizens. In following Williams's answers to these questions in his poetry and prose, and in exploring and attempting to account for the shape of the concerns voiced in those questions, the work of John Dewey emerges as, if not a guiding principle, then as a vital articulation of the liberal democratic ethos shared and valued by Williams.

As the United States emerged during the early years of the twentieth century as the wealthiest industrial nation in the world and as a global military power, seemingly confirming the ideological assumptions of manifest destiny and legitimating the claims of Americanism, the importance of articulating a vision of the good society as an adjunct to material prosperity and international predominance became increasingly necessary, particularly in the light of the massive social inequities that remained unsolved by industrial and technological development. Dewey helped set the intellectual barometer for American liberals throughout perhaps the most decisive period of American history, from the 1880s through to the 1940s.[1] More than probably any other single commentator of his time, Dewey sought to answer the kind of questions Williams is so keen to consider in "Against the Weather," and if we expand those questions to include all the citizens of a democracy—who, as we shall see, should all be, in the kind of democracy Williams has in mind, artists of one kind or another—then it is Dewey to whom we should turn in order to learn the art of American cultural politics.

In examining Williams and Dewey together, my point is not to unveil a pattern of textual and theoretical correspondences (although this does, indeed, emerge during this study), nor to claim Dewey as a major direct influence on Williams's work (although, again, there are some grounds for such a claim). Neither am I interested in presenting Williams as a systematic political or philosophical writer who uses poetry merely as a platform for socioeconomic arguments. This could not be farther from the case. Nevertheless, as my opening quotation from Williams shows, his concern with the relationship between the aesthetic and the political was a very real one, and, as will become clear, a longstanding and sophisticated preoccupation. The connection between Williams and Dewey is, then, as I see it, not so much one of influence as of ideological confluence.[2] Williams and Dewey both inherited the moral values of the Victorian middle classes—self-reliance, a strong and proud work ethic, and a loyalty to place and to family. Rapid industrialization had, by the early years of the twentieth century, largely supplanted these values with rootlessness and bureaucracy. Williams's and Dewey's social progressivism is characterized by an ambivalence toward both the past and the future, at once rejecting the stifling gentility and prejudice (usually associated with imported European values) that accompanied nineteenth-century virtues of selfhood, work, and family, yet recognizing, in the face of growing social fragmentation and alienation, the need for some kind of stability and security with which to anchor society and to protect individual liberty from growing capitalist incorporation.

This refusal to hold on to the past and concern for the future reveals in the work of both men a constant struggling to attain a middle ground, a sense of balance and control over forces that seem uncontrollable and hopelessly unstable. The desire to preserve the good without falling into a nostalgic conservatism, and to promote a radical alternative to corporate America without dismissing the advantages of modernity, is articulated by Williams and Dewey through a vocabulary of holism, organicism, and mediation, which attempts to bond seemingly inconsistent elements within a logic of interdependency. An important objection to reading Williams alongside Dewey might be that their widely differing style makes them incompatible bedfellows, Dewey's famously awkward and lengthy exposition of ideas standing in severe contrast to Williams's skill in poetic compression. Yet Williams's lexicon is unmistakably a Deweyan one: "embodiment," "contact," "invention," "faith," "imagination," "field of action," "no ideas but in things." These are some of the terms of Williams's optimistic, pragmatic, experimental, progressive democratic poetics, terms that resonate with the confidence and vitality that Dewey brought to American liberal political culture during the first half of the twentieth century.

The inherently optimistic focus of Dewey's, and Williams's, belief in a melioristic reconstruction of America that bypasses social revolution, however, often fails, it seems, to grasp or refuses to accept the complexity and intractability of the socioeconomic power structures they seek to change. Where a concrete analysis of the institutions of domination—whether academic, literary, or social—would seem most appropriate, Williams and Dewey instead often tend to rely on generalizations about the inherent promise of American democracy, of America as an endless experiment in pushing the limits of human potentiality, of the need to recognize and promote community and communication; of the desirability of individual liberation through education and unalienated labor. While these are, of course, excellent aspirations for any democratic nation, as tools for social critique they are often insufficient, despite their potency as ideals, to cope with the

practical problems of political and social life. What should not be forgotten, however, is the rhetorical force of Progressive liberalism and the power, in the cultural
and intellectual spheres, if not necessarily in the political, of its message. Faced, as
liberals increasingly were faced throughout the 1920s and 1930s, with the impossible choice between fascism and communism, progressives understandably made
much of their middle ground, of the possibility of change without bloodshed, of
cooperation over conflict, and of communication over censorship.

Dewey and Williams are typical of middle-class progressives in their powerful sense of responsibility, coupled with the constant anxiety that the relative privilege that goes with liberal respectability cannot adequately fulfill this responsibility. Williams's and Dewey's radicalism has clear boundaries, it will push so far but
then stops, limited by the practical imperatives of their respective social positions,
positions that rest on the very principles of self-reliance, industry, and family loyalties which they were in many ways seeking to reconstruct.[3] This is not to say
that their radicalism is therefore hollow, but it is seriously constrained. Such constraint is, of course, the dilemma of liberalism's desire to balance rights and duties,
to combine the clean sweep of social change with the hard won benefits of existing structures. Williams and Dewey often spoke in defense of the underprivileged
and underrepresented, but there can be a residual sense of exoticism attached to
their paeans to cultural pluralism which, perhaps, says more about their romanticism and tendency toward empathic projection than their ability to grapple with
complex social problems. In this sense, Dewey's educational experiments, and
Williams's calls for a common language, could be read as imposed upon, rather
than developed from or facilitated by, the materials of the environment. Balancing tradition and innovation can lead the traditional element in the equation to
become inadvertently dominant through a form of political unconscious,
whereby the ideological framework that supports professional life is used to colo-
nize so-called minority groups and interests in the name of social responsibility.
This is, of course, not Williams's nor Dewey's intention at all, and it is a contradiction they work hard to resolve, since without a fully inclusive egalitarian polity,
the notion of a democratic culture remains in the realms of the unattainable.

Williams and Dewey speak the language of American democracy with a lack
of equivocation not shared by many of their contemporaries (Williams's long-
running argument with his friend Ezra Pound comes to mind, not to mention his
antipathy toward T. S. Eliot's views). Their largely unshakeable faith in the guiding principles (while, notably, not the reality) of their national character shapes
their entire respective outputs. Their desire to recharge the dissipated power of
these principles, and to enact through them a cultural critique based on exemplary deeds, (or, to use a different idiom, performative utterances), is shot through
with a radical intent fraught with difficulties and contradictions. What I wish to
examine is the nature of this American language of democracy as spoken by
Williams and Dewey, the strategies through which they attempt to liberate this
language from the hands of corporate capitalism, and how they envisage the outcome of this liberation for American culture and politics. In their work are

embedded, exemplary democrats that they are, the aspirations and limitations of a progressive liberalism. The question remains, however, of what value to assign to the travails of this liberalism, of what can be salvaged from the project of experimental, creative democracy and of political, avant-garde literature. One of the great blind spots caused by characterizing Williams and Dewey as American democrats is that this appellation can serve to conflate national origin and political ideology into some sort of being-in-and-for-itself, effectively eliminating the political bite so obviously present in the works themselves. How far Williams and Dewey may have de-fanged themselves, through their appeal to principles so successfully absorbed into the ideology of modern capitalism, is a question that will shape this study.

The kind of cultural criticism developed by Williams and Dewey derives from a convergence of romantic anticapitalism, civic republicanism, and Jeffersonian radicalism. Fortified by the Progressivist faith in creative evolution, the beneficence of science, and confidence in the gradual dissolution of temporary blockages to social improvement, such a brew, of varying strength and consistency, was imbibed by a host of American intellectuals broadly placed within the pragmatist tradition; for example, the so-called Young Americans—Van Wyck Brooks, Randolph Bourne, Waldo Frank, and Lewis Mumford—and Marxists such as Max Eastman, Sidney Hook, and C. Wright Mills. While the grounds for agreement in terms of specific objectives, terminology, and priorities never cohered into a broad-based or organized program, the fundamental assumptions remain constant: the need for a thoroughgoing revaluation of American culture and society, rooted in the traditions and values of America itself; the centrality of key areas of debate, namely, the role of art, the impact of science and technology, the importance of education, the significance of community; and the relation between notions of individuality, identity, and the emerging mass society. That many, if not all, of these issues were articulated in their most authoritative form by Dewey is indicative of his prominence as a public intellectual and of his influence as a social commentator as well as an academic philosopher. (Eastman, Bourne, and also Williams's friend and subsequent editor Louis Zukofsky number among Dewey's students at Columbia.) That the tenor of the debates over community, science, education, and so on, is, by and large, so consistent suggests the extent of Dewey's intellectual influence.

Williams belonged to this generation, shared its inherited values and suffered its anxieties. Placed in the context of international modernism, Williams, in the presence of the cosmopolitan Pound, Eliot, Joyce, and the rest, was often portrayed, as Pound never let him forget, as the provincial, unsophisticated country doctor with artistic ambitions his circumstances could not fulfill. Williams is the one who stayed at home. Yet most Americans, poets or otherwise, stayed at home. It is when Williams is read alongside his contemporaries and neighbors that it becomes clear exactly how involved he was in the ongoing debates concerning American culture and society—not as an outsider but as a citizen. While many of Williams's broadsides and much of his poetry—notably *Paterson*—are undoubtedly responses to transatlantic modernism (and most specifically to Pound), this response is not individual and idiosyncratic so much as it is backed by, and saturated with, the idioms and values of a discourse of cultural exploration and criticism, which only one living and working daily in the United States could have absorbed and responded to with such urgency and force.

Implicit in the grander claims of Dewey's pragmatism and Williams's modernism is the belief that in transforming the role and structure of philosophy and poetry, by making them responsive to social reality, they will achieve a substantive transformation of that social reality itself. This makes sense in terms of a contextualism—shared by Dewey and Williams—that sees intellectual and creative activity as an inevitably social act: a poem or statement, by virtue of its presence, shifts, however slightly, the position of everything else. Yet there is more to Dewey's and Williams's progressivism than that; namely, they believe that the influence of expertise, method, technique, craftsmanship—however it is variously described—upon society at large can implement a fundamental alteration in the habits, abilities, and desires of the people. On the poet, claims Williams, "devolves the most vital function of society: to recreate it—the collective world—in time of stress, in a new mode" (SE, 103). Dewey and Williams, like other liberal intellectuals of their time, are primarily concerned, not with the internecine squabbles of professional elites and political ideologues, but with America in its entirety, and with the relation between the usefulness of knowledge and its application in the renovation or resuscitation of the polis.

Assuming that present conditions do not conform to the ideals of democracy, and even assuming that these ideals can be consensually defined, who is authorized to make changes on behalf of society in order to align the ideal with reality? From where does the transformative impulse legitimately arise? From below, or from above? Since democracy cannot theoretically accommodate notions of intrinsic social stratification—class—it becomes very difficult to figure, when democracy is not working, who has the right to speak for whom. If the mass of the population is unable, because of undemocratic conditions, to speak for itself, who can do so without the emergence of a patrician elite? Such broad political and cultural perplexities have serious ramifications concerning how professional middle-class intellectuals such as Dewey and Williams perceive their roles as cultural critics. For example, despite their rejection of imposed standards of valuation—usually denigrated with recourse to the familiar Old World bad, New World good dichotomy—there is an assumption made by Dewey and Williams that right-thinking people will see things their way, and that others must be properly educated in order to liberate themselves from their inability to do so. This view, of course, itself implies some sort of standard from which right-thinking can be derived. For Dewey, this feeds into his articulation of a program of assisted self-empowerment, and for Williams, into his understanding of the role of poetry and of the kind of audience he writes for. As Jeffrey Walker observes of Whitman, such a democrat "must either cultivate in his fallen audience the ethical awareness of the true American, or he must demonstrate to them the true American's ethical authority and legitimate claims to leadership, so that the national destiny may be fulfilled."[4] Following this argument, the democratic standard, as somehow already "true," is not imposed but discovered. While this remains latent in the mass of the population, it is the job of those who can manifest its quality to do so as representative Americans. The purpose of a democratic poetry (or any other work for that matter) becomes the demonstration of its resistance to the undemocratic as evidence or testimony of what can be done.

That said, the democratic poet is, nevertheless, at odds with the prevailing undemocratic culture, which presumably stands as a false America in opposition to the democrat's truth. This democratic poet therefore often betrays an ambivalent attitude toward the unregenerate mass that is, at the same time, considered as the potential audience for the poems, because the mass, in its lack of differentiation, threatens to absorb and deny the free and individual voice of the poet. The irony of this situation is that you probably need to be a democrat in order to understand the democratic poem, since otherwise the screen of false consciousness will prevent its message from reaching you. Faced with this series of complications, the poet will find it increasingly difficult to know how to pitch the poem. Does it ascend above the homogeneity of the mass in order to save itself, or descend to earth in order to redeem society? Williams, it could be said, tries to do both, which entails a rather complex maneuvering of positions. He claims common speech as the ground for a democratic poetry, but common speech rendered as poetry. This may not result in poetry in any traditional sense, but it is poetry and, egalitarianism aside, often "difficult" poetry. So Williams counters by arguing that the mass must learn how to gain access to the materials contained in this difficulty. But how? By learning how to read. And who will teach this skill? The democratic poet. So it goes on, the poet stepping alternately inside and then outside of society, accepting and then denying responsibility, willing and then fearful of making contact with that which makes up the substance of the reality in which the poem is supposed to reside.

The prospect of describing a democratic art, let alone a truly democratic society, thus very quickly becomes more complex and problematic than it first appears. The clarity and precision Williams and Dewey seek for this description is soon muddied in execution, the mud coming from the social reality they wish to cultivate. The means by which they attempt to scrub clean (to use Williams's metaphor) that which has become ragged and dirty—America as an idea and an ideal, as the site for a true democracy in every sense—and the extent to which they succeed or fail, is the subject of what is to follow.

Chapter 1 explores the contours of Dewey's language of democracy, his faith in communication and community as the ground for a liberal polity. Williams's conceptions of the role of the poet and of poetry, I argue, grow out of this language, ambivalent as he often is toward the practicality of such a model when faced with institutionalized state power. Chapter 2 addresses the question of what art itself should be in a democracy, and focuses on Williams's and Dewey's commitment to an organicist notion of aesthetic experience as the consummation of democratic freedom. I suggest that it is Dewey's aesthetic theory which properly stands at the heart of his social philosophy. Williams's experimental improvisations of the 1920s, likewise, provide a methodological base for his subsequent attempts to create an indigenous democratic art. Chapter 3 looks at the problem of how to create and nurture citizens for the kind of aesthetic nation Williams and Dewey have in mind; in other words, their interest in education. Chapter 4 considers the consequences of Williams's emphasis on the local environment as the bedrock of a democratic art. Drawing on the liberal values voiced by Dewey and the Seven Arts group, Williams presents an argument for an alternative linguistic and financial economy founded on reciprocity and contact. Chapter 5 focuses on the 1930s, during which time the amelioristic philosophy of process held by liberals such as Williams and Dewey comes under increased pressure from both Left and Right. Both men's work, subsequently, becomes more socialistic in tenor and commitment. The final chapter deals with Williams's ambition to write, in *Paterson,* a democratic epic, the consolidation of his commitment to a civic poetry. The pervasiveness of Williams's Deweyan pragmatic liberalism is examined as it contributes to the aesthetic and social vision of the poem, the evident strains within the text revealing, I suggest, the extent to which the optimism of Progressivism buckles under pressure from the often barbarous consequences of corporate capitalism in America.

ONE

ARTICULATING DEMOCRACY

---

a metaphysical mathematics of the incommensurable

I shall use the words America and democracy as convertible terms.
—Walt Whitman

"Doctor," asks an unnamed voice in *Paterson*, "do you believe in / 'the people,' the Democracy? Do / you still believe—in this / swill-hole of corrupt cities? / Do you, Doctor? Now?" (P, 132). The voice is prodding in its insistence, challenging with its alliterative drumming and short, stabbing questions. There is a sense of betrayal, or at least of disappointment, that the Doctor's beliefs have not been borne out by actual conditions. Well, the voice seems to ask, what have your grand ideas amounted to? The accentuation of "the people" and the capitalization of Democracy emphasize this half-mocking tone, which sounds very much like a challenge from below, from someone who perhaps has to live in the "swill-hole" of a corrupt city. The challenge is made against a respected public servant, someone who moves amongst the people but nevertheless remains separate, someone whose training and expertise has made him necessary, but at the same time, an outsider. "Do you still believe?" implies that there was a time before the corruption of cities, a time when it was possible to believe in "the people." Like Peter, the Doctor's faith is questioned three times. The emphatic "Now?" is urgent, the pressure of the present will allow for no evasion.

What can the Doctor say in reply? Are, as Whitman claims, America and democracy really convertible terms? What kind of language is capable of cleansing swill-holes of corruption as the Doctor would bathe a wound? Embedded in the self-doubt of Book 3 of *Paterson* as it is—"Give up / the poem. Give up the shilly- / shally of art. // What can you, what / can YOU hope to conclude- / on a heap of dirty linen?"—the passage insists on attention. Its concerns are central to Williams's ambitions as a poet and to a crisis of liberal republicanism: what does

9

democracy mean in the modern world? To whom do its values apply? In following Williams's response to these questions it is necessary to understand what democracy in America might promise, where the power of its ideals meets the exigencies of everyday life. Williams's poetic vision is bound up with a certain conception of what it means to be an American and a democrat, and it is a conception shared by his class and promoted by its apologists. John Dewey is one of the most prominent, most vocal, and most determined exponents of this understanding of the American tradition. So, what does it mean to believe?

THE RHETORIC OF LIBERALISM

Dewey follows Marx in overturning the Hegelian notion of man as a subjective manifestation of the state by asserting that society is founded on the primacy of the individual, that the identity of the community is the sum of the individualities which constitute it. This communal basis of the individual is the essential swerve away from a justification of bourgeois individualism, which rests on the separation of the political and the social. Dewey and Marx insist on the full participation in the political state by each member of society, so that individual and society are inseparable and define the existence of each other: such a democracy is, for Marx, "the true unity of universal and particular," a democracy that "starts from man and makes the state objectified man."[1] There is a strong echo of Emerson in this statement, who suggests in "Politics" that "To educate the wise man, the State exists; and with the appearance of the wise man, the State expires. The appearance of character makes the State unnecessary. The wise man is the State."[2] Indeed, in an ideal democracy, the notion of the state being separate from the individual is an anachronism. Dewey does not expect the state to expire, but instead to be indistinguishable from the citizens who, through their communal relations, embody the state. Emerson places his emphasis on "the influence of private character," and is generally less convinced of the necessity for social organization than Dewey. As George Kateb observes, "Emerson would be an anarchist if he could."[3] While Dewey maintains the Emersonian, processual conception of the self, and endorses Emerson's stress on the primary democracy of face-to-face transactions, he is far more preoccupied with, and less skeptical of, broader communal and social organization than Emerson ever was. Where the thought of Dewey, Emerson, and Marx does converge is on the fundamental stress that democracy is, as Dewey sums up, "a way of personal life" which should not be conceived as a form of government external to, and different from, the individual.[4]

For Dewey, democracy is "a moral idea and so far as it becomes a fact is a moral fact." Democracy "is a reality only as it is indeed a common-place of living." This moral faith "in the capacity of human beings for intelligent judgment and action" so long as "proper conditions are furnished," however, is not without its problems. The "faith in human nature in general" to live democratically seems to conflate nature, morality, and democracy as the core of human existence.[5] If this is so, if living democratically is somehow human nature, why do "proper conditions" need to be furnished? If the conditions have not been furnished already, how do we know what they are, and even if we did, who would do the furnishing? Dewey's appeal to "human nature in general" relies on an undefined and assumed quality of concern for certain communal values that has its root in our nature itself. If this were the case, would not all human beings be innately democratic? While it may be possible to have degrees of democracy, depending on "conditions," proper or otherwise, is it possible to have degrees of nature?[6] If nature is being, is it correct to say that democracy is being also? In short, if democracy is bound up with human nature, how do we know if we are living democratically, since we would have to step outside of our nature in order to see what it was? The only appeal, it seems, is to faith:

> Democracy is the faith that the process of experience is more important than any special result attained, so that special results achieved are of ultimate value only as they are used to enrich and order the ongoing process. Since the process of experience is capable of being educational, faith in democracy is all one with faith in experience and education. All ends and values that are cut off from the ongoing process become arrests, fixations. They strive to fixate what has been gained instead of using it to open the road and point the way to new and better experiences.[7]

Again, where does this lead? If the process of experience overrides results, surely there are no results, only process. Yet Dewey does not abandon results, he saves them to enrich and order the process. How would results be identified if they are not recognized as such, and how could something antithetical to process be of "ultimate value" to it? In a processual world, what does "ultimate" mean? Furthermore, if everything is in process, how do we know what is and is not capable of being educational, and, assuming that this process is natural, why should it be necessary to use nature to teach naturalness? Behind these difficulties is Dewey's unwillingness to consider American society as it stands as fundamentally contradictory, at the level of ideology, to his definition of democracy. Faith in the process of democracy, education, and experience assumes that there is no obstacle or blockage so strong that the evolutionary drive of progress cannot overcome. It is here, despite their shared conception of the nature of a "true" or "ideal" democracy, that Dewey and Marx part company, because where Marx recognizes the intractability of vested interests to social change, which must lead necessarily to political and social revolution, Dewey holds on to the elasticity of social forms, and optimistically appeals to a power structure he hopes is amenable to moral suasion and logical exposition.

Dewey's use of the word experience is intended as a challenge to the mind and matter dualism, which privatizes experience as a property of the mind separate and independent from the material world. For Dewey, human nature is a constituent part of nature, that is, the entire existent universe. Human life may be distinct from other forms of natural existence, but it is not separate, it does not inhabit a different place from the rest of nature. Experience is, then, even in its most introspective forms, "*of* as well as *in* nature":

> It is not experience which is experienced, but nature—stones, plants, animals, diseases, health, temperature, electricity, and so on. Things interacting in certain ways *are* experience; they are what is experienced. Linked in certain other ways in another natural object—the human organism—they are *how* things are experienced as well. Experience thus reaches down into nature; it has depth. It also has breadth and to an infinitely elastic extent. It stretches. (EN, 13)

Language, for Dewey, is also of and in nature, "a natural bridge that joins the gap between existence and essence" (EN, 133). What makes a "substratum of organic psycho-physical actions" into "identifiable objects, events with a perceptible character," is their "concretion in discourse" (EN, 135). Thus, even when the individual is most wholly occupied with the "private realm of events," "he is only turning his attention to his own soliloquy," which is itself "the product and reflex" of communication with others. "If we had not talked with others and they with us, we should never talk to and with ourselves. Because of converse, social give and take, various organic attitudes become an assemblage of persons engaged in converse" (EN, 135). Language is social in origin, and since understanding or thought is concretized in language, then thought, subjectivity, derives from society also. Language, thought, and society are all aspects of experience and are therefore all of and in nature. Each is dependent upon, and constituted by, its organic relationship to the others.

Dewey's view of liberal democracy is that, in Richard Rorty's words, "although it may need philosophical articulation, it does not need philosophical backup." While this suggests that, for example, the conception of the individual might correspond to and confirm a political model, it does not follow from this that politics is being justified by or grounded on any foundational principle of individualism. What it simply means is that the practice of politics is put first and political theory or philosophy is tailored to suit, to articulate, what goes on in practice.[8] But how do we arrive at the politics? Where does democracy come from? Just because we call our social organization democratic, does this make it so? Is democracy, asks Dewey in "Philosophy and Democracy" (1918), "a comparatively superficial human expedient," or "does nature . . . sustain and support our democratic hopes and aspirations?"[9] If democracy is constructed, "how then shall we construe and interpret the natural environment and natural history of humanity in order to get an intellectual warrant for our endeavors . . . ? [H]ow shall we read what we call humanity . . . so that we may essay our deepest political and social problems with a conviction that they are to a reasonable extent sanctioned and sustained by the nature of things?" (PD, 48). In short, is democracy born or made, natural or cultural? Dewey's answer is, not surprisingly, both/and. Democracy is cultural insofar as it is the result of human interaction, something made. It is natural inasmuch as culture is itself part of nature, and to the extent that the world accepts the forms of human action made from its substance: "All deliberate action of mind is in a way an experiment with the world to see what it will stand for, what it will promote and what frustrate" (PD, 48-49).

Dewey goes on to explain the keywords of the democratic faith—liberty, equality, and fraternity—in terms of this naturalistic empiricism. Under this dispensation, liberty means "a universe in which there is real uncertainty and contingency," a world that is always "incomplete and in the making," and that is thus accessible to change as need or desire arise. "To such a philosophy any notion of a perfect or complete reality, finished, existing always the same without regard to the vicissitudes of time, will be abhorrent." Time itself will be thought of as "a field of novelty, of real and unpredictable increments to existence, a field of experimentation and invention" (PD, 50). This does not mean that there are no limits to expansiveness because "there is in things a grain against which we cannot go." Yet it is in the making of experiments and fresh efforts that, through mistakes and frustrated efforts, we "discover what that grain is .... For it is the grain which is rubbed the wrong way which more clearly stands out." Liberty, then, is the exploration of what is humanly or naturally possible. As part of the openendedness of the world, human beings are in accord with nature by recognizing their own openness to change within the "field of novelty" (PD, 51).

A democratic articulation of equality involves for Dewey a dismantling of foundational concerns with "supreme reality or ultimate and comprehensive truth." Such concerns expose philosophy's commitment to the undemocratic notion "that inherently some realities are superior to others," which "works out practically in support of a regime of authority or feudal hierarchy." This "metaphysics of feudalism" is "an apologetic for the established order" in that it supports the notion of "an indefensible seat of authority," however differently this may be called (PD, 51). The preoccupation with a "single, final and unalterable authority from which all lesser authorities are derived" has left democracy "at an immense intellectual disadvantage," because, Dewey argues, the people are too empirical "to be lent to deification." When a philosophical basis for democracy has been attempted, "it has clothed itself in an atomistic individualism," which has reduced equality to a "mathematical equivalence," a quantitative rather than a qualitative measure. Equality means for democracy that the world is not to be thought of "as a fixed order of species, grades or degrees. It means that every existence deserving the name of existence has something unique and irreplaceable about it, that it does not exist to illustrate a principle, to realize a universal or to embody a kind or class." Individuality means "a world in which an existence must be reckoned with on its own account, not as something capable of equation with and transformation into something else. It implies, so to speak, a metaphysical mathematics of the incommensurable in which each speaks for itself and demands consideration on its own behalf" (PD, 52–53).[10]

Given that democratic equality means individuality, fraternity can be understood as continuity, that is, "an association and interaction without limit." Without the corrective of fraternity, equality or individuality is "centrifugal," and "tends to isolation and independence." For Dewey, "what is specific and unique can be exhibited and become forceful or actual only in relationship with other like things" (PD, 53). Liberty, equality, and fraternity are thus considered by Dewey to be in accord with an organic view of the world. Philosophy and politics cohere as processual, experimental forms of experience arising through the interaction of human beings with their environment.

In grounding social life in the "process of experience," Dewey rightly histori-cizes democracy, but in conceiving of democracy as a moral idea based on a "faith in human nature," he abstracts it again, undermining the opportunity for evalua-tion and critique of current institutions and beliefs. In naturalizing democracy, Dewey makes it impossible to view democratic ideology *as* an ideology, and is in danger of falling prey to what Sacvan Bercovitch describes as "a process of symbol-making through which the norms and values of a modern culture . . . [are] ra-tionalized, spiritualized, and institutionalized—rendered the vehicle, as the Amer-ican *Way*, both of conscience and of consensus."[11]

Louis Hartz famously made the same point back in 1955, albeit from a less critical perspective: without a feudal past a society can have no truly revolutionary tradition since in being born equal its citizens lack a heritage of reaction. In such a society, liberalism is considered a "natural" phenomenon, and this society "has within it, as it were, a kind of self-completing mechanism, which insures the uni-versality of the liberal idea."[12] Dewey's vision of democracy, as codependence and as the free flow of experimental discourse, takes little account of the kind of social conflict that can tear communities and nations apart. Nor does he consider the place of values and norms that do not conform to his natural democracy. The no-tion of adaptability considers all conflict to be negotiable, and Dewey's meliorism relies upon a universal acceptance of the liberal ideals of social responsibility and interdependent individualities, based on a shared faith in human nature that is largely without historical verification.

Dewey's rejection of dualisms undoubtedly seeks to break down artificial re-strictions and undermine the powers which might benefit from polarizing, for ex-ample, theory and practice, fact and value, and hierarchically arranging one term over the other. Nevertheless, by replacing dualistic categories with the notion of a fluid continuum, Dewey removes the possibility of developing a negative critique of ideologically sanctioned dualisms since, on Dewey's terms, everything seems organically related and mutually supporting. This is perhaps one reason why the notion of class conflict is conspicuously absent from Dewey's social criticism, since the idea of exclusively defined and antagonistic terms such as ruling class or working class would be considered an inappropriate way of describing America's fluid social composition. This may be true, and Dewey certainly considers a Marxist perspective inadequate and inappropriate for America, yet without a vo-cabulary of separateness, and therefore of alienation, society's inequalities can look more like imbalances than built-in structural elements of socioeconomic stratifi-cation. All we see is that along the continuum some people are more or less free than others, some more or less wealthy, and so on. In a society in which most members prefer to consider themselves to be middle class, class consciousness refers merely to a vague sense of belonging, which elides the very real and intractable divisions within American society.[13]

Dewey's organicism leads him to characterize social conflict as an undesirable and avoidable imbalance within the social whole. Conflict does not occur "because the interests of the individual are incompatible with those of his society, but because the interests of some groups are gained at the disadvantage of, or even by the suppression of, the interests of other groups."[14] While this assessment acknowledges inequality, it does not consider conflict to be a structural problem, but merely a question of a maladjustment of group dynamics:

> We need to observe, first of all, the causes of social conflict, to find out what groups have become too dominating and have come to exercise disproportionate power, as well as to identify the groups that have been oppressed, denied privilege and opportunity. Only by making an accurate diagnosis can we hope to prevent social infection and build a healthier society. We must devise means for bringing the interests of all the groups of a society into adjustment, providing all of them with the opportunity to develop, so that each can help the others instead of being in conflict with them.[15]

The therapeutic slant of Dewey's holistic diagnosis is clear, although exactly how dominant groups might be persuaded into relinquishing their power remains unexplained. It seems that Dewey is relying upon some kind of moral imperative that, once demonstrated, will reveal the necessity of inter-group reliance: "We must teach ourselves one inescapable fact: any real advantage to one group is shared by all groups; and when one group suffers, all are hurt. Social groups are so intimately interrelated that what happens to one of them ultimately affects the well-being of all of them."[16] Where, we might ask, is the evidence that the advantage of one group benefits all, or that suffering is shared around? Dewey's conception of democratic community needs the notion of interdependence and equilibrium to work because such a community must be founded on shared values. The prospect of contending ideological positions within a single society is incompatible with a harmonious community. Conflict is therefore refigured as a sickness or "infection" that must be objectively (that is, not ideologically) cured: reformers should "*dispassionately* determine which needs of their society are not being *reasonably* met."[17] Such a strategy of rational problem solving, believes Dewey, would be "immeasurably more profitable" than any kind of social or political revolution, but profitable for whom?

Dewey shares with Marx the belief that it is philosophy's job not merely to interpret the world but to change it. This entails the recognition that all human activity is formed by social institutions, and that it is these institutions that must be transformed in order to liberate the creative potential of society's members. For Marxists, however, as Richard J. Bernstein has observed, Dewey's philosophy fails to take full measure of capitalism's power, his faith in creative intelligence being "naive because he underestimates the powerful social, political, and economic forces that distort and corrupt this 'ideal'." Taking Dewey's faith in the reconstruction of social institutions through educational reform as typical of his pragmatic optimism, Bernstein reflects that "our schools are and will continue to be a reflection of a larger society in which they function. No capitalist society will tolerate a school system that is designed to overthrow it."[18] This may be true, though Dewey's contextualism seems no more vulnerable to the distortions and corruptions wrought by capitalism than is a dialectical analysis, which, like the pragmatic perspective, should be only too aware of its own historical contingency. Nevertheless, even given his criticisms, Bernstein maintains that it would be "disastrous if we discarded what stands at the center of the pragmatic tradition." This is the importance of the theory of inquiry, the "critical understanding of the norms by which any idea or hypothesis is to be tested and evaluated."[19]

The problem with Dewey's notion of community is that it assumes a shared set of moral and institutional coordinates. Such a notion, as C. Wright Mills argues with some force, constitutes nothing but a "set of images out of a fairy tale: they are not adequate even as an approximate model of how the American system of power works. The issues that now shape man's fate are neither raised nor decided by the public at large. The idea of a community of publics is not a description of fact, but an assertion of an ideal, an assertion of a legitimation masquerading . . . as fact."[20] The optimistic ideal of a community of publics is founded, writes Mills, on three mistaken assumptions: that there is a natural harmony of interests between individuals, that before public action there will always be rational public discussion, and that public opinion will always prevail. The first of these assumptions, Mills goes on, has long since been replaced, firstly with the Utilitarian doctrine that harmony must first be created by reform before it can work, then by the Marxist notion of class struggle. The assumption that public discussion will precede public action has been undermined by a belief in the necessity for experts to decide delicate and complex issues. The third assumption, that public opinion will prevail, has been undermined by the "great gap now existing between the underlying population and those who make decisions in its name."[21] From Mills's point of view, then, the notion of publics is an outmoded form of nineteenth century idealism, "a projection upon the community at large of the intellectual's ideal of the supremacy of intellect," a projection that explains away ignorance, irrationality, and apathy as merely "an intellectual lag, to which the spread of education would soon put an end."[22]

Dewey's operational paradigms for democratic community are the academic and scientific communities, much as Williams's notions of communal interaction are rooted in the shared interests of the medical profession and of mutually aligned artistic groups (organized around little magazines, small presses, and social gatherings). As largely self-sustaining micro-communities, these groups, based on shared idioms and expertise, undoubtedly enjoy a level of mutual respect, freedom, and interaction that does not easily translate to the wider social sphere. Furthermore, this shared expertise, necessarily specialized, can often lead to detachment from general affairs due to a belief in objectivity and impartiality. Such groups do not generally engage, as organized bodies, directly in political debate or protest. As Mills writes, from the point of view of the elite, those who "clamor publicly" can be easily identified as "Labor", "Business", "Farmer", and so on. Those not so easily recognized "make up 'The Public'," which is "composed of the unidentified and the non-partisan in a world of defined and partisan interests. It is socially composed of well-educated, salaried professionals, especially college professors; of non-unionized employees, especially white-collar people, along with self-employed professionals and small businessmen." In this "faint echo of the classic notion," the public consists of the middle classes, often identified as "the unattached expert," who, although well informed, has never taken a clear-cut, public stand on controversial issues which are brought to a focus by organized interests. These are the "public members of the board, the commission, the committee. What the public stands for, accordingly, is often a vagueness of policy (called open-mindedness), a lack of involvement in public affairs (known as reasonableness), and a professional disinterest (known as tolerance)."[23]

The danger of what Mills calls the "rhetoric of liberalism" is that its emphasis on minimizing conflict and promoting harmony can easily become a form of ideological domination that legitimizes exploitation and the inequities of the status quo in the name of freedom and democracy. Dewey is well aware of this danger and attempts to counter this kind of corporate or state liberalism by stressing the radical credentials of democracy as a moral ideal, an ideal that will not brook abuse of the inalienable rights of man.

Since democracy is not for Dewey a form of government alone, but a way of life, it must be capable, like any natural form, of adaptation to different conditions in order to survive. Dewey endorses Jefferson's belief that "Each generation has a right to choose for itself the form of government it believes the most promotive of its own happiness" (Jefferson quoted in FC, 174–175). To live democratically is thus to shun externally imposed structures that might serve to threaten the well-being of the polis. As "a moral standard for personal conduct" (FC, 155), democracy can function as a radical force for social transformation, providing in its principles of inherent and inalienable rights the justification for an attack upon that which impedes individual freedom:

> The fundamental principle of democracy is that the ends of freedom and individuality for all can be obtained only by means that accord with those ends. . . . The end of democracy is a radical end. For it is an end that has not been adequately realized in any country at any time. It is radical because it requires great change in existing social institutions, economic, legal and cultural. A democratic liberalism that does not recognize these things in thought and action is not awake to its own meaning and to what that meaning demands.[24]

Democracy, then, is a moral ideal that must be advanced through inquiry and experimentation. To the extent that capitalist institutions have co-opted the language of democracy and reduced its radical promise to ideology, this ideal remains unrealized and adversarial.

THE NEAR SIDE OF REALITY

In his influential 1966 essay on Williams, J. Hillis Miller claims that Williams's poetry goes "beyond subjectivism and dualism." The "distinction between subject and object" disappears, Miller goes on, taking with it the "profound abysses of subjectivity . . . and the limitless dimensions of the external world" which constituted the Romantic poetic legacy of the nineteenth century. If something exists at all in Williams's work, observes Miller, "it dwells in the only realm there is, a space both subjective and objective, a region of copresence in which anywhere is everywhere, and all times are one time."[25] While Miller is, I believe, on the whole correct in his assessment of Williams, there are some fine but important distinctions to be made if we are to fully grasp what Williams is attempting to achieve. Firstly, to go "beyond" subjectivism and dualism suggests that Williams has somehow cracked the subjectivism and dualism questions once and for all. Williams does not move beyond dualism, he simply rejects it, as does Dewey, as a viable way of understanding the world. As for subjectivism, there are strong vestiges of a subjectivist viewpoint throughout Williams's work, suggesting that he had trouble relinquishing the primacy of the subjective self, supposing, of course, that he wished to in the first place. We will return to this below.

A second misconception arises from the acceptance of Williams's abandonment of dualisms. Miller claims that, in Williams, the subject-object distinction disappears. To remove dualistic thinking is not necessarily the same thing as eliminating distinctions, nor does one logically flow from the other. Rejecting polarized opposites does not have to result in homogeneity. Williams constantly emphasizes clarity and precision in the delineation of things and words as things. For Williams, it is of the utmost importance to know where one thing ends and another begins. This is measure. It is not dividing experience, objects, or thought into separate realms, but recognizing the diversity of differences between heterogeneous forms. That these forms all exist, as Miller writes, "in the same realm," is undoubtedly true, yet this realm is not simply "both" subjective and objective at the same time, it is a common space in which subjective and objective interact, converse, and transform one another. Without distinctions, such relationships would be impossible, since without separation there can be no contact. The "region of copresence" is not an Emersonian oneness but a field of action, and all fields have boundaries determined by the extent of free movement available to the inhabitants. Contact between differences enlarges the repertoire of possibilities and expands the field, extending the boundaries and defining the localized character of experience. Like Dewey, Williams is attempting to conceive of "a *via media* between extreme atomistic pluralism and block universe monisms."[26] While things cannot exist in isolation this does not mean that each thing is not uniquely itself. "Only if elements are more than just elements in a whole," writes

Dewey, "only if they have something qualitatively their own, can a relational system be prevented from complete collapse" (EN, 75). This kind of interdependent individualism allows for a more socially aware form of autonomy than is available through Emersonian self-reliance, and is closer to what Donald Pease has called, in relation to the Whitmanian self, a "mass logic" in which "the masses free or 'untie' the individual from bondage to his own person," so that he "both completes himself, hence knows perfect liberty, and experiences himself completed by everything, hence knows democratic equality."[27]

Miller's observation that "anywhere is everywhere" is an accurate characterization of Williams's democratic ontology of space, Miller's nod to the Whiteheadian interpretation of relativity Williams uses to bolster his adoption of Dewey's phrase "the local is the only universal." In a sense, Whitehead writes in *Science and the Modern World*, "everything is everywhere at all times. For every location involves an aspect of itself in every other location. Thus every spatio-temporal stand-point mirrors the world."[28] While anywhere is everywhere, each "anywhere" is nonetheless a specific, ascertainable "stand-point." Each stand-point is understood in terms of its relationship to every other point. Identity and knowledge, argues Williams, are grounded in an understanding of this relationship: "Before any of the arguments begin they must be placed, for from place, a place, begins everything—is in fact a place. Synchronously occupied by everything and at the same time space itself—nothing but. Before science, philosophy, religion, ethics—before they can begin to function—is a region unsusceptible to argument" (EK, 130). Gaining knowledge can thus only be achieved by recognizing the limits of the knowable, which involves "a certain positioning of the understanding . . . in which the thinker places himself on the near side of reality—abjures the unknowable and begins *within* a certain tacitly limited field of human possibility to seek wisdom" (EK, 132). While we can only "live in one place at a time," this limitation is not a fixed boundary—merely tacit—and "only through it do we recognize our freedom."[29]

This freedom is that of the individual as placed uniquely within the democratic field of co-dependent citizens: the "man who has 'worked' or has seen at least from a position of place purely, in that he shares this not by gifts of family like an aristocrat (a great advantage, position—but dangerous to the mind since it involves a confusion, the lesser *seeming* to hold the greater). A commoner might be greater if he feel a community in *this* and so an *addition* to his consciousness and not a division of it among all in common" (EK, 134). The man who works to place himself as an equal adds to the democracy of the community because his contribution and his position is made out of lived conditions, rather than inherited, which would separate by distinctions made by birth rather than by agency.

Williams's model of location as the ground for democracy is, however, like Dewey's conception of an ideal democracy, far from being a description of the world, or even America, as it actually is. What passes for democracy in America "is certainly antagonistic to this realization of place. It hates it, tears down fences that delineate, is jealous of differences,—distrusts all elevations of the realization of intense place, sets a premium on placelessness" (EK, 134). The leveling tendency inherent in this modern reading of democracy seeks to reduce the many to the one, to rationalize existence and obliterate differences. Williams's conception of democracy as a radical demonstration of independence must be in constant dispute with the homogenizing tendency of bureaucratized democracy since the differences that he celebrates are the markers of achieved independence: individuality, unique identity, the open ended potentialities of the unmonitored creative act. By obscuring Williams's anti-dualism as a dissolution of difference, Miller misses the point of why Williams formulated his anti-dualistic position, which is at root politically motivated. Miller makes Williams's use of relativity sound like relativism, which dampens the impact of Williams's insistence that democracy is grounded in the freedom to *be* where one is, at that moment, free to define that being, the limit of that freedom (and an essential limit) being the recognition and acknowledgment of the freedom and equality of every other element within the field to likewise define itself. The "strange lack of tension" Miller sees in Williams's work can only be noted if the political dimension in Williams is ignored. The very real tension in Williams's writing is due to the fact that ideal and real, mind and matter, the one and the many, and so on, are dualisms Williams can well do without, but he has to contend with them at all times as manifestations of rational domination and reified consciousness. Enabling differences to be maintained as mutually interactive and fluid agents, rather than as polarized and divorced opposites, is the core of Williams's poetics and politics, the need to insist upon and to enact this process involving him in the project of positing a workable aesthetic democracy.

The case for Williams as a romantic idealist has been well argued by Carl Rapp and reiterated by Donald W. Markos.[30] Rapp provides a convincing reading of Williams's early rite of passage poem "The Wanderer" (1914), arguing against the predominant view that the narrator, obviously Williams, through immersion in the Passaic River, is purged of his desire for transcendence and accepts the resources of the local urban environment. Rapp claims that while Williams "*is* purged of his yearning for transcendence, [this is] only because he achieves it. He *does* give up his private consciousness or ego, but only because that ego or consciousness has suddenly expanded to the point where it now contains everything within it."[31] Rapp goes on to back his claim by quoting a letter from Williams to John Thirlwall of 1955:

> The mind always tries to break out of confinement. It has tried every sort of interest which presents itself, even to a flight to the moon. But the only thing which will finally interest it must be its own intrinsic nature. In itself it must find devices which will permit it to survive—physical transportation to another planet will not help, for it will still be the same mind which has not been relieved by movement. (SL, 330–331).

Rapp suggests that the "merger of mind and world" revealed in "The Wanderer" leads, in Williams, "to the higher recognition that mind itself is the ultimate object of knowledge. If the phenomenal world is really epiphenomenal with respect to mind, empathy plays into or gives away to the egotistical sublime."[32]. Comparing Williams with Wordsworth, Coleridge, and Hegel, Rapp concludes that for an idealist, "in one way or another, the concept of transcendence supersedes that of immanence."[33]

While Williams's romantic belief in the necessary freedom of the creative imagination is beyond doubt one of the overriding concerns of his work, Rapp's argument allows little space for the equally important stress in Williams on the materiality of things and of language. For example, Rapp claims that "the imagist poem has little or nothing to do with the intrinsic importance of the things themselves. Rather it signalizes a momentary intensification of the mental powers of the poet."[34] Markos has responded, correctly I believe, by recognizing a tautology in Rapp's reading: "if the mind is not constrained by the intrinsic qualities of those phenomena it uses as occasions to display its own power or to objectify its emotions, then every poem winds up meaning the same thing."[35]

The confusion here is partly due to an understanding of idealism that casts it as antagonistic to materialism. For example, while Hegel is known as an idealist, as Richard J. Bernstein has pointed out, this can be "extraordinarily misleading," since if we define idealism as the opposite to materialism "then Hegel is certainly *not* an idealist" because the whole thrust of his philosophy is toward the concrete, toward showing that "what may appear to be 'other' than *Geist* is really spiritual in its true nature." What Hegel seeks to achieve "is an *Aufhebung* of the dichotomy of ideality and materiality. If we are to discover the working of *Geist*, we must understand its concrete working in the 'material' of the world."[36] Rapp, in countering materialist readings of Williams has, in understanding idealism within a dualistic material/ideal paradigm, failed to register Williams's own attempted *Aufhebung* of ideality and materiality. Williams's desire to biologize the imaginative and intellectual powers of the individual and to humanize the social institutions that control those powers—science, philosophy, education, and business—is closer to Whitehead's organicism (as Markos points out) and Dewey's pragmatism than a traditional reading of Hegelian idealism. There is unquestionably a lot of Hegel in Williams, just as there is in Dewey, but the emphasis needs to be made that it is Hegel's radical challenge to the idealist/materialist dualism that most usefully serves to characterize Williams's poetic project, which is, as is Dewey's philosophy, inherently social in orientation.

The importance Williams places on the independence and primacy of the imagination does not have to lead to subjectivism. Imagination is, for Williams, the interaction of subject and object in space and time, not a transcendent subjectivity that exists for and of itself. The "confinement" of the mind Williams speaks of in the letter to Thirlwall does not refer to the hopeless inaccessibility of the world, which leads, in Rapp's view, to empathy giving way to the "egotistical sublime." While Williams writes that the mind must find devices that will permit it to survive "in itself," these devices are to be used to engage with what lies outside the mind. In the arts, for example, "lie resources which when we become aware of their existence make it possible for us to liberate ourselves" (SL, 331).

When Williams adds that "it is in the mind, not on the moon, we must find our relief," he is referring to the mind's ability to relate, through perception, cognition, and expression, to what is separate to it: "The first thing you learn when you begin to learn anything about this earth is that you are eternally barred save for the report of your senses from knowing anything about it. Measure serves for us as the key: we can measure between objects; therefore we know that they exist" (SL, 331). What is reported by the senses is measured by the mind, but the standard of measurement itself is established by the tool used, which in the case of poetry is language. And language, as Williams would accept, is social. Rapp's mistake in characterizing Williams as an idealist is in undervaluing his stress upon language as the concrete site for subject-object interaction. As Dewey points out, while inner experience, "a realm of purely personal events that are always at the individual's command . . . implies a new worth and sense of dignity in human individuality," failure to recognize that this world of inner experience "is dependent upon an extension of language which is a social product and operation" can lead to subjectivism, solipsism, and egotism (EN, 136–137). Language connects the mind to the world as part of that world, and what is present in language is not the immediacy of sense impressions, but the "report," the "measure." "Immediacy of existence," writes Dewey, "is ineffable. But there is nothing mystical about such ineffability; it expresses the fact that of direct existence it is futile to say anything to one's self and impossible to say anything to another. Discourse can but intimate connections which if followed out may lead one to *have* an existence" (EN, 74). The possibility of having an existence is what Williams means by finding and using "devices" that permit the mind, or individuality, "to survive." "Things in their immediacy are unknown and unknowable," Dewey goes on, "not because they are remote or behind some impenetrable veil of sensation of ideas, but because knowledge has no concern with them. For knowledge is a memorandum of conditions of their appearance, concerned, that is, with sequences, coexistences, relations. Immediate things may be *pointed to* by words, but not described or defined" (EN, 74–75).

By placing oneself "on the near side of reality," as Williams explains, and beginning "*within* a certain tacitly limited field of human possibility," it can become possible to "recognize our freedom." Language is this field, and the freedom is freedom to describe what can be known. The process of doing this is communication, and the communicative model followed by Dewey and by Williams as the most appropriate for democracy (and, to a large extent, constitutive of democracy), is that of the conversation.

THE VOICE OF POETRY IN THE CONVERSATION OF AMERICA

What is perhaps most distinctive about conversation as a mode of discourse is its elasticity. Conversations, unlike arguments, avoid any confrontation and conflict that might threaten to break off communication. Conversations are more likely to

be meeting places than battle grounds.[37] In contrast to the goal-oriented, problem-solving argument, a conversation can be unresolved, inconclusive, an end in
itself, in Michael Oakeshott's words, an "unrehearsed intellectual adventure."[38]
For Dewey, this adventure creates culture through communication, the development of meaning through the articulation of thought. It is this "power to attrib-
ute meaning to events—that is, the power of talking about them—that saves us
from just being more events, caught in their flux, hurried along with them,
caught among them and buffeted to pieces in their stress."[39] Language thus becomes "the beginning of any liberation from necessity" (CE I, 125), a way of
transforming the way we live:

> When communication occurs all natural events are subject to reconsideration
> and revision; they are readapted to meet the requirements of conversation,
> whether it be public discourse or that preliminary discourse termed thinking.
> Events turn into objects; things with a meaning. (EN, 132)

The meaning created through conversation is not the unmediated transmission of
concepts or information, since the receptor must interpret the discourse of the
other, which is inherently strange and must be negotiated: "Where there is speech
there are two, each of whom remains to some extent to the other a bare brute
event, something to whose acts and words meaning can be imputed but who is
not himself a transparent meaning" (CE I, 125–126). Understanding is thus a
communal activity, a form of reciprocity that forms the structures of meaning that
make up the polis. Events that are not given meanings "are accidents and if they
are big enough are catastrophes" (CE I, 129). The creation of meaning through
communication is thus seen as a form of social bonding through which community is strengthened against the threat of disruption. As a process of making, of
constructing the public sphere, communication is analogous to art—the presentation of communication resulting in meaning-laden objects.[40]

     This is what Dewey means when he understands conversation as a way of
making "events into objects; things with a meaning," and what Williams suggests
in A Novelette (1932) when he sees conversation as design. Williams realizes that
the textual space is not the immediate manifestation of thought—"the actual sentences of conversation simply do not exist in literature—and can never do so;
Since they have doffed their actuality" (N, 289)—but he knows also that creativity resides in communication, in breaking down the unidirectional "special meaning" uniquely understood by the thinking subject by presenting this meaning in
language, making it available in "the reciprocity of communication." Once
thought exists as an object, having "only the effect of itself," it has become involved in the conversation between thinking and doing, mind and world, word
and word, and is thus "pure design," and therefore "real" (N, 287).

     The kind of republic of letters Williams is after reveals itself in his many
works in which different genres and voices find themselves in the same text: the
relationship between improvisational writing and exposition in Kora in Hell,

between poetry and prose in *Spring and All* and *The Descent of Winter;* the collection of documents and creative re-readings in *In the American Grain;* the dialogic space of essays such as "The Basis of a Faith in Art"; and the collision of contending discourses and formal strategies that make up *Paterson.* Williams's lyric poems also often read as one half of a conversation with an unseen partner, the language of the lyric broken by the outbursts of some other voice.

The "excellence" of conversation, writes Oakeshott, "springs from a tension between seriousness and playfulness": without seriousness it would "lack impetus," yet through participation "each voice learns to be playful, learns to understand itself conversationally and to recognize itself as a voice among voices. As with children, who are great conversationalists, the playfulness is serious and the seriousness in the end is only play."[41] Seeing conversation as pure design, Williams understands this relationship between the playful and the serious, poetry being "real" only when it has "the effect of itself"—a kind of purposive purposelessness that subverts means-end rationality and points toward the possibility of the aestheticization of experience Dewey calls for in works such as *Art as Experience.*[42]

Unfortunately, while this conception of conversation as a form of cultural subversion makes for a convincing proposition, it does not account for how it might function at the level of social reality. Conversation as a paradigm for democratic life will hold up as a viable communal adhesive only so long as there is a shared set of values, principles, and norms that informs the community. When society is characterized more by irreconcilable conflict than by consensus, by powerful ethnic, racial, and class divisions than by a shared identity, and by a plurality of tongues and idioms than by a common language, how valid is reference to the conversation of mankind? Conversation, the exchange of language, both creates community and is at the same time dependent in advance on the existence of a community as the conversational space. This interdependence leaves Dewey and Williams struggling to find a ground for their communication-based social criticism. How can one find, let alone speak, a common language when there is no commonalty? If there is no commonalty, the idea of a common language very quickly becomes an imposed standard, which contradicts the processual notion of language creation through conversation.[43] It seems that "the actual sentences of conversation" have "doffed their actuality" not just in literature but also in life. Modern capitalist society, in breaking up local communities and homogenizing individuality, has, Dewey accepts, "immensely widened the scope of associational activities," but "at the expense of the intimacy and directness of communal group interests and activities" (FC, 176). Association may be natural, but association alone does not make a community: "Electrons, atoms and molecules are in association with one another. Nothing exists in isolation anywhere throughout nature. Natural associations are conditions for the existence of a community, but a community adds the function of communication in which emotions and ideas are shared as well as joint undertakings engaged in" (FC, 176).

The kind of community Dewey has in mind draws on Jefferson's proposal for local self-governing units "small enough so that all its members could have direct communication with one another and take care of all community affairs" (FC, 176). The prospect of "face-to-face associations" may, Dewey believes, "offset if not control the dread impersonality of the sweep of present forces" (FC, 176). Expecting the virtues of a close-knit, small town community to offset the effects of massive industrialization, urbanization, population growth, and so on, however, seems rather like asking a mule to drive an express train. Despite his constant insistence that America should recognize its transformation into a modern corporate state and find ways to work within it, Dewey's model for viable communal life remains largely a nineteenth-century rural one. Mills observes that Dewey's "peculiar" and "complex" meaning of "social" is "not peculiar or complex when viewed against a small town of artisans or a farming community."[44] Dewey's conception of action, argues Mills, is not political action, it is "the conduct of an individual in non-rationalized spheres or types of society. It is conduct that makes decisions about situations that have not been regulated." While this conduct is appropriate "on the edge of structures, such as frontier types of society," in a rationalized social context Dewey's concept of action is hopelessly out of step.[45]

Again, as we have already noted, Dewey does not have a complex vocabulary of power which could work through the difficulties of entrenched political conflict and struggle. The fact is, he does not think he needs such a vocabulary because social problems, as Dewey understands them, are not created and perpetuated by an inherently unjust social and economic system (which would make them inaccessible to reform), but are at heart problems of imbalance and inefficiency. This "manipulative active" standpoint, writes Mills, presents no difficulties in the areas of technology or within a biological framework. To generalize such a category "into the fields of political movements," however, "ignores power issues, doesn't see them, defines issues around them, but never directly in their middle." This evasion of the political is accomplished, explains Mills, in five ways:

> (a) by continual selection of concrete examples which are in a power context or even clearly inter-human, (b) by becoming very formal, highly abstract in its unitary model of thought, "adjustment," "control of environment," (c) by refusing to formulate concrete socio-political ends, (d) by an infinitely pluralistic view of society, (e) by methodizing *all* such problems: *i.e.,* rendering them, formally, soluble by "intelligence."[46]

Underwriting Dewey's faith in a problem-solving scientific method is the assumption of a "relatively homogeneous community which does not harbor any chasms of structure and power not thoroughly ameliorative by discussion. Always there must be the assumption that no 'problems' will arise that will be so deep that a third idea-plan would not unite in some way the two conflicting plans. But this model of problem posing does not concern itself with two social interests in a death-clutch."[47] A homogeneous community is also the prerequisite for the initial assessment of what constitutes a social "problem," since without a shared recognition of unsatisfactory situations how could a problem be solved with nonpartisan objectivity? The argument becomes a circular one: community is the necessary environment for a method of problem solving that would be unnecessary if such a community existed.

The need to believe in the natural, organic harmony of small town life, as inadequate a foundation for social and political reconstruction as it is, remained a powerful ideal for Dewey and for many urban Americans in the early twentieth century, many of whom, including Williams, had experienced in their own lifetimes the dismantling of such communities by the encroachments of corporate capitalism. Williams's persistent advocacy of the local as the ground for creativity, while often used as a broader reference to the need for rejecting European traditions in favor of indigenous materials, is also a defense of Jefferson's proposed small self-governing units and Dewey's "face-to-face associations," a defense of participatory democracy. In 1946, after receiving a typically patronizing and pedantic letter from Ezra Pound, Williams countered by asserting his belief in the local environment, quoting from Dewey's *Freedom and Culture* that "[v]ital and thorough attachments are bred only in the intimacy of an intercourse which is of necessity restricted in range . . . "[48] In political terms what this means for Dewey is that "[d]emocracy must begin at home, and its home is the neighborly community" (FC, 176).

What, or perhaps more pertinently, where, is such a neighborly community to be found? In *The Great American Novel* (1923), uneasily balancing satire and sentimentality, Williams portrays the Southern mountain folk who live "untouched by all modern life. In two centuries mountain people have changed so little that they are in many ways the typical Americans" (GAN, 220). There is heavy but curious irony in Williams's mock National Geographic observation, since the mountain people's isolation from modern life must make them the most untypical of Americans. Such isolation "makes people fiercely individualistic" (GAN, 217), but it is a kind of deformed and inverted individualism brought about by such extreme solitude. As Williams famously observed in "To Elsie," "The pure products of America / go crazy—" (SA, 131). Lack of commerce with the world results in inbreeding which corrupts individuality to produce a degenerating sameness: "[A]t bottom the mountain mother is always the same" (GAN, 218). The portrayal of the independent spirit and natural vitality of the mountain folk as ideal American types is thus itself inverted to suggest a critique of American society whose citizens are wilfully isolated, individualistic at the expense of cultural commonalty, and deeply suspicious of anything that lies beyond the immediate domestic domain. Ma Duncan's homespun wisdom does more than evoke a simple recognition of the evils of capitalist greed; its hackneyed sentimentality, and the deliberate division Ma makes between herself and "folks"—the me and not-me—reveal an abdication of responsibility funded by a denial of communal ties. America's myth of small self-sustaining communities based on pioneering "natural" men and women appears here as little more than a case of wilful avoidance of reality.

Ma Duncan is the mouthpiece for a view of America as lost potential, a conventionally nostalgic protest against the postlapsarian wilderness left after the very rugged individualists the mountain woman herself epitomizes have extracted its natural wealth and moved on:

> I wish you could have seen the great old trees that used to be here. If folks was-n't so mad for money they might be here and a preachin' the gospel of beauty. But folks is all for money and all for self. Some day when they've cut off all the beauty that God planted to point us to him, folks will look round and wonder what us human bein's is here fur -.(GAN, 219)

Surely the day when folks wonder what they "is here fur" has already arrived, and it is only Ma Duncan's isolation that prevents her from realizing it. She is out-moded, an anachronism in modern America. Her protest, however true, reaches no one because her reclusive tribe speaks only to and for itself.

Williams's uncertainty over whether to valorize or satirize Ma Duncan and her fellows suggests that he is far from comfortable with the "neighborly commu-nity" model of democracy and the plausibility of a genuine cultural conversation of equals. Through his medical practice, Williams was only too aware of deep so-cial divisions and gross inequality, yet this social awareness did not lead him to re-ject, just as Dewey did not reject, the principles of liberal democracy which, in the hands of arch individualists, had obviously contributed to, or at the very least seemed to do little to assuage, the injustices of the society built in its name. While this is perfectly legitimate, the gap between principle and fact being no grounds for abandoning the principle, the deep unease created by this gap separating America as a notional "perfect democracy" and the reality of America as an impe-rial capitalist nation state generates a powerful ambivalence in much of Williams's writing, an urgent, occasionally shrill, thinly veiled nationalism alternating with an incisive and canny understanding of the cruelty, hypocrisy and cynicism that freights such national hubris. It is upon this ambivalence that many of Williams's poems are built.

A MONGREL PLURALITY

"Language," writes Emerson, "is a city to the building of which every human being brought a stone; yet he is no more to be credited with the grand result than the acelaph which adds a cell to the coral reef which is the basis of the conti-nent."[49] Language is here conceived as that which constitutes the *civitas*; it is the medium through which individuals become interdependent citizens. It is through participation in public discourse that democracy is built, and no one voice or group of voices can be in ascendancy if this discourse is to continue. As a conse-quence of this, however, it seems that the individual contribution must be sub-sumed into the throng and must to some extent become indistinguishable within it. The strain here between the recognition that society is constructed out of indi-vidualities and that, in the process that individuality is negated, must be felt at the core of any liberal democracy. Furthermore, if the public sphere consists of the sum of all of its parts, then the kinds of voices that can be heard will determine the kind of society there is.

This strain is striking in a poem such as Williams's "It is a Living Coral" (CP1, 255–258), which concerns the Capitol building in Washington, D.C., the acme of official democratic culture. This white neoclassical monument to American government, and its art collection, become for Williams the space for an examination of national self-representation. As a synecdoche for democracy, the building is, like coral, an organic structure constructed through accretion, capable of growth and expansion. The Capitol is, indeed, able "to expand // and contract with / variations // of temperature"; it can withstand outside pressure and internal disruption. While the capacity for shock absorption is a desirable and perhaps necessary property of any healthy political system, as with coral, the tendency to spread and grow can lead to domination and a choking off of alternatives not compatible with the principal life form. While democracy is positively a living coral, then, it is also "a trouble," partly due to its being "artificially fettered" by an outmoded and inappropriate classicism which forces a semblance of unity and harmony, the one from the many. Representing freedom through formal totality can ultimately serve to negate that freedom, suggesting a latent impulse toward domination. We might remember Theodor Adorno's observation that by "imposing its harmony from without, classical art flouts the truth of that harmony," which is to expose, despite itself, "reconciliation as violence."[50] Williams is presumably aware of this danger, making sure to include the fact that, perched atop the Capitol's containing dome, liberty stands armed.

What the Capitol seeks to formally gather and absorb, however, the poem is determined to unravel. It seeks, in effect, to represent the Capitol as a testament to the failure of the very totalizing logic the building is constructed to achieve. The seamless story of American ascendancy offered by the art in the rotunda is broken in the poem's unfolding, a mess of proper names and decontextualized details run together into a long slither of cubist observation that has been refracted through the prism of the American poet claiming his democratic liberty to challenge and refigure worn out forms.

"This scaleless // jumble is superb // and accurate in its / expression // of the thing they would destroy -." As with the poem's title, the pronoun has no distinct object — "they" might refer only to Generals Marion and Lee, but it more likely refers broadly to all the historical figures, to Congress and the Commission, to the artists; in short, to all agents of government. Further, is this a straightforward recognition of the Capitol's unashamed display of rebel defiance and victory, or is it, more subtly, a marvel at the way that the desire for harmony and unity is undermined even as it is constructed? On top of this, "the thing that they would destroy" is temporally confusing: does this mean the thing they *intend* to destroy, or have already destroyed? And what is "the thing"? Is it plurality, unity, democracy, colonial oppression? Or, if the poem is itself Williams's Capitol, enacting what it is—if *it* is a living coral, the embodiment of national characteristics.- then is "this scaleless // jumble" in fact the triumph of the poem over the tyranny of official culture? This ambiguity generates its own trouble, extracts the many from the clutches of the one, and enables Williams to hold celebration, criticism, and artistic power in place. Such ambiguity also allows for complicity, since if the poem is a Capitol, it is also an embodiment of national identity, and must be held accountable for the values it enshrines. In this sense, even as the poem refigures democracy in a new form it is recapitulating the traits of the old. The next lines of the poem continue to press this difficulty.

"Baptism of Poca- / hontas" is a direct reference to John G. Chapman's painting of that name, the first of four commissioned pictures to hang in the rotunda in 1840. The painting depicts the Indian woman's renunciation of her racial and cultural identities as she kneels, in a clear invocation of the Virgin, with bent head, clasped hands, and benign expression, dressed in white, in a church surrounded by pious Virginians and skeptical Indian relatives. An interpretive pamphlet published to accompany the work in 1840 reinforces what is already clear in the picture: passivity leads to assimilation and survival, while resistance must result in removal and extinction. Both, of course, are facilitators of absorption, of an actual disappearance and reappearance as myth. Pocahontas becomes Rebecca and founds a line of prominent Virginians, her scowling kin are made by Andrew Jackson to go away. It is no accident that Williams snaps the word Pocahontas on the line break, the only time in the poem he does this. Other names run on and run together; Pocahontas is divided, literally taken apart. That the importance of the official reading is such that the painting cannot be relied upon to carry it alone but needs written backing, remains into the twentieth century. Williams makes a point of including the "little card / hanging // under [the painting] to tell the persons // in the picture." There must be no misunderstanding or doubt as to who is whom. The card is a measure of government mistrust of the people's ability to read correctly, and for Williams the card is as revealing of interpretive containment as the painting itself and the building that houses it.

In the context of the Capitol, "coral" is likely to be read as signifying the white exposed skeletal structure of the building and the institution of government it represents. But coral is also conventionally used as a word describing qualities of redness, often of blood. This doubleness of coral as both white and red shadows the poem and the building itself, which contains a racial image repertoire of predominantly Indians and whites (there are notably few African Americans represented in the Capitol).

"It is a Living Coral" was published in 1924, while Williams was researching his book of historical reinvention, *In the American Grain*. Nineteen twenty-four was also, of course, the year of the National Origins Act and the Indian Citizenship Act, the culmination of years of incremental moves to, on the one hand shut down immigration from predominantly Catholic and Jewish south and east Europe and from Asia, and on the other to finally bring Indians into the nation as citizens. Together, these laws sought to stabilize the parameters of possible Americanness, preventing the dominance of "alien" influence and incorporating the now harmless minority of "natives" as a necessary part of what it means to be indigenous.[51]

Like the burning arrows Mrs. Motte uses to remove the British, Pocahontas is consumed by the republic as an act of revolutionary identity-formation. Williams is typical of his time in celebrating Indianness as coterminous with authentic Americanness and in seeking to identify with the unreconstructed "wildness" of the aboriginal. Where he differs from the nativist justification of racial separation based on irreducible difference is in his embracing of miscegenation not as absorption of the passive into the dominant but as a necessary mongrelization of culture, of language, and of identity. The unpredictable consequences of such cross-fertilization means that no white totality can ever fully guarantee its own legitimacy, identity is never entirely self-evident, the trace of redness is always written into coral and its hybrid accretions must continue to erupt to the surface. As with racial and national identity, so with language. In troubling the reading of the Capitol's version of history, in embracing a mongrel national identity, and in drawing blood from the coral, Williams does what de Tocqueville worried about so much with regard to language in a democracy, which is to give "an unwanted meaning to an expression already in use. This . . . practice is most dangerous to the language," he goes on, since, "When a democratic people double the meaning of a word in this way, they sometimes render the meaning which it retains as ambiguous as that which it acquires." For de Tocqueville it is a "deplorable consequence of democracy" that "there is no common appeal to the sentence of a permanent tribunal that may definitely settle the meaning of the word."[52] For Williams it is this very unsettled quality that allows him to challenge received values, to add his mongrel cell to the reef, to make it say things it is not expected to say, to resist the establishment of permanent tribunals that may definitely settle not only the meaning of the word, but the self-identity of the American.

Sacvan Bercovitch believes that the valorization of heterogeneity in America can easily become "a function of hegemony":

> The open-ended inclusiveness of the United States was directly proportionate to America's capacity to incorporate and *exclude*, and more precisely to incorporate by exclusion. The culture seemed indefinite, infinitely processual, because as America it closed everything out, as being Old World and / or not-yet America. And vice-versa: the process by which it closed out everything un-American was also the spur toward an ideal of *liberal* inclusiveness, a vision of *representative* openness that eroded traditional barriers of nationality, territory, language, and ethnicity, and eventually, perhaps, would erode even the barriers of race and gender—which is to say, would open the prospects of liberalism to women and blacks as it had to the Irish, the Jews, and the far-flung regions of Alaska and Hawaii.[53]

So how can the conversation be kept going when the erosion of barriers necessary to create a common language ends up by obliterating the identities, customs, and traditions that accompany those barriers? Under such conditions, what would there be left to talk about? If community is based on communication, does this mean that what is distinctive about ethnic, racial, gender, or class subgroups must be smoothed away in order for community to exist? This is surely what Williams sees embodied in the Capitol, and his desire for an American poetry written in the local idiom is faced with this dilemma. If grounded in the local, will it be possible for anyone outside of the locality to understand the poem? "I wanted to write a poem / that you would understand" writes Williams in "January Morning" (CPI, 103), "For what good is it to me / if you can't understand it? / But you got to try hard-." The vernacular of the last line is simple and direct but nonetheless syntactically broken: short words to be understood, picked up from the street. Who is Williams writing for? Residents of Rutherford, or New Jersey or New York, the Eastern Seaboard, the USA, or any reader at all? And exactly how hard must this reader try in order to understand? Is it the peculiarities of form, the strangeness of subject, the obscurity of the idiom, or the actual language itself that might prove incomprehensible? To an extent, Williams is referring to any act of communication and the need to cross the boundary from subject to object. He is also stressing that he considers his poem to be different from, and therefore less recognizable than, what is usually considered to be poetic. There is also, however, an implicit suggestion that the very words themselves may be strange, not at all common. In a nation of many tongues, what is a common language? In such a nation, every word must be clearly articulated and turned over, given a chance to be understood and learned. This effort of comprehension means that what community there might be amongst disparate groups is no easy achievement and must be deliberately worked at; the common ground must be slowly built up, constructed rather than found as given.

For first-generation Americans, the idea of an inherited American tradition or American language made little sense. For Williams, and for other poets such as his friend Louis Zukofsky, Jefferson's proposal of permanent revolution, the perpetual redefinition of meaning and purpose, offered an attractive political model for self-generated, improvised linguistic construction. Williams heard and spoke Spanish, French, and English at home; Zukofsky's family spoke only Yiddish at home.[54] Zukofsky's sister, despite arriving in America at sixteen and living until she was eighty-five, was not alone in never becoming a U.S. citizen, largely due to the fact that all her life she could speak only a few words of English. Given that citizenship meant learning at least some English, the relationship between national identity and linguistic proficiency, between community and communication could be problematic and politically exclusionary at the very least.

Finding a voice from such a marginalized position requires a much greater sense of self-consciousness than it would for a native speaker—becoming American means self-becoming and self-creation in quite a literal way, since language must be made or chosen. Mary Oppen remembers that Zukofsky "had to choose his way of speaking English, as his family did not speak it, and his mother and sister never left the Bronx. I think Louis chose the accent of John Dewey; when Louis was at Columbia, Dewey was a leading figure and a great influence there.

Students who graduated from Columbia in that period, in many cases, had what was recognized as a Columbia accent."[55] If Count Hermann Keyserling's account is anything to go by, Zukofsky made a pertinent choice. Dewey, Keyserling claims extravagantly, is "the most representative, the most important American living." Dewey is "representative of the inner aspirations and possibilities of the nation. Thus, one has every reason to believe that he who understands the type of Dr. John Dewey understands 'the' American as far as he differs, as a general type, from other nations."[56]

The common language Williams and Dewey believe should form the basis of the conversation of America is a language based on the moral values of a democracy of interdependent individuals. This kind of cultural pluralism is grounded on a shared tone and timbre yet coupled with a recognition of, and a respect for, individual voices. Dewey rejected the notion of the melting pot and saw the prospect of a multiracial and multiethnic America as the only viable option, and as a valid model for international relations. "If there is to be a lasting peace," claimed Dewey in 1916, "there must be a recognition of the cultural rights and privileges of each nationality, its right to its own language, its own literature, its own ideals, its own moral and spiritual outlook on the world, its complete religious freedom, and such political autonomy as may be consistent with the maintenance of general social unity."[57] While supporting Horace Kallen's conception of American civilization as an orchestra, Dewey points out that it is essential that "we really get a symphony and not a lot of different instruments playing simultaneously. I never did care for the melting pot metaphor, but genuine assimilation *to one another*—not to Anglosaxondom—seems to be essential to an America."[58] In Kallen's argument Dewey detects and is wary of "an implication of segregation geographic and otherwise. That we should recognize the segregation that undoubtedly exists is requisite, but in order that it may not be fastened upon us."[59] For Dewey, the premium should be on harmony between different groups and interests, and he cannot accept a cultural pluralism that does not promote interaction and communication between groups. In order to prevent America splintering into discrete units of self-contained and self-interested subcultures, the moral values of democracy must be shared by all in order to override the local exigencies of class, race, ethnicity, gender, and so on. What these values amount to are "friendly and helpful intercourse between all and the equipment of every individual to serve the community by his own best powers in his own best way."[60]

The problem with a notion of social harmony that maintains difference is that there needs to be some common meeting point between cultures. In order to achieve this a shared idiom must be found. Or imposed, such as Williams's view of the Capitol, as a whitewash over national and racial difference. Dewey understands this, and therefore advocates that immigrants should have "not only the opportunity but the obligation to learn the English language."[61] How this can be expected to work without enforcing an assimilation to "Anglosaxondom" is unclear, and despite Dewey's antagonism toward agencies of Americanization, it is hard not to conclude that compulsory English lessons are, in fact, an easy and

obvious way of not only acculturating immigrants, but of breaking down the social cohesiveness of immigrant communities and clearing away the cultural heritage (often radical) of the Old Country. Furthermore, like Zukofsky's sister, not
learning English excludes recalcitrant immigrants from the political process altogether. Social harmony can cut both ways.

Communication, for Williams, has less to do with the intelligibility of words
than with the form in which they are arranged. While he is not interested in the
pressure of centuries of inherited tradition bearing down upon the present —
"You must begin with nothing" (VP, 98)—neither could or should the past be
pasted over with a homogenizing "English", which in America belongs to no one.
The new forms Williams is grasping for are available in the New World precisely
because there is and should be no national language that will pin down meanings
once and for all. In this sense "Art is a country by itself" (VP, 251), a country that
communicates not through "a logical recital of events" but through "that attenu-
ated power which draws perhaps many broken things into a dance giving them
thus a full being" (KH, 16–17). As a nation of many broken languages, America
could be this country by itself, speaking not through a system of imposed correspondences between words and things (a "pastime of very low order," like "the
coining of similes" [KH, 18]) but through a much keener power "which discovers
in things those inimitable particles of dissimilarity to all other things which are
the peculiar perfections of the thing in question" (KH, 18). In the country of art,
citizens speak the language of the imagination, a language derived from the specific circumstances of each individual. The music made by this national orchestra
is not performed from a prewritten score—Dewey's compulsory English—but
created on site by the interaction of instruments :

> [O]ne does not attempt by the ingenuity of the joiner to blend the tones of the
> oboe with the violin. On the contrary the perfections of the two instruments are
> emphasized by the joiner; no means is neglected to give to each the full color of
> its perfections. It is only the music of the instruments which is joined and that
> not by the woodworker but by the composer, by virtue of the imagination. (KH,
> 19)

Dewey is concerned with harmony, but Williams's music is of a kind that does not
recognize any previously agreed upon values, aesthetic or otherwise; the imagination may hear music where Dewey hears only noise. For Williams, the country of
art is truly democratic; on the level of the imagination "all things and ages meet in
fellowship. Thus only can they, peculiar and perfect, find their release" (KH, 19).

Art is a country by itself because it accepts the sovereignty of no master. This
does not mean that art is to remain aloof from society. Quite the contrary, the
forms of art "arise from the society about [the poet] of which he is (if he is to be
fed) a part—the fecundating men and women about him who have given him
birth. Let me insist, the poet's very life but also his forms originate in the political,
social and economic maelstrom on which he rides. At his best he translates them

to new values fed from the society of which he is a part if he will continue fertile."[62] While art, then, arises out of conditions whether they be good conditions or bad, what is important for Williams is the artist's ability to construct "new values" from circumstances. Social transformation is not a prerequisite for art, yet art, it seems, is one of the prerequisites for social transformation. Williams's organic metaphors make clear the interdependence of artist and society: the latter fertilizes the artist and what springs forth is a "translation" of the maelstrom into new forms.

Williams's conversation of mankind conveys meaning through its form, as design, rather than through its message. This aestheticization of communication bypasses the problem of intelligibility and accessibility by postulating a translinguistic space where shape, sound, color, and movement create a communal culture from the fragments of lived experience. While this is not a Deweyan harmony—"All is confusion"—as a conception of modern social existence it reaches beyond the hierarchies of the feudal past and the restraints of a scientist social control toward a new order of consonance, a pluralism of forms united in their abandonment of inherited clutter: "Destruction . . . comes before creation . . . We must be destructive first to free ourselves from forms accreting to themselves tyrannies we despise. Where does the past lodge in the older forms? Tear it out . . . We can't go back to it politically. How then otherwise?"[63] This is a version of Jefferson's endorsement of each generation's right to choose a government most promotive of its happiness. Williams advocates the establishment of America as an aesthetic state, but, as he says, there is much to be destroyed before construction can begin.

TWO

AESTHETICS AS A FIELD OF ACTION

And in a dying world, creation is revolution.

—Waldo Frank

Imagination is the chief instrument of the good.

—John Dewey

Dewey and Williams are both at their most romantic when arguing for the liberating and transformative power of the aesthetic as a counterweight to modern industrial culture. Grounded in romantic organicism and a nostalgia for an imagined prior unity of cultural and political life, industrial capitalism is presented as the fracturing, decentering agent of inexorable social collapse. The source of social and individual reinvigoration is the creative imagination, which must be recognized as the means through which a radical democracy can be achieved. This is not, unlike Pound's contortions of Jefferson and Mussolini, an appeal for the emergence of a heroic genius but for an awakening of the latent aesthetic sensibility in the common people. For Dewey and Williams, as for earlier romantic anticapitalists such as William Morris, "the cause of Art is the cause of the people," a form of political activism through which the alienated world gives way to the aesthetic world, where art and life, culture and society, become interwoven and inseparable.[1] Williams's interest in the meaning of democracy, then, is not something distinguishable from his aesthetic concerns. For Williams the work of art should embody the possibilities of democratic liberty in its form, providing an index of human creativity through which other kinds of work might be measured. Since the work of art is made out of historically and socially contingent local materials, it stands as evidence of the powerful activation of everyday life by the force of interaction with the artist. Art is the consummation of individual liberty and serves for Williams and for Dewey as the paradigm for democratically fulfilled potential.

The kind of union with the world sought by Dewey and Williams is prima-rily based on relatedness. An important trope for Williams is that of marriage (and its obverse, divorce, which remains a constant threat), a transactional and contractual metaphor for notions of choice, commitment, and responsibility, of contact and communion. To marry is to bond the self with the other within the constraints of an institution, the boundaries of which are established by custom and a mutual acceptance of duties. Freedom is contingent upon the limits of the contractual space, which are designed for the protection and the preservation of the union. Marriage is also a pertinent description of Williams's paratactic formal experimentation, words being discrete objects that commune with other words within a relational field, each transformed and gaining significance by virtue of their connectedness and context.[2] Just as the wedding of individual elements ani-mates Williams's aesthetic of contact, the convergence of the biological and socio-cultural imperatives of marriage as communally generative is not far from Dewey's mind when he is thinking about art. It is telling that when Dewey attacks the in-stitutions of "high" culture for being deliberately removed from everyday affairs he uses the metaphors of celibacy and divorce to convey the aloof and sterile precincts of a culture disengaged from the people. Certainly, for both men the no-tion of isolation is inimical to cultural and personal well-being and is presented as, at the very least, unhealthy and perhaps even as unnatural. What is clear is that, if art is somehow to be the embodiment of democracy, it cannot be a separate sphere of activity but must move into the world of which it is a part and embrace it. It cannot be a higher realm but of a piece with everyday life even as it seeks to transform that life. Such a conception of art cannot shun the fallen world or re-treat into its own untouchable autonomy but must become entwined with the forces that might destroy it. A democratic art, then, is far from an art of alienation or withdrawal. It is, in fact, as Williams and Dewey conceive it, an art of con-frontation and possible transformation. It does not hold up a mirror to the world, it *is* that world, fraught with contradictions and imperfections, a process, an act, a force, as Williams would say, like electricity pulsing through the culture, a power.

THE UNIVERSAL HUSBAND

What the notion of marriage enables is a drawing together of subject and object through the reaching out of the imagination, a kind of imaginative empiricism that recognizes feeling not as separate from intellect but as a form of cognition, as a part of the process of knowing.[3] By force of the imagination, a form of will and desire, objects become charged with significance. As Williams writes in *Spring and All,* this is not a "beautiful illusion," a subjectively derived mirage, but an ex-perienced reality, reality being, in effect, not the object or the person alone, but the marriage between them which, as Coleridge envisioned, "dissolves, diffuses, dissipates, in order to recreate. . . . [The imagination] struggles to realize and to unify. It is essentially vital, even as objects (as objects) are essentially fixed and dead."[4]

At its most potent, this creative bonding of self and other can enable Williams to declare that "I am the universal husband" (EK, 33), hungry for connection, wedded to all things in a mutually transformative union. While marriage can serve to release the energy of the imagination, however, because it involves a responsiveness to what is outside the self, it must also function as a form of limitation. In bonding with the real, Williams must acknowledge the accompanying restriction of liberty that connectedness entails. Williams wants a revolution in language grounded in actuality, in experience. This is what he identifies as the achievement of the French Surrealists, an "ability to knock off every accretion from the stones of composition" (N, 280). While the Surrealists provide for Williams an exemplary model for what he himself seeks to do, their work is of no use to him in practical terms because "it is their invention: one." The imagination must work with the material its own specific location offers; Williams must see what is before him: "Theirs [the Surrealists'] is a simplicity of phrase emphasizing the elusive reality of words. Mine is in pink pants, she hanging my coat in the closet" (N, 281).

The domesticity of Williams's inspiration is, for him, both a necessity and a burden; necessary in that to remain faithful to the actuality of his experience he must accept the form this experience takes, burdensome to the extent that his romantic notions of the artist often strain for something more exotic, more in keeping with the wild and unrestrained life he believes the imagination needs. To a large extent, this conflict between responsibility to the fidelity of experience and the recognition of, at times, the paucity of that experience, becomes the main dialectical force in Williams's work, as he constantly attempts to balance duty—to family, profession, and his conception of art—and complete individual freedom.

In a poem such as "Danse Russe" (CP1, 86–87), the poet flirts with the excesses of the romantic self—the primitive, naked narcissist singing, "I am lonely, lonely. / I was born to be lonely, / I am best so!"—with the shades drawn while his family sleeps. The wry self-mockery of the poem and the provisional "If" with which it opens cannot fully dispel the sense of containment it transmits, expression and frivolity squeezed into this small private space where no one will see. The alternative, however, a primal oneness of man and nature, is not without its problems for Williams. In "Pastoral 2" (CP1, 45–47), for instance, the poet desires to abandon the restrictions of civilized bourgeois family life, yet is fearful of exposure to the brute force of wild nature. Addressing nature, the poet complains that "you never tell / The cause of this terror / That strikes me back / Feverishly upon petty business." The quotidian demands of everyday life—"Saving the sick, / Getting shelter, food / And delights for my dear family"—are here portrayed as a kind of retreat or shelter from true being, yet despite the "terror," the desire to escape responsibility remains, the poet longing to fling off his clothes and "crawl in naked / There among you / Cold as it is!"

It is not, however, complete and utter fear of exposure to nature that prevents this communion. The familial and social structures and loyalties built as protection from the cold have become confining; the fortress has become something of a prison, "this hide / I have drawn about myself" as a "shield" has "bound me more subtly / Than you have imagined." Thus, while Williams is wary of the atomizing and alienating consequences of divorce from the world, marriage to the "not-me" seems to challenge the freedom it also makes possible. The bonding that constitutes marriage also binds, union also demands responsibility and sacrifice. In "Idyl" (CP1, 49–50), the poet's wife "comes out / And tucks me in." She brings with her "our baby" and puts him "In the bed beside me." Moving over to make room for the child, the poet thinks of "the freezing poor" and considers himself "Happy— / Then we kiss." The wife brings responsibility with her, limiting movement (tucking in) and forcing the poet to shift position to accommodate to his family duties. Wheeling on the freezing poor—those exposed to the force of nature in a way that the poet of "Pastoral 2" longs for but will not risk—as a measure of his good fortune does not seem to be an adequate means of judging happiness, and the kiss is more a gesture of resignation than of union and contentment.

Despite the uneasiness of these poems, marriage nonetheless remains a useful trope for Williams, because it enables him to prevent conflict becoming a crisis. Rather than face the problem of the irreconcilability of art and life, of wandering desire and family responsibility, he can contain and explain the incompatibility of contending forces through the notion of a contractual bonding that remains flexible enough to allow for transgressions. These transgressions stand for moves toward liberation, a liberation that is not so much a permanent escape from convention and responsibility as it is a temporary excursion away from total constraint. In returning to the demands of the marriage contract, Williams is attempting to prove, through the act of wandering and return, that the contract can accommodate and is amenable to a certain amount of change and adaption.

For Stanley Cavell, a successful marriage is only achieved after a separation, which implies that the connection is already there but not necessarily recognized: "[O]nly those can genuinely marry who are already married. It is as though you know you are married when you come to see that you cannot divorce, that is, when you find that your lives simply will not disentangle."[5] In terms of the self-world split, this suggests that the division is not an ontological fact, but a way of thinking and being that can be changed, a willed connection with the world that suspends skepticism in favor of a chosen union which must be constantly reaffirmed in order to banish unreasonable doubt and alienation. The fact that the connection is a decision and not a given makes the self responsible for maintaining contact. The knowledge of divorce, of separateness as a constant possibility, defines the marriage as one of differences held together by a reciprocal arrangement. As Cavell suggests, the awareness of separation must be recognized "in order that an intimacy of difference or reciprocity [can] supervene. Marriage is always divorce, always entails rupture from something."[6]

As a theme around which Williams can play variations of attachment and separation, marriage, then, functions as a recognition of the need for institutions to stabilize social relationships, so long as these institutions remain flexible enough to allow for individual transgressions of a limited kind. As a metaphor for the scope of artistic creativity, marriage represents an institutional frame analogous to the structuring notion of "art," a boundary concept within which freedom of movement can be enjoyed and measured. So long as the limits of this concept are not rigid and are not completely transgressed, the activity can continue to be called art. Furthermore, if the limits are overstepped, the activity, emerging from the institutional boundaries of art, might be called a critique of art. Either way, the concept itself is necessary as a means of understanding the art-related activity. Modernist art might be disrespectful of the limits of the institutional setting within which it is defined but it cannot move too far away from the security of the definition provided by the institution itself, since, as problems arise when marriage becomes divorce, when ties are deliberately and permanently broken, there will be no way to describe the resulting separation except by negation. Art that loosens itself from the institution of art to such a degree that it becomes unidentifiable as art must, of necessity, be described as something else: as life, or labor, or mass production.

At this point, the question becomes one of how to redefine the institutional or conceptual perimeters of behavior without erasing what is specific and desirable within the original concept. How can social relationships be transformed without the removal of what has been learned and accepted in terms of social responsibility? How can the function of art be broadened and radicalized without the eradication of what is unique to art? Such problems are particularly pressing in the ambitious kind of democracy Williams and Dewey imagine for America. In such a democracy, where freedom and equality are such that the socioeconomic divisions between individuals and the categorical distinctions between art and life are eliminated, does art disappear? And if it does, does it matter? If we accept, as Williams and Dewey accept, that American democracy as it exists is not a true democracy, but a society based on inequality and lack of freedom, then the institutional distinctions and hierarchies that serve to uphold the status quo, as undemocratic, must be removed. Without these institutions, however, it becomes very difficult to describe what society or art would look like.

While Williams and Dewey recognize the need for the transformation of American life in order to bring about a radically participatory democracy, there remains plenty about America as it exists that they want to preserve, despite Williams's enthusiasm for creative destruction. Just as marriage maintains the distinction between partners even in union, they wish to maintain the distinctiveness of the aesthetic even as they desire everyday life to become charged with the liberating power of the aesthetic. And just as Williams, in poems such as "The Young Housewife," "Woman Walking," "Good Night," and "Young Love," presents sexual infidelity, actual or imagined, as a form of circumscribed individual freedom within the safety (so long as it remains clandestine) of the social contract of marriage, so the liberal critique of American society exercised by Dewey and Williams invariably, despite its libertarian wanderings, returns to the bosom of the middle-class culture it at other times appears to seek to escape.[7] While it would probably be less complicated to call for an absolute revolution of values, whether in art or in life or both, the fact is that Williams's and Dewey's pragmatic acceptance of the contingency of art and life means that there can be no stepping outside the fabric of existing conditions. When Dewey and Williams reject such ideas as party political ideology or literary tradition they do so because such ideas imply foundational claims external to local conditions. For both Dewey and Williams the process of critique is enmeshed in circumstances and must move within them. There can be no blank slate upon which to write a new reality any more than there can be an atomistic individual who can be understood outside his or her social interactions. Neither can there be an art that is comprehensible outside of the conventions that describe it as art. This does not mean that invention or change cannot occur, but they must come out of what is already there. If the aesthetic is the site for social transformation, then, how does it obtain its power within a rhetoric of liberalism that seeks to preserve and protect even as it attempts to initiate change? Furthermore, how does art stay married to a world that appears to insist on divorce?

THE BEGINNING OF ART

Art, for Dewey, denotes "any selective activity by which concrete things are so arranged as to elicit attention to the distinctive values realizable by them." Understood in this way, art and aesthetic appreciation "are not additions to the real world, much less luxuries." Rather, they represent "the only ways in which the individualized elements in the world of nature and man are grasped."[8] Art, then, is a way of experiencing the world as a formal arrangement of phenomena, or at least this is what art should be. Unfortunately, the modern preoccupation with science-driven technology, technical training, professionalization and specialization has been "disastrous" in its tendency to fix ideas and attitudes. Drawing upon Whitehead, Dewey agrees that "the celibacy of the medieval learned class has been replaced by a celibacy of the intellect which is divorced from the concrete contemplation of the complete facts."[9] This celibacy of the intellect, Dewey goes on, has found its way into the galleries and histories of art, effectively removing art from the vicissitudes of everyday life and sequestering it in the rarefied and privileged sphere of "high" culture, a cold, hard place safe from the profanities of the world.

This "museum conception of art" (AE, 12) effectively shuts art off "from that association with the materials and aims of every other form of human effort, undergoing, and achievement" (AE, 9). In such a walled-off environment, art cannot possibly, according to Dewey, hope to have any relevance to our lives. The task as he sees it is to "restore continuity between the refined and intensified forms of experience that are works of art and the everyday events, doings and sufferings that are universally recognized to constitute experience" (AE, 9). On these terms a work of art, for Dewey, is more properly described as a product than as an object, the latter term contributing to the sense of rupture between active creation and passive appreciation. "Object" implies a state of existence free from the processes of making, whereas to consider art as a product acknowledges that the actual work of art resides precisely there, in the doing, "what the product does with and in experience" (AE, 9). As Williams consistently argues, culture "isn't a thing: it's an act . . . if it stands still, it's dead" (SE, 157).

We must see ourselves and the artwork, according to Dewey, as engaged participants within the entire range of human activity that constitutes our culture, as agents in "the events and scenes that hold the attentive eye and ear of man, arousing his interest and affording him enjoyment as he looks and listens" (AE, 10). Such a form of engagement can serve to move us away from the museum conception of art and present us with the aesthetic potential that resides in the "sights that hold the crowd" (AE, 11): a fire engine rushing by, a machine digging up the earth, men working high above the ground, the grace of the ballplayer— notably scenes of urban communal activity. If these examples from Dewey conflict with our notions of what art might be and where it might be found, this is because of our narrow conception of the aesthetic which has filtered off "art" from life, and idealized the former at the expense of the latter. If fine art is placed on a pedestal, Dewey argues, it is not surprising that most people avoid it as above them, preferring more accessible diversions such as movies, jazz, comic books, and sensational newspaper stories: "When, because of their remoteness, the objects acknowledged by the cultivated to be works of fine art seem anemic to the mass of people, esthetic hunger is likely to seek the cheap and the vulgar" (AE, 12). Such distractions are a disservice to human culture, which needs to benefit from the life-enhancing potential in fine art; the culture will suffer while art remains a commodity or a form of interior decoration for a cultivated elite: "As long as art is the beauty parlor of civilization neither art nor civilization is secure" (AE, 346).

This final statement is a powerful attack on art as the adorning legitimation of the status quo and brings to mind the kind of view held by Williams's "It is a Living Coral," where the art of the Capitol building is seen as an ossification of culture and which has turned the process of democracy into a museum of treasured but redundant relics. While fine art may seem bloodless to the mass of people, however, Dewey's examples of the cheap and vulgar suggest a curious stance toward what might constitute aesthetic experience. It is reasonable to ask, perhaps, what makes a fire engine, a building site, or a ball game latent aesthetic experiences while watching a movie or listening to jazz are mere diversions. Dewey's examples of vulgarity are all what today would be called "mass" or "popular" cultural forms, and this is clearly what separates them from the events "that hold the crowd." The implication is that brute events have the capacity for generating aesthetic experience while comic books cannot, by their very nature as cultural chewing gum, yield such an experience. For a cultural critic highly resistant to the division between intellectual and bodily experience, Dewey betrays here a suspicion of the sensual pleasures of what he is prepared to dismiss, rather highmindedly, as mere commodity culture.

Williams certainly found aesthetic sustenance in the sights that hold the crowd, one of his most anthologized poems, "The Great Figure" (CP1, 174), of course, taking as its subject the experience of a fire engine flying through the city streets. These everyday urban experiences are an important part of Williams's distinctiveness as a writer and his view of mass culture, likewise, while certainly not defended as being of the same significance as "high" culture, suggests a more celebratory and even defiant mood among the "mass" than Dewey's conception of it as a pacifying diversion. In *The Great American Novel*, Williams, like Dewey, recognizes the "esthetic hunger" that finds sustenance where it can. Indeed, America satisfies this need "in strange and often uncatalogued ways" (GAN, 200). Just as Dewey observed a general desire for aesthetic experience, Williams sees the attraction that "Jazz, the Follies, the flapper in orange and green gown and war-paint of rouge" hold for so many people, for "impossible frenzies of color in a world that refuses to be drab" (GAN, 200). While a refusal to be drab is something, Williams is prepared to admit that this kind of surface flamboyance is not adequate because it does not nourish. It is less like eating than peering through the shop window: "Human souls who are not living impassioned lives, not creating romance and splendor and grotesqueness—phases of beauty's infinite variety—such people wistfully try to find these things outside themselves; a futile, often destructive quest" (GAN, 200).

As with Dewey, it is hard to see from Williams's diminished view of popular entertainment exactly what might be wistful about it. How does he know that flamboyant revelers do not lead impassioned lives, that they do not create and enjoy the "phases of beauty's infinite variety"? There remains an assumption that such cultural "frenzies" must somehow be raised to a more distinguished level for them to have meaning, that writing a poem about the movies, or jazz, or baseball, as Williams did, is qualitatively different and better than participating in the activities themselves. Despite the democratic argument about the latent power of everyday experience and culture as an act, there is in both men, it seems, a real skepticism regarding the actual value of what "ordinary" people get up to. Nevertheless, Dewey and Williams both are careful not to dismiss popular cultural forms outright; what they argue is that such forms are not, in Dewey's term, "consummatory," but merely "cheap and vulgar." Such forms serve to distance individuals farther from the possibility of "life-enhancing" activity because, since they are mostly confection, they generate greater needs than they can ever deliver. As Williams writes, "[It] is not enough to agree and assert when the imagination demands for satisfaction creative energy" (GAN, 200). However, he goes on to say that the very hunger itself is a good sign, that the love of flamboyance and spectacle is a demonstration of faith in the possibility of creativity: "[It] is a shout of delight, a declaration of richness. It is at least the beginning of art" (GAN, 201).

The problem with this view of popular culture as a debased or undeveloped version of artistic fulfilment is that it is in danger of undermining the democratic pluralism that supposedly underpins Dewey's and Williams's critique of institutionalized "high" art. Only someone educated and acculturated to discern and appreciate the "fine" aspects of "high" culture would be comfortable making disparaging remarks about jazz, film, and so on. Are not these forms part of the very democratic communal culture Dewey and Williams seem to be advocating? There appears to be something of a contradiction here between rhetoric and belief, a latent paternalism that calls for broader access and participation in cultural production, but only for so long as the products conform to preestablished notions of what constitutes art in the first place.[10] While it can be argued that mass culture derives from and contributes to the false consciousness of a society incapable of perceiving its true relationship within the machinery of capitalist power, surely the alternative argument, that mass cultural forms are capable of retaining residual counterhegemonic strategies of resistance, is equally sustainable and more pertinent to Dewey's and Williams's point of view. They both hint at such a possibility, Dewey seeing the potential in the urban scene and Williams noting the "beginning of art," yet in seeing popular art forms as the potential for something else—presumably for an art more highly evolved and unified—they betray their need to legitimate art in terms of its conventional, value-laden identity as autonomous, as more (or other) than life. While calling on the materials of everyday life to be the generative stuff of a democratic art, these materials will, it is hard not to conclude, once this stuff is made into art, simply become absorbed into the special place outside of everyday life that art allegedly occupies.[11] The need that Dewey and Williams see for the transformation of what art means and what it does, in these terms, appears to be more of an argument for wider access and participation than for a radical overturning of the category of art itself. This is certainly not a bad argument but it does preserve the idea of the aesthetic as a form of "higher" experience to which all other experiences aspire. Nevertheless, Dewey does make it clear that the question of what constitutes a democratic culture "is not a matter of an increased number of persons who will take part in the creation and enjoyment of art and science" (ION, 100). It is, in fact, a qualitative question about "whether work itself can become an instrument of culture and of how the masses can share freely in a life enriched in imagination and esthetic enjoyment" (ION, 101).

Dewey's remarks on mass culture are thus part of a larger criticism of social conditions that prevent most of those "engaged in the outward work of production and distribution of economic commodities" from having any "share—imaginative, intellectual, emotional—in directing the activities in which they physically participate" (ION, 104). Indeed, he can think of nothing "more childishly futile" than "the attempt to bring 'art' and esthetic enjoyment externally to the multitudes who work in the ugliest surroundings and who leave their ugly factories only to go through depressing streets to eat, sleep and carry on their domestic occupations in grimy, sordid homes." Any interest in art and the aesthetic must develop into an "alert interest in the conditions which determine the esthetic environment of the vast multitudes" (ION, 103). It is, in fact, the job of "sociologists, psychologists, novelists, dramatists and poets to exhibit the consequences of our present economic regime upon taste, desire, satisfaction and standards of value"

(ION, 103–104). Under these terms, issues of what constitutes the aesthetic are inseparable from, and cannot be dealt with outside of, the political ramifications of the transformation of what is meant by terms such as work and experience.

The sense of potentiality latent in everyday life is central to Dewey's thought and is bound up with his understanding of experience and the aesthetic. As his comment on the cheap and vulgar suggests, Dewey does not believe that every experience is intrinsically aesthetic. What he does believe, along with Williams, is that every experience has the potential to become an aesthetic experience. An experience with aesthetic quality, a consummated experience, is what Dewey refers to as *an* experience, but before we get to an experience, it is necessary to clarify what experience in general means to Dewey.

Dewey most concisely sums up his conception of experience in "The Need for a Recovery of Philosophy" (1917).[12] In his view, experience should not be seen as either a form of knowledge separate from life, as established by precedent, as wholly subjective, as made up of discrete units of data, or as antithetical to thought. Rather, experience is commerce with the world in all its forms, "an affair of the intercourse of a living being with its physical and social environment."[13] Experience, for Dewey, is experimental and projective, "pregnant with connections" and intrinsically bound up with thought: "reflection is native and constant."[14] The world is not a picture that we behold but an environment that we inhabit. Experience is interaction.

What Dewey calls having *an* experience is the process of consciously working with the elements involved in this interaction. To have an experience is to organize and guide experience, to attempt to understand it and derive meaning from it, to bring its potentialities to fruition. For Dewey, to accomplish this is to achieve aesthetic value; such an accomplishment is, he believes, most apparent and most fully realized in works of art. From experience to an experience is a movement from biology to the aesthetic, or from nature to culture, and Dewey makes this movement without resorting to a dualistic model of art and life. Ontology is of a piece with aesthetics, emphasizing the simultaneity and interdependency of existence and creative action. Life goes on not merely in an environment but because of it: "No creature lives merely under its skin; its subcutaneous organs are means of connection with what lies beyond its bodily frame, and to which, in order to live, it must adjust itself, by accommodation and defense but also by conquest" (AE, 19). Life is an endless series of negotiations of needs and desires, a continuous falling out of equilibrium and of recovering it through effort or by chance. The creature never returns to its prior state, but learns and grows during its passage through disparity or resistance. If art, then, is the result of a process of successful negotiations with the world, it is a kind of provisional resolution of experience, not an end in itself nor predictable in the form that it will take. In a sense, the creation of art is a triumph of agency over chaos. "The world is full of things that are indifferent and even hostile to life," writes Dewey, but if life is to continue there must be an overcoming of conflict, a transformation into "differentiated aspects of a higher powered and more significant life" (AE, 20). Such "biological commonplaces" are much more than that, "they reach to the roots of the esthetic in experience" because they reveal a basic drive toward form and order. Life is more than just flux and chance because form is achieved "whenever a stable, even though moving, equilibrium is reached" (AE, 20). Order is not imposed from without but is made from "the relations of harmonious interaction that energies bear to one another" (AE, 20). Only when this order is achieved can the stability exist that is essential to living, and when order comes after a period of disruption or conflict "it bears within itself the germs of a consummation akin to the esthetic" (AE, 20).

Art, then, stands as supreme testimony to the kind of order possible in the world. It is the bringing together of disparate elements and experiences into form. While art is the consummation of this process, all activity should, as Dewey conceives it, aspire to the condition of artistic creativity. If all experiences have the potential to become aesthetic experiences, by implication it seems likely that all experience can become art. This is certainly a position Williams would endorse to the extent that his democratic faith allowed that anything could be material for a poem. He would also accept, as a good modernist, that there can be no a priori identifying formal characteristics that mark art off as art. Culture (or art) is an act, not a thing, and as such it is the process that, like the experimental ethos of scientific method, governs artistic procedure, not pre-scripted goals. Such a model of artistic and cultural practice makes a great deal of sense for Dewey and Williams from a democratic point of view since it is analogous to the democratic process itself. The idea of culture in an Arnoldian sense has little to offer a democratic society, as both Dewey and Williams recognize in their criticisms of imported European conventions of aesthetic value based on hierarchy, status, and detachment. In America, where there need be no obeisance to precedent, the raising of experience to the realm of the aesthetic should brook no impediment. Unlike an elite model of culture, however, a democratic aesthetic ought not be altogether comfortable with the idea of "raising" experience to a higher level. As Dewey's and Williams's remarks on cheap and vulgar forms of mass culture suggest, there remains a resistance to unpalatable forms of activity which would still undoubtedly be described as "low". To take the democratic line seriously, it might be argued that just as the vulgar can be transformed into art, the aesthetic experience can equally easily become debased. The "people" can also easily turn into a "mass" or a mob. A fluid society greases the wheels of social improvement but also opens the way for possible chaotic insurgency from the bottom.

A democratic aesthetic, then, is not without its problems. While separating cultural production from everyday life would save it from possible dilution or vulgarity it would only reconfirm the values of class and privilege that attend traditional notions of high art. To ground cultural production in the everyday, as Williams and Dewey wish it to be, runs the risk of simply reproducing the inadequacies and inequalities of the status quo. When there is no known vantage point from which to survey society—no cultural high ground—how is cultural criticism possible?

Extricating the democratic artist from this dilemma is a task Williams realizes he has to face. "How in a democracy, such as the United States," he wonders, "can writing . . . be at once objective (true to fact), intellectually searching, subtle and instinct with powerful additions to our lives? It is impossible, without invention of some sort, for the very good reason that observation about us engenders the very opposite of what we seek: triviality, crassness and intellectual bankruptcy. And yet what we do see can in no way be excluded" (SE, 118). What kind of "invention" is capable with dealing with "the unmitigated stupidity, the drab tediousness of the democracy, the overwhelming number of the offensively igno-rant, the dull nerve" of America—which "cannot be escaped" and is "there in the artist's mind"—without abandoning the prospect of a democratic art altogether? This, Williams admits, is "one of the major problems of the artist" (SE, 119), and his solution is not without difficulties. "To be democratic," he goes on, that is "local (in the sense of being attached with integrity to actual experience)," the artist "must for subtlety ascend to a plane of almost abstract design to keep alive. To writing, then, as an art itself" (SE, 118–119).

This sounds less like a prescription for democratic art than a retreat to a priv-ileged art for art's sake philosophy. To an extent, this is what Williams is saying, but for him there is nothing inherently elitist or otherworldly about the notion of the autonomy of art. He does, however, hang on to the idea of rising above in order to keep art safe. Much as Adorno argues, Williams sees it as the social re-sponsibility of art to be autonomous, imbued with and created from the stuff of actual conditions, but strong enough to repel the detrimental influence those con-ditions may have upon its form.[15] A "pure" art is not, for Williams, pure in that is untouched and untouchable, but pure in the sense that it is simply itself, "not a dray horse carrying something for an alien purpose" (EK, 117). While art is un-doubtedly, as far as Williams is concerned, part of the world, it is its very presence, not its message, that is the source of its power. "A work of art can have, justifiably, no such meaning without doing itself violence. It has, justly, no 'meaning'. It is a work of art. And that, on the other hand, is precisely its significance" (EK, 119).

Armed with this notion of the autonomy of "pure" art, Williams can direct his sights toward the acquisitive mentality of industrialists such as J.P. Morgan, who attempt to harness the cultural capital of "high" art—and in doing so, serve to elevate it even higher—by founding "collections, museums and schools." Such ex-ercises in aggrandizement are "all useless" because they merely consolidate social and economic inequality, making the work of creating an indigenous democratic culture that much harder. As Dewey argues, while "imagination is concerned pri-marily with pecuniary success and enjoying its material results, the type of culture will conform to these standards" (ION, 106). Men such as Morgan, sneers Williams, "like to feel themselves King," importing "the effects of the great of the past whose crowns of light they think to borrow" (EK, 121). Outside these citadels of privilege, the modern pure art work, "the ultraviolet side of the spectrum of the categories of the intelligence," is "stripped to penetrate" the refined and curated world of the purchased, safely sealed off aesthetic aristocracy (EK, 121).

Williams is precisely the kind of "intellectual" Dewey conceives of as being necessarily involved in the "remaking and redirection of social forces and conditions" (ION, 109). Unlike the many American critics during the 1920s "engaged in devising modes of escape," whether by fleeing to Paris or to an imagined golden age, and in so doing achieving their liberty "in direct ratio to their distance from the scenes of action," Williams dug in (ION, 101). He was aware of what Dewey calls the "gap" that "isolates the intellectual worker from the wage earner," a gap symbolic of the "split between theory and practice" which is "as fatal to culture on the one side as on the other" (ION, 109). Williams articulated this gap as the divorce, or loss of contact, between the individual and the world of other things and other people, and knew as well as Dewey that without bridging the gap "what we call our culture will continue to be, and in increased measure, a survival of inherited European traditions, and that it will not be indigenous" (ION, 109). And by extension, we might add, following the logic of Dewey's conflation of Europe and class division, such a culture will not be democratic.

WRITING THE PAGELESS ACTUAL

Against the museum conception of art, as we have seen in Dewey, stands the prospect of art as experience. What might such an art look like? How might it function as an attack on the "triviality, crassness and intellectual bankruptcy" of capitalist-funded "official" culture? Williams's improvisational piece, *A Novelette* (1932), is suggestive of potential avenues open to writing "as an art itself." For the strategies utilized in *A Novelette* do not simply seek to demonstrate a fusion of life and art as an experience; the work itself must also necessarily be taken as that experience, as the incarnation of aesthetic consummation. It is necessary to recognize this distinction between demonstration and incarnation because it is integral to Williams's project that the writing should not be seen as a reconstructed, retrospective telling of its subject matter, a form of displacement from the real, but as the immediate realization of itself as the experience. Cecelia Tichi, in her useful discussion of *A Novelette,* obscures this point somewhat when she says that Williams heightens the tempo of modern times by "setting the work in a late 1920s flu epidemic."[16] Yes, Williams does convey the acceleration of life in this work, but he does not choose the epidemic as the setting, as Tichi implies; rather, the crisis is where he finds himself at the time of writing. It is beyond choice, a setting he must work with rather than decide upon. The scene is not a vessel into which the artist pours the subject matter, it is the matter "in the raw," as Dewey says (AE, 10), with which the artist must work.

Under extreme pressure from the epidemic and also in the midst of marital problems, January 1929 was indeed a time of multiple anxieties for Williams, yet it seems that it is the very intensity of the situation that provides the motor force driving him to write: "It is that a stress pares off the inanity by force of speed and a sharpness, a closeness of observation, of attention comes through" (N, 273). A difficult situation is thus turned around and seen as of value because of the necessity for a concentration of energies. Dewey writes that an environment "that was always congenial to the straightaway execution of our impulsions would set a term to growth as surely as one always hostile would irritate and destroy" (AE, 65). By an impulsion, he means "a movement outward and forward of the whole organism" (AE, 64). Every experience begins with an impulsion, but to become an experience the impulsion must be realized "by instituting definite relations (active relations, interactions) with the environment" (AE, 64). The only way an impulsion "can become aware of its nature and its goal is by obstacles surmounted and means employed" (AE, 65). Without resistance from its surroundings, the self cannot become aware of itself, "it would have neither feeling nor interest, neither fear nor hope, neither disappointment nor elation" (AE, 65). It is, then, the very resistance put up by the environment that enables the correct moves to be judged and made toward a creative and productive conclusion:

> Impulsion from need starts an experience that does not know where it is going; resistance and check bring about the conversion of direct forward action into reflection; what is turned back upon is the relation of hindering conditions to what the self possesses as working capital in virtue of prior experiences. As the energies thus involved reinforce the original impulsion, this operates more circumspectly with insight into end and method. Such is the outline of every experience that is clothed with meaning. (AE, 66)

The crisis of the flu epidemic, read through Dewey, is a form of resistance that challenges Williams's functional success as a doctor and as a poet. As it multiplies illness which he must cure, the epidemic shrinks the amount of time left for Williams to spend writing. But by taking the conditions of the epidemic on their own terms, allowing himself to be shaped by need, yet refusing to relinquish his hold on the original impulsion (to cure, to write), Williams directs the situation toward the resolution of a text formed by the shape of his responsibilities. It is this kind of interaction between Williams's impulsion and the restrictions imposed upon him that enables him to observe acutely, in a moment of repose:

> Where the drop of rain has been, there remains a delicate black stain, the outline of a drop marked clearly on the white paint, in black, within which a shadow, the smoothest tone faded upward between the lines and burst them, thinning out upon the woodwork down which rain had come. In the tops of the screws the polishing powder could be seen white. (N, 273)

And then to recognize how such observation is made possible:

> Thus the epidemic had become a criticism—to begin with. In the seriousness of the moment—not even the seriousness but the single necessity—the extraneous dropped of its own weight. One worked rapidly. Meanwhile values stood out in all fineness. (N, 273)

There are times, however, when Williams fails to achieve the fusion of environment and creative action. Dewey observes that experience "is limited by all the causes which interfere with perception of the relations between undergoing and doing. There may be interference because of excess on the side of doing or of excess on the side of receptivity, of undergoing. Unbalance on either side blurs the perception of relations and leaves the experience partial and distorted, with scant or false meaning" (AE, 51). The drive toward forming an experience can fail, and Williams accepts failure: "On the oak leaves the light snow lay encrusted till the wind turned a leaf over—." Pause. "No use, no use. The banality wins, is rather increased by the attempt to reduce it" (N, 274). Later, a moment of affirmation of the need for intense action and struggle—"I blunder not at all. But the difficulty is immense, not to be solved by quietness, but by greater fracture. In the haste, stillness: it is fused" (N, 294)—is followed immediately by the frustration of losing such a moment. "Try as I will the thing comes only when I have one stocking on, the telephone is ringing, my mind is full of difficulties and you have asked me a question. In a flash it comes and is gone" (N, 294).

Williams writes such failures into the text because even the inability to pull together what Dewey calls "the perception of relations," although it is not a consummatory experience, is nonetheless part of the process toward such an experience, part of the flow of the impulsion. Resistance, even when it overcomes, is part of the learning process and must be faced rather than ignored: "Better to learn to write and to make a smooth page no matter what the incoherence of the day, no matter what erasures must be sacrificed to improve a lying experience to keep ordered the disorder of the pageless actual" (N, 275).

To write life, the "pageless actual," is to acknowledge conflict and disorder as well as moments of order, to work sometimes blindly with the "incoherence of the day." As Williams writes in *Kora in Hell*, "That which is known has value only by virtue of the dark. This cannot be otherwise. A thing known passes out of the mind into the muscles, the will is quit of it, save only when set into vibration by the forces of darkness opposed to it" (KH, 74). Dewey makes this same point in *Experience and Nature*:

> The visible is set in the invisible; and in the end what is unseen decides what happens to the seen; the tangible rests precariously upon the untouched and ungrasped. The contrast and the potential maladjustment of the immediate, the conspicuous and focal phase of things, with those indirect and hidden factors which determine the origin and career of what is present, are indestructible features of any and every experience. (EN, 45)

It is the task of perception to grasp the relation between doing and undergoing in an intelligent and meaningful way in order to maximize order—the creative, productive response. Doing and making is artistic, argues Dewey, "when the perceived result is of such a nature that its qualities as perceived have controlled

the question of production. The act of producing that is directed by intent to produce something that is enjoyed in the immediate experience of perceiving has
qualities that a spontaneous or uncontrolled activity does not have. The artist embodies in himself the attitude of the perceiver while he works" (AE, 55). Perception is not just a function of the eye; the whole organism sees. The senses do not
act in isolation but are co-ordinated and inform one another. "In an emphatic
artistic-esthetic experience, the relation [between the senses] is so close that it controls simultaneously both the doing and the perception. . . . Hand and eye,
when the experience is esthetic, are but instruments through which the entire live
creature, moved and active throughout, operates" (AE, 56).

Seen from this perspective, it is insufficient to view Williams's improvisations
as simply automatic writing or as uncontrolled, spontaneous outbursts.[17] The improvisations may not have been revised to keep a "lying appearance" of contrived
order, but they find their form immanently realized, in the making. As Williams
writes, "The compositions that are smoothed, consecutive are dis-jointed. Dis-
jointed. They bear no relation to anything in the world or in the mind" (N, 275).
This is a position Williams maintained throughout his career. In *I Wanted to Write
a Poem* he is clear about the intrinsic order of art. Rejecting the idea of free verse,
Williams asserts that "All art is orderly" (IWWP, 75). This does not just mean
classical forms of order, but refers to an order commensurate with the environment from which the work derives. A poem's movement "is intrinsic, undulant, a
physical more than a literary character."

> When a man makes a poem; makes it, mind you, he takes words as he finds
> them and composes them—without distortion which would mar their exact sig-
> nificance—into an intense expression of his perceptions and ardors that they
> may constitute a revelation in the speech that he uses. It isn't what he says that
> counts as a work of art, it's what he makes, with such intensity of perception that
> it lives with an intrinsic movement of its own to verify its authenticity. (IWWP,
> 90–91)

Perception is made into an expression and an expression is formed out of the
medium of the "speech that [the poet] uses." In distinguishing Williams's improvisations from purely therapeutic or automatic writing, Dewey's important
distinction between discharge and expression is useful to bear in mind. "To discharge is to get rid of, to dismiss; to express is to stay by, to carry forward in
development, to work out to completion" (AE, 67–68). An act of discharge has
no medium, it is self-exposure rather than self-expression; an act of expression is
intrinsically connected to a medium, in Williams's case, "the speech that he
uses."

What Williams says about the poem's movement is also of interest regarding
Dewey's theory of expression. What the artist makes "lives with an intrinsic movement of its own to verify its authenticity," the poem manifesting itself and its significance through the temporal process of writing/reading. Williams's decision in

A Novelette, and also in *Spring and All,* to write something every day bears out this intention to allow the extended act of making reveal the form of the work. Dewey writes that

> [T]he act of expression that constitutes a work of art is a construction in time, not an instantaneous emission. . . . [T]he expression of the self in and through a medium . . . is itself a prolonged interaction of something issuing from the self with objective conditions, a process in which both of them acquire a form and order they did not at first possess. (AE, 71)

In a distinctly Thoreauvian passage of *A Novelette,* the interaction Dewey speaks of between the self and objective conditions is readily apparent, as Williams finds in the thawing and freezing of water a natural form of movement and stasis akin to the stop-go process of his writing:

> Frozen ground cracks open. A tree with a split that admits water will show fresh wood when it freeze
> A stone is darker when wet than when dry. Water falling free in the air is, however white.
> The pipe emits steam which, freezing, coats the roof with ice, which, melting runs from the roof edge and freezing, forms icicles there, which, melting, the water drips in the sun and catches the light as it falls. (N, 295)

These observations are necessary, says Williams, not for scientific or practical purposes, nor for their wit or originality, but to release them from such categories, which rob them of their actuality as common things and nail them down as information, data "stripped of freedom of action and taken away from use" (N, 295–296). Williams's interaction with his environment is transactional: his perception and expression bestow significance on things even as these things provide for him a trope for writing. Self and environment are inseparable, the act of writing seen as a means of liberating common things from the cramping, meager significance bestowed upon them by a limited and dull stance toward everyday existence. The role of the artist, then, is partly that of a liberator, emancipating the latent power of the common world of things: "[A]ll the information that is static in the liberal arts and sciences can, by intelligent understanding, be made active" (N, 296). Like Thoreau's natural etymology, which demonstrates the interpenetration of word and thing, Williams's commerce with the world thickens experience, swelling the load of the words as they follow the form of their meaning, the sentence freezing and melting, pausing and moving, illuminated by the sun, which catches the particles shifting from steam to water to ice: different, but structurally the same H2O. Thus with objects, perception, writing: these are points along a transformational continuum strung together by the experiential constant. Dewey makes the equally Thoreauvian point that "experience is not a veil that shuts man off from nature; it is a means of penetrating continually further into the heart of nature" (EN, 5).

The sense of totality recognized at the consummation of an experience might be construed as suggesting that a final resolution and closure is possible, some sort of "oneness" that will render all subsequent experience purposeless. For Dewey this is not the case at all; in fact, each ending generates a new beginning: "Every closure is an awakening, and every awakening settles something" (AE, 174). The world is more than chaos but less than total order; it is capable of transformation from one state to another but absolute wholeness and unity are impossible to achieve. It is, however, not a pointless goal to pursue as "an ideal, an imaginative projection" (CF, 14). The ideal of wholeness is the horizon of meaning and value in life and provides an aspirational framework which is future oriented but based in the experience of the present. Thus, no experience, however resolved, is self-sufficient enough to be used as a given by which to model and judge future experience. "The consummatory phase of experience," writes Dewey, "always presents something new" (AE, 144). It is through the imagination that present action is guided toward the possibility of achieving an anticipated goal, an imagination charged by the ideal of perfection: "[A]ll possibilities . . . are ideal in character" since "all endeavor for the better is moved by faith in what is possible not by adherence to the actual." The actual may be the limit of the knowable but it is not necessarily the limit of thought. Neither does this faith in the possible guarantee any definite result: "The outcome, given our best endeavor, is not with us. The inherent vice of all intellectual schemes of idealism is that they convert the idealism of action into a system of beliefs about antecedent reality. The character assigned this reality is so different from that which observation and reflection lead to and support that these schemes inevitably glide into allegiance with the supernatural." (CF, 17)

Dewey's talk of ideals, then, does not contradict his assertions concerning the materiality of experience and the significance of environmental influence, but it removes the possibility of any kind of determinism creeping into his thought by asserting the power of the imagination to create new possibilities from its environment. Such possibilities, when achieved, constitute a growth of meaning. There is no end to this process because "the bounding horizon . . . moves as we move" (AE, 197). An experience is a consummation in itself but it should not be conceived as *the* experience, the end of the line.

Imagination, writes Dewey, is "the only gateway" through which the meanings of prior experiences "can find their way into a present interaction." It is "the conscious adjustment of the new and the old is imagination" (AE, 276). The gap between past meaningful interactions and the here and now, if it is not bridged by the imagination, will result only in "recurrence, complete uniformity," "routine and mechanical" experience (AE, 276). Because of this gap, furthermore, "all conscious perception involves a risk," since "it is a venture into the unknown," which does not just assimilate the past into the present but also "brings about some reconstruction of that past" (AE, 276). Imaginative activity thus always has something of the pioneering spirit about it, acting on faith in the ideals it can hope to realize through its interactive situation. Thomas M. Alexander's gloss on Dewey's notion of the imagination is illuminating here: "Imagination is nothing other than the ability to grasp the meaning of the present in terms of a possible situation which may be realized because its ideal possibility has been grasped and used to mediate the situation and direct action."[18] The ideal, importantly, is not fanciful, but, as Dewey asserts, is "made out of the hard stuff of the world of physical and social experience" (CF, 33–34).

Williams's thoughts on writing and imagination in *Spring and All* share many of the concerns of Dewey's aesthetic theory. The root of their common attack on art as it is normally conceived is, as we have seen in Dewey, the problem of a "spectator theory of knowledge," which severs the person from experience, encouraging a passive and disengaged perception of the world. This is the root of their shared disdain for mass culture, "the cheap and vulgar" which offers sustenance but merely adds another layer to the screen separating act from meaning. There is, argues Williams, "a constant barrier between the reader and his consciousness of immediate contact with the world" (SA, 88). This barrier, in writing, "if not [in] all art," is not accidental, it "has been especially designed" to divide "sense and the vaporous fringe which distracts the attention from its agonized approaches to the moment. It has always been a search for 'the beautiful illusion.' Very well. I am not in search of 'the beautiful illusion'" (SA, 89). Williams is clear here that it is not individual dullness that has erected the barrier. It has been "designed" especially in order to alienate the individual from the world. Williams thus sees his writing not as a sophisticated and obfuscating communication with the few who will already understand but as the revolutionary force that will break down the barrier and liberate understanding for all readers. This is a writing with democratic ambitions at its core, emancipatory in rhetoric and intention.

Williams is addressed, he claims, to the imagination, but as with Dewey, this is not imagination as in "fancy", some kind of pure subjectivity superior and separate from everyday reality. Rather, the imagination is a form of dynamic energy that unites rather than divorces subject and object: "To refine, to clarify, to intensify that eternal moment in which we alone live there is but a single force—the imagination" (SA, 89). In a particularly Whitmanian passage Williams extends the range of this synthetic power to include the reader:

> In the imagination, we are from henceforth (so long as you read) locked in a fraternal embrace, the classic caress of the author and reader. We are one. Whenever I say, "I" I mean also, "you." And also, together, as one, we shall begin. (SA, 89)

Thus, the force of the imagination, in generating self-expression from the materials it has made contact with, extends outward from the individual to achieve communion with the reader. Reading itself becomes a form of immediate contact; it is itself an experience that connects the self with the world. Communication between reader and writer generates new meanings and is thus a form of creative community building, making connections rather than severing them: "In the end, works of art are the only media of complete and unhindered communication between man and man that can occur in a world full of gulfs and walls that limit community of experience" (AE, 110). Williams's concern with process, with the movement of substances from gas to fluid to solid, with the relationship between the aesthetic and the domestic, between words and things, influenza and poetry—these are not separate from democratic politics for Williams but are the very stuff of politics. They are concerns over the articulation of a way of life further liberated in the act of articulation, continuously energized by imaginative engagement. The imagination is the agent for the dissemination of power: power to break down barriers preventing contact, to create new forms (of art, of communication, and thus perhaps of social organization).

The power of the imagination to reconstruct the past for the future in the present, to enable learning and growth through what Dewey calls "the conscious readjustment of the new and old" (AE, 276), is also present in Williams. "The reader knows himself," writes Williams, "as he was twenty years ago and he has also in mind a vision of what he would be, some day. Oh, some day! But the thing he never knows and never dares to know is what he is at the exact moment that he is. And this moment is the only thing in which I am at all interested" (SA, 89). To live in the present is to embody the accumulated experience of the past-as-present, "the eternal moment." The future, likewise, is immanent in the present in the sense that the fire is in the wood. After all, how else is the potentiality of experience to be realized except in the act of realization, which must necessarily be actual, experienced, not nostalgic or hoped for activity. The past can be remembered, and memory is always a present act, a misprision of the past in the present. The past is always becoming its future, hauled as it is through time by present memory. Unless we can step outside our skins and see time as an object, then the time must always be now. The imagination is the force of contact, which makes all experience in time hang together.

To stand facing the petrified authority of a dead past, to feel it as a solid and unyielding mass pressing upon the present, is a terrible thing for Williams. He takes it as his task, as the task of American culture, to destroy this burden, and his rhetorical apocalypse in *Spring and All* is ruthless in its ambition: "now we come to dedicate our secret project: the annihilation of every human creature on the face of the earth." Only then "will the world be made anew" (SA, 91). The pressure of tradition is great, however, and without driving the creative imagination at full throttle, the new, because of the tendency to revert to ingrained habit, will be constructed in the shape of the old: "EVOLUTION HAS REPEATED ITSELF FROM THE BEGINNING" (SA, 93). Habit is unconscious and reflexive, the mind is unengaged and action is performed without intent: it is without conscious purpose and meaning, going nowhere. The kind of blind acceptance of established cultural forms attacked by Williams is explained by Dewey in *Experience and Nature*.

By habit, by conditioned reflex, hens run to the farmer when he makes a cluck-ing noise or when they hear the rattle of grain in a pan. When the farmer raises his arms to throw the grain they scatter and fly, to return only when the move-ment ceases. . . . But a human infant learns to discount such movements; to become interested in them as events preparatory to a desired consummation; he learns to treat them as signs of an ulterior event so that his response is to their meaning. He treats them as means to consequences. The hen's activity is egocen-tric; that of the human being is participative. The latter puts himself at the standpoint of a situation in which two parties share. (EN, 140)

To adhere to traditional standards is, for Williams, to live like Dewey's chickens, to repeat unquestioningly the conditioned actions triggered by the farmer of con-vention. Under such conditions evolution will, of course, repeat itself. The imag-ination is, however, the springtime child, participative and engaged; it alone is un-deceived and can make the world anew by creating situations "in which two parties share" because "someone has written a poem" (SA, 92), or, in more Deweyan language, consummated an anticipated potentiality in an experience.

The aesthetic, then, drives all change, defies all convention. The museum conception of art is, for Williams and Dewey, a sorry excuse for aesthetic agency whereby imagination is merely the hired hand of an economic elite that seeks only to further adorn its palaces of profit. What passes for culture among the rest of so-ciety are the impoverished and alienated responses of a people successfully shut off from their own imaginative powers. Williams's and Dewey's arguments for the emancipation of the creative energies latent in everyday experience are an attack on the idea of art as an institution jealous of its privatized cultural power. The point of this attack is not to democratize museums or to widen access to "high" culture. It is to expose the extent to which individual experience has been de-based, how work has become severed from any purpose save the most primitive instrumentality, and how the pleasures of communication have been replaced by the commodified surfaces of vacant spectacle.

The strength of Williams's and Dewey's case for the liberation of creativity is that it does not see the debased forms of "mass" culture as the end but as a begin-ning. Their faith in democracy is such that they do not fall prey to a deep pes-simism in the face of a culture of incorporation. They see that the future of American democracy is in the creativity of its citizens and that these citizens may be downtrodden but they are not defeated. As a latent force, imagination can be tapped, not to find new forms of cultural anaesthetic, but in order to transform the habits and conventions of everyday life. In this, the aesthetic is truly at the core of Williams's and Dewey's cultural politics. If democracy is corrupted, it is the force and vision of the creative imagination, or intelligent understanding, that will enable its reconstruction. Williams's improvisational writing seeks to embody this emancipation of the imagination. Part of the task of energizing democracy is to reach out and make available the tools of emancipation. Williams was never shy of didactic commentary in his work and clearly saw its function in part as a form of education in how to greet the "new world naked" (SA, 95). His aesthetics of marriage, of contact, of mutual responsibility between writer and reader, individual and society, is grounded in the belief in the transformative powers of art. Dewey literally took his similar aesthetic views to school; for Williams the writing itself could become both textbook and playground of a creative democratic education.

THREE

LEARNING DEMOCRACY

Education that does not bear on LIFE and on the most vital and immediate problems of the day is not education but merely suffocation and sabotage.

—Ezra Pound

I see with joy the Irish emigrants landing at Boston, at New York, & say to myself, there they go—to school.

—Ralph Waldo Emerson

In the late 1920s, Williams, sketching out ideas for a book that was to be a series of speculations and ruminations concerning the nature of knowledge, art, and education, suggested that "John Dewey and others appear to look for a solution to the problem of education in psychology and sociology—in philosophy then. They might do worse than to seek it in poetry" (EK, 7). As we have seen, Dewey's interest in aesthetics was to manifest itself most decisively in *Art as Experience* only a few years later, in 1934. Williams read the book when it came out, but his own commitment to the notion of an experientially based, socially transformative art was already well thought out. The stack of notes Williams was working on, which he notably dedicated to both "My country, right or wrong" and "TO MY BOYS" (EK, 2), sought to articulate some of the possible avenues an experiential aesthetics might take within a democracy. Sending the manuscript to Kenneth Burke, Williams was perturbed to find that Burke saw the work as deeply indebted to John Dewey. Williams responded that "[I]f I could convince myself or have anyone else convince me that I were merely following in the steps of Dewey, I'd vomit and quit—at any time. But for the moment I don't believe it—the poetry is offered not too confidently as proof" (SL, 138). As a poet, Williams certainly has the edge on Dewey (who did, in fact, write verse, though not for publication), but his defensiveness in the letter to Burke suggests, perhaps, an awareness on Williams's part of the importance Dewey's ideas played in formulating some of his own ideas. Williams's unwillingness to associate himself with Dewey has a lot to do with Williams's suspicion of scholastic elitism and disciplinary rigidity, which he believed unnaturally restricted the imagination's freewheeling explorations. Such a view is, of course, completely at one with Dewey's own position; it is, in fact, at the heart of Dewey's antifoundationalism. Williams could have done worse than listen to Kenneth Burke. But why a book on education?

Dewey is perhaps still best known as an educationalist, though what is often regarded and criticized as "Deweyan" education is usually far from Dewey's actual position. Over and above the misconceptions concerning Dewey's theory of education, however, is the fact that his work in this field has been bracketed and separated from his roles as philosopher, social theorist, and public intellectual. Such a separation of realms is so contradictory to Dewey's project that it serves to undermine not only his theory of education but the potential efficacy of the pragmatist world view. A similar objection might be made about the reception of Williams's writing, which is often characterized, as is Dewey's philosophy, as anti- or unintellectual, some critics, as Brian Bremen has recently suggested, still reading "No ideas but in things" as simply meaning "no ideas."[1] Williams himself was not unaware of this perception of his work. To Kenneth Burke in 1947 he wrote that

> the trouble as between me and the "placed" critics is that they think I am fooling or rambling or at best uninformed. To put it in its "academic" light: ignorant. I *am* ignorant but only of inessentials, *[sic]* I haven't had time in my life to bother too much with them.
>
> But I am neither uninformed nor unguided in the essential matters that concern me as a poet. Rather the others are infants to me and the more so because of their "training," their learning. (which has taken up so much of their time).[2]

As Williams's final sentence suggests, there is more, as far as he is concerned, to being informed than mere learning or training.

To understand why both Williams and Dewey have been considered anti-intellectual, it is necessary to view their work as moving outside the perimeters of what, by the late 1940s and through the 1950s, had become the dominant paradigms in academic philosophy and literary studies: logical analysis and the New Criticism. Whatever else might be said about the methodologies of these paradigms, their emphasis was on the containment of information within their own fields, and as such served to consolidate and justify the professions of philosophy and literature on their own terms as legitimate academic fields. Analytical philosophy and New Criticism saw their tasks as obtaining insights into the nature of structurally discrete units: a proposition or a text. They did not consider it part of their brief to extend their findings into the world in terms of any kind of socially transformative activity. Dewey and Williams, in contrast, conceive of their work very much in terms of what it can do, not just as theory or text, but what it may be able to achieve in the world. Indeed, they cannot imagine a philosophy or a literature that is not engaged directly with the doings and sufferings, to use Dewey's words, of everyday life.

Gail McDonald's observation that Pound's and Eliot's pedagogic impulses stem from the desire to have poetry recognized as a serious occupation which can offer "substantive contributions to the real world," might also be made about Williams.[3] The challenge to classical education by the growing authority given to science, technology, and business in the late nineteenth and early twentieth centuries shifted the emphasis of scholarship onto professionalism, efficiency, and utility. In such a climate, it is not surprising that poets sought to define and justify their discipline in terms comparable to other, verifiably productive professions. Pound, Eliot, and Williams, in different ways, promote the poet as an agent of culture building; in McDonald's words, they claim "to reform poetry so as to re-establish its authority and to re-authorize poetry so as to reform civilization."[4] The premium placed upon learning by Eliot and Pound is well known, but Williams's supposed anti-intellectualism has hampered a serious reading of his position on education and epistemology.

Williams, of course, did not receive a formal literary education, yet his participation in the growth in scientific and practical studies, which accompanied the expansion of higher education in America in the late nineteenth and early twentieth centuries, places him in a significant position from which to articulate a scientifically derived poetics. While Pound and Eliot sought to distance themselves from the emerging culture of professionalism by avoiding academic careers (even as they took on the terms of professionalism to bolster their positions as poets), Williams, as a medical student, was right at the heart of it. Burton Bledstein has described the values and goals that characterized the new research universities and science departments as "the testing ground for the kind of world an energetic middle-class sought to create for itself." Such a world was driven by "[c]areerism, competition, the standardization of rules and the organization of hierarchies, the obsession with expansion and growth, professionals seeking recognition and financial rewards for their efforts, administrators in the process of building empires."[5] This was the era of scientific management, with its emphasis on efficiency and planning, rationalization and time-motion studies, and Williams was within its orbit, F. W. Taylor receiving an honorary doctorate from the University of Pennsylvania the year Williams graduated from there.

Gerald Graff writes that the "new academic professional thought of himself as an 'investigator' devoted to advancing the frontiers of knowledge through research, and his loyalties went to his 'field' rather than to the classroom dedication that had made the older type of college teacher seem a mere schoolmaster."[6] The advocacy of scientific method as a standard of excellence stresses specialization and expertise, both in order to measure competence and to get results. Scientific method, of course, is central to Dewey's philosophy and his educational theory, but for Dewey science and its applications have little to do with establishing standards, narrow specialization, or a professionalism geared to career and market forces. Williams's support for scientific advance and innovation is also clear, yet in *The Embodiment of Knowledge* his bête noire, along with philosophy, is science. What is at issue for Williams, and for Dewey, is the definition of science and the consequences that the compartmentalization of knowledge into "fields" has for education. What Williams and Dewey seek to do is to redefine and reclaim science and scientific method as a means of achieving democratic change that can be applied to any area of inquiry and creativity. The use of such a method could transform, Williams and Dewey believe, how American culture is made, not to build careers but to shape everyday life. To understand Dewey's ideas on education and Williams's belief in poetry as a form of imaginative empiricism it will be useful to begin with Dewey's conception of science.

For Dewey, science is not a body of knowledge but a way of producing knowledge. Science is about taking no belief for granted: "Our attitude becomes scientific in the degree in which we look in both directions with respect to every judgement passed; first checking or testing its validity by reference to the possibility of making other and more certain judgements with which this one is bound up; secondly, fixing its meaning (or significance) by reference to its use in making other statements."[7] To think scientifically, for Dewey, is but a refined version of any procedure for establishing a belief, and like any reflective thought, proceeds through five steps: recognizing a felt difficulty or problem, locating and defining the difficulty, suggesting a possible solution, considering the proposed solution, and carrying out further observation and experiment in order to accept or reject the suggested solution.[8] The movement from problem to solution is inevitably influenced by context: "past experience, received dogmas, the stirring of self-interest, the arousing of passion, sheer mental laziness, a social environment steeped in biased traditions or animated by false expectations, and so on."[9] For a more precise solution to the problem at hand, such factors must be regulated, and this is the job of science. Science "does not depart from the factors employed in the reflective examination of any topic so far as introducing new operations is concerned, but only in supplying the conditions of increased control and care under which to carry on these operations."[10] Scientific method, then, is a way of approaching thinking, a method of reaching accurate conclusions, which produces freedom: "Genuine freedom . . . is intellectual; it rests in the trained *power of thought*, in ability to "turn things over," to look at matters deliberately, to judge whether the amount and kind of evidence requisite for decision is at hand, and if not, to tell where and how to seek such evidence."[11]

For democracy to benefit from science, the scientific method must be disseminated as a form of liberation. As a method it "has proved fruitful in any subject—that is what we mean when we call it scientific. It is not a peculiar development of thinking for highly specialized ends; it *is* thinking so far as thought has become conscious of its proper ends and of the equipment indispensable for success in their pursuit."[12] These "proper ends" imply a moral and ethical purpose to the application of scientific method. The "experimental notion of truth that reigns among the sciences, technically viewed," must be carried over "into political and moral practices, humanly viewed."[13] As a democrat, Dewey believes that ordinary men and women should understand and be able to apply scientific method to direct the affairs of society. This way of thinking and doing should not be mystified and cordoned off by a specialized elite into "fields": democracy is "an absurdity where faith in the individual as individual is impossible; and this faith is impossible when intelligence is regarded as a cosmic power, not an adjustment and application of individual tendencies. . . . To put the intellectual center of gravity in the objective cosmos outside of men's own experiments and tests, and then to invite the applications of individual intelligence to the determination of society is to invite chaos."[14]

The pedagogic impulse is often present in Williams's work, though it takes a form much less direct than, say, Pound's ABC's and How To books. Aside from *The Embodiment of Knowledge*, the volume of fragmentary notes Williams showed Kenneth Burke in 1932, (but which did not find a publisher until 1974), works such as *Kora in Hell, Spring and All*, and *In the American Grain* function partly as demonstrations, as practical exercises in liberating thinking. In *Kora in Hell* and *Spring and All*, Williams develops a kind of call and response narrative between presentation and interpretation, or between prose and poetry, the text doubling back on itself to call attention to, and to question, its form and function. The improvisations of *Kora in Hell* are accompanied by passages of "opaque commentary" (KH, 16) which are at once part of, yet also separate from, the "main" text, at once a parody of explicatory analysis and a demonstration of what insights "commentary" might be able to produce. The desire to understand and order information, confounded by the free play of the improvisational writing, pulls the reader to the commentary, the aid to "meaning", which turns out to be as oblique, despite a more considered tone, as the passage it follows. The awareness that there are (usually, but not always) two parts to each improvisation, nonetheless, transforms, through their relational proximity, the reading of each. Writer and critic inhabit the same textual space, the "commentary" feeding off the "primary" text, and feeding into it also.

In *Spring and All*, the cross-cutting of poetry and prose acts as a means of demonstrating what it is to write, to create form from fact, to make the "jump from prose to the process of imagination" (SA, 133). Prose is, according to Williams, a "statement of facts concerning emotions, intellectual states, data of all sorts—technical expositions, jargon, of all sorts—fictional and other," while poetry is "new form dealt with as a reality itself" (SA, 133). The very fact that *Spring and All* contains statements such as this suggests that Williams intends the reader to be taken through some sort of crash course in modernist poetics. The poems of the volume are visually striking when placed within a prose context, the white space around them exposing the "new form" that has been wrought from the "statement of facts." These are not illustrations of a theory so much as they are incarnations of a writing practice, the consolidation of a way of thinking and doing. As in the "text" and "commentary" of *Kora in Hell*, the reader must consider relationships between different modes of discourse not through reference to other, "primary," texts to which Williams's exposition is "secondary", but simply through the experience of reading *this* text, the text that is its own explication, *Spring and All*.

In the American Grain, likewise, has clear didactic ambitions. It is a reader in American history, a dissertation on the uses of history, a collection of scattered observations, a polemic, a satire, a statement of national identity. At the same time, it is none of these things absolutely. As we will see in the next chapter, this text, like *Kora in Hell* and *Spring and All,* confounds categorization, and the reader must periodically reconsider the claims being made by the text. The kind of history lesson offered by Williams's book is a lesson in the explosion of certainty, which, like his other genre-defying texts, is achieved not through the mechanisms of scholarly analysis and the establishment of truth claims but in the grain of the language itself and the destabilizing experience of reading.

So, if Williams is teaching, what is it his readers learn? For one thing, that "[t]he fixed categories into which life is divided must always hold . . . but not as dead dissections" (SA, 138). Poetry and prose, writing and criticism (and, in *The Embodiment of Knowledge,* other, wider categories of knowledge and experience), follow different logics and codes yet the existence of difference does not, for Williams, constitute a priori a hierarchy, so long as each is "energized by the imagination" (SA, 138). The criticism Williams is making is that fixing categories and collecting data has become an end in itself. The use to which this data might be put is not considered by its collectors: "There is proficiency in dissection and a knowledge of parts [,] but in the use of knowledge—" (SA, 139). Knowledge "is placed before a man as if it were a stair at the top of which a DEGREE is obtained which is superlative . . . nothing could be more ridiculous" (SA, 139).

To collect and classify without imagination is to work on the principle of simple accumulation, which privileges quantity over purpose; quantity is the purpose. The resulting store of information serves, for the store holder, as a source of power over those who have acquired less. This is power solely for the purpose of domination. "The inundation of the intelligence by masses of complicated fact is not knowledge" (SA, 139). A true education "would begin by placing in the mind of the student the nature of knowledge—in the dead state and the nature of the force which may energize it" (SA, 139). What is important for Williams is not so much what the material of knowledge is, but the process of knowing, the "nature of the force." Once this force is known and grasped, any material may be utilized. Like Dewey, for Williams education is about learning critical intelligence. The form of Williams's writing is the embodiment of the imaginative process and as such functions as the transmitter of intelligence. Williams's formal experiments, his textual conversations between presentation and interpretation, give space to contending ways of writing and thinking, coaxing out of the linguistic interplay of styles the "nature of the force," the imagination (a way of critical thinking, a form of action), which, Williams believes, once its effect "upon life" is realized, will effect "the emplacement of knowledge into a living current" (SA, 140).

It is the need to demonstrate the importance of education as a way of life, inseparable from the "living current" of the world of everyday things and feelings, that forms the argument of Williams's most sustained writing on education and (anti-) epistemology, *The Embodiment of Knowledge.* Williams, as we have seen, along with Dewey, attacks the idea of education as a form of processing students by feeding them information. This is not learning for Williams, and leads to the young "quite correctly" concluding "that a life of action outside of academic walls is preferable to continued purposeless amassing of data within" (EK, 3). The kind of education Williams believes in is one that teaches a way of being and knowing that draws the individual into the world in its complexity, not one that categorizes and separates information from experience, thinking from doing. "Specifically it is not the purpose of colleges just to teach the steps to a 'profession,' to make itself into a mechanical master to apprentices in rather cultured trades. Its purpose should be to lead the mind to heights of understanding" (EK, 4). The emphasis throughout *The Embodiment of Knowledge* is on clarity, on the need for a piercing of vagueness by a "light, a bolt even, through the chaotic murk of information" (EK, 4). This is the light of understanding, an active, illuminating force that might be shone upon any object.

ONE VAST CLASSROOM

The kind of scientific method Dewey believes in is the obverse of the rationalizing impulse engendered by business and management interests. Dewey's notion of science belongs to the broader reformist movement of the 1890s and early 1900s, well characterized by *The Dial's* credo of 1916 to "meet the challenge of the new time by reflecting and interpreting its spirit, a spirit freely experimental, skeptical of inherited values, ready to examine old dogmas and submit afresh its sanctions to the test of criticism."[15] Such a program yoked issues in education and literary study with broader social concerns. Take, for example, the issue of 11 April 1918, which offered Dewey's "Education and Social Direction" alongside Charles A. Beard's "University and Democracy," and Van Wyck Brooks's influential "On Creating a Usable Past." This was, in Richard Rorty's words, the "heroic period of Deweyan pragmatism" when the university was a "privileged sanctuary of attempts to reconstruct the American social order."[16] The kind of power Dewey's ideas had in inspiring a generation of young progressives is captured by Alfred Kazin in *On Native Grounds*. Dewey, writes Kazin, "created a moral hero for the times, the progressive teacher; he even proposed a heroic milieu, the new experimental classroom. . . . He so indoctrinated the principle of education and 'creative doing' that he became the leader of a group of minds who regarded themselves as teachers and Progressive America as their classroom. He imparted a new freshness, a sturdy and mature optimism, to the best spirits in contemporary society." With America as "one vast classroom," Dewey "rose to their leadership by projecting in every classroom a miniature society. He did more than give a new philosophy to education; he transformed the very concept of learning into a new and exciting principle of life," and "words like *school, experience, energy,* suddenly became revolutionary even by implication."[17]

The issue of education, of course, is central to any debate concerning the nature of democracy. Education can be interpreted as a means of enhancing the liberty of the citizenry and reducing class distinctions, or as a way of protecting against the excesses of popular rule and streaming citizens into roles appropriate to their abilities. What is at issue is the question of what can and cannot be expected of an educated citizen, a question that turns on the definitions of both democracy and of freedom. The rise to prominence of scientific and professional standards of assessment and value was met by the reform movement with a creative misreading of these standards. Dewey embraced the promise of science and efficiency, but the meaning he gave them bore little resemblance to the rationalizing tendencies of the growing management class. This kind of reconstruction of the dominant ideology to fit a progressive agenda enabled liberals such as Williams and Dewey to keep hold of the authority and forward-looking experimentalism of the sciences, while attempting to guide the insights of the scientific approach into other areas. Science, for Dewey, is a liberating force because it enables clarity of understanding and provides concrete evidence, which can overthrow unproven habit, prejudice, and outworn tradition. This kind of scientific testing means that, if applied to all areas of life, every experience becomes a learning experience, and every assessment a potential act of political emancipation. As Dewey sees it, it must be the job of social institutions, including schools, if these institutions are to fulfil their function as agents of democracy, to encourage this kind of thinking: "Government, business, art, religion, all social institutions have a meaning, a purpose. That purpose is to set free and to develop the capacities of human individuals without respect to race, class or economic status. And this is all one with saying that the test of their value is the extent to which they educate every individual into the full stature of his possibility."[18]

The interests of writers such as Williams and Pound and progressive educationalists such as Dewey converge in a shared vocabulary that unites experimentation and method in education and literature with social and political transformation. While Williams, certainly, did not always share Dewey's faith in the tractability of institutional forces, he did have an unshakable belief in the liberating power of art, which had its source in the individual's capacity to learn and change. He never doubted that this capacity could be awakened and encouraged by the knowledge art could embody. Ezra Pound may not have been much of a liberal, but Williams would have agreed with Pound's observation to one of his former school teachers in 1922 that "[i]t's all rubbish to pretend that art isn't didactic. . . . A revelation is always didactic."[19] What Williams, Pound, and Dewey all believe, albeit in differing forms, is that art and education should be socially useful and effective without becoming tools of the business system. It had to be clear that terms such as scientific method, accuracy, and efficiency meant free experimentation and clarity, rather than deterministic utility. The field of education became a crucial arena within which the fight against bureaucracy and the profit system took place. The university and school as primary agents of socialization are thus enormously vulnerable to pernicious interests. Pound is characteristically scathing of a university system "warped by the profit system, by a bureaucracy of education, the bureaucrat being a man who avoids 'dangerous' knowledge, who can almost indefinitely refrain from taking, officially, cognisance of anything whatsodamnever that is likely to disturb his immediate comfort or expose him to the least inconvenience or ridicule."[20] Less aggressive than Pound, but making the same point, Eliot writes that "more invidious than any censorship is the steady influence which operates silently in any mass society organized for profit, for the depression of standards of art and culture."[21] Apart from Eliot's concern with standards, it is unlikely that Williams would have much to disagree with here.

The growing interest in social control in America during the early years of the twentieth century fueled the growth of curriculum development in schools, "curriculists" such as Franklin Bobbitt and W.W. Charters being heavily influenced by scientific management, social measurement specialists, and the eugenics movement.[22] For such men, social control meant more than simply educating students in the forms of social organization and meaning necessary to community life; it was a means of closing down access to what Pound celebrated as "dangerous knowledge." As Michael W. Apple notes, "education in general, and the everyday meanings of the curriculum in schools in particular, were seen as the essential elements in the preservation of existing social privilege, interests, and knowledge, which were the prerogatives of one element of the population, maintained at the expense of less powerful groups."[23]

Maintaining this position depends upon establishing a normative standard from which to measure levels of social belonging. In the early years of the twentieth century, the means of assessment was governed by national consolidation and ideological acculturation (as opposed to assimilation). Marvin Lazerson's example of schools in urban Massachusetts is instructive. By 1915, he claims, two central themes had emerged. One, drawing upon the reform impulse of the decades between 1870 and 1900, "saw education as the basis for social amelioration. The school would reach out and uplift the poor, particularly through new techniques to teach traditional moral values." The second theme, increasingly prominent after 1900, "involved acceptance of the industrial order and a concern that schools mirror that order." The school's major function became the "fitting of the individual into the economy. By the teaching of specific skills and behavior patterns, schools would produce better and more efficient workers and citizens, and they would do this through a process of selection [testing], and guidance." These developments, Lazerson suggests, transformed the idea of equality of educational opportunity in America since "they made segregation—by curriculum, social class, projected vocational role—fundamental to the workings of the school."[24]

The standard appealed to is, unsurprisingly, middle-class, white Anglo-Saxon protestant, pre-industrial, pre-urban, small town America. In these terms, democracy and community mean homogeneity and like-mindedness, and these are the values men such as Bobbitt and Charters sought to bring to the heterogeneous, multicultural, multiethnic urban world of modern America: theirs is the myth of the melting pot. This is not to say that they were unaware of, or insensitive to, the problems thrown up by such a new situation. Indeed, it was the recognition of the need for the development of a sense of group identity and belonging that led Bobbitt to suggest that the job of the curriculum worker should be determined by the local community in which the school is situated.[25] Dewey would no doubt approve of this, but where Bobbitt departs from Dewey, and where his approach betrays a distinctly conservative agenda geared to the production of normative and cognitive consensus, is in the emphasis on the dissolution of individual difference within the group:

> How does one develop a genuine feeling of membership in a social group, whether large or small? There seems to be but one method and that is, *To think and feel and ACT with the group as part of it as it performs its activities and strives to attain its ends.* Individuals are fused into coherent small groups, discordant small groups are fused into the large internally-cooperating group, where they *act together* for common ends, with common vision, and with united judgment.[26]

While the rhetoric here is communitarian and democratic, the suggestion is that group consciousness can only be achieved by melting down individual interests, burning off impurities or "discordant" elements, to produce an undifferentiated, pure community. While Dewey also advocates a common subject matter as a means of creating social cohesion, he sees this as a way of enlarging the repertoire of possible experiences for each member, rather than a reduction to general consensus:

> The intermingling in the school of youth of different races, differing religions, and unlike custom creates for all a new and broader environment. Common subject matter accustoms all to a unity of outlook upon a broader horizon than is visible to the members of any group while it is isolated. . . . A society which is mobile and full of channels for the distribution of a change occurring anywhere, must see to it that its members are educated to personal initiative and adaptability. (DE, 88)

This kind of community is one of interaction, not of melting down, yet the hope of dissolving cultural differences through institutional influence persisted. The early American sociologist Edward A. Ross optimistically and yet, typically, with an air of dubious nostalgia, looked to education as a means of national consolidation: "To nationalize a multitudinous people calls for institutions to disseminate certain ideas and ideals. The Tsars relied on the blue-domed Orthodox church in every peasant village to Russify their heterogeneous subjects, while we Americans rely for unity on the 'little red school house.'"[27]

It is doubtful that Ross is thinking of immigrant or African American citizens when he uses the phrase "we Americans." His sense of what it means to be an American is already established, and based on the model of the nineteenth century rural town which, unlike many large cities, probably did once have a little red school house. The standard here is implicitly accepted as the natural state of Americanness, which must be protected. For Dewey, by contrast, the notion of a standard is inherently undemocratic, since it is a form of external authority that restricts individual liberty. Yet external authority there was, as the school system expanded and became increasingly bureaucratized. Preparing students for their place in a corporate industrial society took precedence over the kind of participatory ideal Dewey supported, and he came to realize that a democratic education amounted to little without a thoroughgoing transformation of society: "The concept of education as a social process and function has no definite meaning until we define the kind of society we have in mind" (DE, 103).

The radicalism of Dewey's program lies in the rejection of the kind of society he does not have in mind: a society based on divisions between mind and body, theory and practice, culture and utility; dualisms that serve to create and justify structural social divisions between working class and leisure class.[28] From this basis, two separate kinds of education arise: manual training and academic education. Dewey insists that such divisions are undemocratic and must be removed by a wholesale reconstruction of philosophy, education, and social ideas (DE, 341):

> The price that democratic societies will have to pay for their continuing health is the elimination of an oligarchy—the most exclusive and dangerous of all—that attempts to monopolize the benefits of intelligence and of the best methods for the profit of a few privileged ones, while practical labor, requiring less spiritual effort and less initiative remains the lot of the great majority. These distinctions will ultimately disappear the day that, under the influence of education, science and practical activity are joined together forever.[29]

In philosophy, Dewey argues that all knowledge is fundamentally practical—"thinking desire"—and in education, he calls for children to be given the tools of social intelligence. The adoption of these attitudes would do more, he contends, than "involve a superficial adaption of the existing system"; they would bring about "a radical change in foundation and aim: a revolution."[30]

Dewey's educational writings of the early years of the century, particularly his attack on the split between culture and utility, should be placed within the context of the debate over vocational education sparked by the report of the Massachusetts Commission of Industrial and Technical Education of 1906. The report revealed the lack of education and practical training for thousands of adolescents who had become alienated from the school system and found themselves in dead end jobs. The Commission called for a shift in secondary schools from "cultural" to vocational training. A massive campaign for such training followed, supported by the National Association of Manufacturers and the Chamber of Commerce, and resulted in 1917 in the Smiths-Hughes Act which gave federal support to vocational education. Disagreements arose, however, as to whether such an education should be integrated into the existing system or whether a dual system should be set up.

While businessmen came out strongly on the side of a dual system, Dewey opposed it, seeing it as undemocratic class discrimination. The split between theory and practice Dewey so often attacked was, by dual education advocates, promoted as so logical and commonsensical as to be virtually beyond debate. Consider the remarks of scientific management guru F. W. Taylor, in 1912, who confidently reported, "without the slightest hesitation," that "the man who is physically able to handle pig-iron and sufficiently phlegmatic and stupid to choose this for his occupation is rarely able to comprehend the science of handling pig-iron." Indeed, the man "who is fit to work at any particular trade is unable to understand the science of that trade without the kindly help and cooperation of men of a totally different kind of education."[31] While different physical and mental attributes are clearly needed for different forms of labor, the paternalistic arrogance of Taylor's position is equally obvious and troubling.

Dewey was by no means against industrial training, but he stressed that it must be approached democratically in order to be effective: "Its right development will do more to make public education truly democratic than any other agency now under consideration. Its wrong treatment will as surely accentuate all undemocratic tendencies in our present situation, by fostering and strengthening class divisions in school and out."[32] Undoubtedly, "those who believe in the continued existence of what they are pleased to call the 'lower classes' or the 'laboring classes' would naturally rejoice to have schools in which these 'classes' would be segregated. And some employers of labor would doubtless rejoice to have schools, supported by public taxation, supply them with additional food for their mills." Everyone else, however, "should be united against every proposition . . . to separate training of employees from training for citizenship, training of intelligence and character from training for narrow, industrial efficiency."[33] To those who claimed a dual system was more democratic for not forcing culture onto the unwilling, Dewey responded with scorn that "[n]othing in the history of education is more touching than to hear some successful leaders denounce as undemocratic the attempts to give all the children at public expense the fuller education which their own children enjoy as a matter of course."[34]

The vocational training issue brought out the social criticism implicit in Dewey's educational work, with Dewey attacking the "stupefying monotony" of industrial labor. He was unequivocal in his rejection of the present social order: "The kind of vocational training in which I am interested is not one which will adapt workers to the existing industrial regime; I am not sufficiently in love with the regime for that. . . . [T]he business of all who would not be educational timeservers is to resist every move in this direction, and to strive for a kind of vocational education which will first alter the existing industrial system and ultimately transform it."[35] While Dewey had always maintained that workers should have a sense of the significance of their work, the growth of scientific management in the 1890s made it plain that the chance for such self-realization through work would not be possible without workers' control of their labor. In *Democracy and Education* (1916), Dewey concludes that workers' "activity is not free because not freely participated in" and will not be free while the "animating motive is desire for private profit or personal power" (DE, 269, 327–328).

If society needs planning, who makes the plans? The familiar appeal to standards, voiced by curriculists and capitalists, requires, of course, some person, group, or class, to establish what these standards are and how they are to be upheld (or even enforced). Not surprisingly, it is usually those calling for the maintenance of standards who believe themselves to be in possession of the requisite qualities and values necessary to uphold them. The assumption is that there are those who "know better", and defenders of standards tend to be preoccupied with saving something, whether it be a moral principle, an institution, or a language, which is seemingly forever on the verge of collapse. As we have seen in relation to the curriculists, the appeal is often to a model past, a tradition, a fixed point of reference. For Williams and for Dewey, to use historical precedent as a yardstick with which to assess the present is to deny agency and to allow culture to atrophy. Dewey recognizes that "[l]iteratures produced in the past are, so far as men are now in possession of them and use of them, a part of the *present* environment of individuals; but there is an enormous difference between availing ourselves of them as *present* resources and taking them as standards and patterns in their retrospective character" (DE, 86). The tendency to fix history as precedent is not lost on Williams either—"Of course history is an attempt to make the past seem stable and of course it's all a lie" (KH, 41)—and in *In the American Grain* he deliberately works toward a dismantling of historical stability, overthrowing the precedence of received teleological national development in order to grasp the latent revolutionary valence of America's past. (This will be one of the concerns of the following chapter.)

To derive a standard from history, there must be a way to detach oneself from it in order to ascertain its dimensions; it must be other than the present. For Williams and Dewey, since history is a process we all inhabit, this is impossible; we can only engage with history as part of our environment. For Dewey, social control begins with learning to belong to the community and feeling a sense of duty and responsibility toward the group. Within such a situation standards are made and re-made through social interaction, not passed down by some external authority. One of Dewey's persistent critics, and well known "standard-bearer," Irving Babbitt, saw Dewey's emphasis on service as nothing but a "romantic myth" and contended that educators ought to "have less to say of service and more to say of culture and civilization."[36] For Babbitt, "No amount of devotion to society and its supposed interests can take the place of [the] inner observation of the spirit to standards," and the democratic principle of freedom of opportunity is "excellent" only "provided that everybody is to have a chance to measure up to high standards,"[37] If equal opportunity is used as a pretext for lowering standards, it is, says Babbitt, "incompatible with civilization."[38] Needless to say, Babbitt's definition of civilization is based on the classical model.

CURING THE FISH IN THE CLASS

The divorce of knowledge from experience and agency is a dominant preoccupation of both Williams's and Dewey's work, and this is nowhere more marked than in formal education. If it is not located in experience, education can easily become, as Williams claims, nothing but a "chaotic murk of information," which ritualizes rote learning and standardized procedures instead of encouraging experiential processes of learning. Williams uses as demonstration the case of his son Bill's French classes. After a year of living and attending school in France, young Bill, on returning to America, finds his grades falling. The teacher "does not know the language save from the classroom stand" (EK, 8), and does not recognize as legitimate the idiom the child has absorbed firsthand. Subsequently, "the child who has not memorized what the teacher has given him receives a bad mark in French," while another child, "who has the daily drill by heart is rewarded" (EK, 8). The other pupils "cleverly band together immediately after a class to compare notes and get by rote the things *that* teacher wants them to know and which they know she will ask in tests." (EK, 8). This cleverness is not intelligence, it is simply knowing the system, and the boy is "perfectly right" to have contempt for both teacher and pupils. In this Williams has located what is central to Dewey's criticism of conventional schooling: its separation of knowing and doing. In schools, Dewey argues, pupils are too often little more than "theoretical spectators." Indeed, "The very word pupil has almost come to mean one who is engaged not in having fruitful experiences but in absorbing knowledge directly." Instead of cultivating the "intimate union of activity and undergoing its consequences," a process that "leads to recognition of meaning," we have "two fragments: mere bodily action on one side, and meaning directly grasped by 'spiritual' activity on the other" (DE, 140–141).

The situation Williams and Dewey both describe is presented by Robert Scholes as a parable "and perhaps a parody" of all schoolrooms. What the student really learns in class, suggests Scholes, "is to give the teacher what he wants. He seems to be reporting about a real and solid world in a perfectly transparent language, but actually he is learning how to produce a specific kind of discourse, controlled by a particular scientific paradigm, which requires him to be constituted as the subject of that discourse in a particular way and to speak through that discourse of a world made visible by the same controlling paradigm."[39] As a parable, this scenario is certainly a warning against unreflective pedagogy. Yet is it a parody of what actually goes on in schoolroom situations or an argument that all schoolrooms are parodies of educational environments? It is not clear here whether Scholes is dismissing schoolrooms per se or merely the misuses to which education can be put. Both Williams and Dewey are rightly skeptical of education as a form of social control, yet they hold out great hope for the reconstruction of schoolrooms and for the transformative power of what could go on within them.

Scholes is writing in the context of a discussion of Pound's anecdote, in *ABC of Reading,* of Agassiz and the fish. "No man," argues Pound, "is equipped for modern thinking until he has understood" this anecdote, which concerns the professor's insistence that a student describe a fish as his final task in an examination. The student proceeds to present a description "as found in textbooks of the subject," but Agassiz is unimpressed. After producing a four-page essay, Agassiz is still unsatisfied and tells the student to "look at the fish." After three weeks, Pound says, "the fish was in an advanced state of decomposition, but the student knew something about it."[40] Pound's point is obviously that knowledge is acquired through close empirical observation of the thing, a key imagist principle that Williams would undoubtedly endorse. Scholes suggest that, as portrayed by Pound, what the student actually learns is, how to "speak and write Agassizese," how to "produce the sort of writing his teacher wants."[41] While it may be true that this is the effect of any teaching situation, this seems too reductive a conclusion, since it assumes that what the student actually sees will be what Agassiz expects and demands the student to see. Surely the point of empirical observation is that there can be no guarantee in advance of what information the observation will yield. Scholes's reading strikes, possibly unintentionally, a cautionary note, for what he produces from Pound's story of the fish is itself a "specific kind of discourse" guided by its own controlling paradigm.

Yet there is something more to be learned from all of this. While Pound's advocacy of the extension of the methods of biological science into literary study greatly appealed to Williams, with his medical training in precision and objectivity, what is lacking in Pound's account is the agency of the observer. The student writes but does not touch. Williams, who had learned firsthand the procedural methods of medical science, knew that observation should be followed by action. Indeed, at the time Williams was receiving his training, participatory demonstrations or case studies in the hospital were replacing rote learning. As in Pound's example, firsthand observation was the key to medical practice, yet as Abraham Flexner observed in *Medical Education in the United States and Canada* (1910), "The student no longer merely watches, listens, memorizes; he *does*." Observed facts "suggest a line of action"; between "theory and practice" the "mind flies like a shuttle."[42] Wiliam Osler, who brought the new methods to the University of Pennsylvania thirteen years before Williams studied there, claimed that doctors should have "a powerful vision for the minutiae of life," but a vision achieved by being "kitchen and backstair men . . . who know the subject in hand in all possible relationships."[43] What Williams gained in practice is the dimension of Pound's anecdote which he (Pound) forgets to point out: a fish left dead for three weeks is of little use to anyone. The spur to action and engagement Williams learned through medicine colors his notion of education and the purpose of knowledge. For Williams, writing, like medicine, embodies the simultaniety of observation and action, just as the cognitive process of reading likewise should be considered an active, imaginative experience. And like medicine, writing and reading transform, engage, move into the world to produce change, not to view from sterilized, controlled environments. Williams's medical and writing practice are those of a "kitchen and backstairs" man, as the discussion of *A Novelette* in the previous chapter makes clear. The kind of training he attacks as indoctrination stifles individual initiative, and as any doctor knows, failure to act on initiative can be fatal.

Education as socialization, rather than as training in critical intelligence, is the bane of any theory that runs contrary to the status quo, since the administration of such a theory cannot be successful until the institutional and social framework is reconstructed to contain it. Dewey began his work in education believing that the transformation of how the young are taught would lead to the transformation of society. By the 1930s he had come to see that without major political and economic change progressive education would have at best a limited impact. Nonetheless, education as a potentially radical force remained a decisive element in Dewey's vision of a democratic community, a belief in the possibility of local change, at the level of the individual or the school, as a crucial beginning for progressive transformation.

Williams reads the fragmentation of experience into knowing and doing as an infringement of liberty, which leads to the germination of a revolutionary spirit of the individual against authority. This he describes as a characteristic of the "American *position* of the intelligence—the pioneer turn of mind." The individual rejects the system and places him or herself outside the jurisdiction of a corrupting authority: "Youth is right when it attacks those who would lead it and have lost the direction" (EK, 8). The alert child, the one who sees with clarity the futility of the processing that passes for education, must fight a guerrilla war to maintain his or her individuality, circumventing "the harm by use of his own mind" by "double-crossing the teacher from within."

Education in America becomes, on these terms, a battle against curricula designed to indoctrinate class divisions and create an aristocracy of learned, otherworldly scholars. The American "*position*" should be "indirect" and "outside of 'learning'" (EK, 9); that is, not about the stockpiling of information, but an education which is felt and experienced by the individual intellectually, emotionally, and physically. The failure of the American school, and of American culture generally, is that it continues to use the methods formed by the "European medieval aspiration toward a peak, aristocratic striving" (EK, 9). American education must be transformed (the need for change being viewed from within by Williams's subversive pupils) so that it gels with the political goals of American democracy, "towards a useful body of knowledge made to serve the individual who is *primary*" (EK, 9).

Simply because the individual (the pupil) struggles for his or her freedom does not mean that Williams, any more than Dewey, is necessarily advocating a "child-centered" education. The "battle of wits between alert child and the sluggards who have captured him in the name of learning when he was too young to protect himself" (EK, 5) is a "pity," a failure of leadership, not evidence that leadership in itself is bad. The dissatisfaction felt by the child at school is a measure of the fact that the young look for good leadership, "the most desirable thing youth should expect out of its elders" (EK, 4). The fact that it is "almost a sign of intelligence when a boy looks at his high school work with an ironical indifference," is a state of mind "that is dangerous and should not be accepted as final. It is also a burden which children should not be expected to carry unassisted" (EK, 5). Williams looks to the young for the spirit of change and renewal, but places responsibility with the social institutions of democracy, in this case the schools and colleges, which must be "newer, firmer, more inclusive, more flexible—or not at all—for new minds" (EK, 3). The "old purpose must be replaced by a more resourceful, a more liberal, a more fertile breadth of purpose" (EK, 4). This involves a symbiotic relationship between the institution and the individual which will break down the rigid system that splits education into the oppositions of the curriculum and the child. Williams sees "God" as the deposed figurehead of a failed teleological system that structures education from point zero, along a developmental continuum to the completion at the "peak," the attainment of something called knowledge, or secularized God-substitutes such as Science and Philosophy. The "scientific-philosophic mistake was in placing a mythical end to research at some remote future—toward which striving was inaugurated—comparable to a very identical 'heaven' of mystical understanding, or the heaven of the stars presuming the unknown to be a fact" (EK, 50).

Science and philosophy, as colonized fields of knowledge owned by experts, "come between men and men, men and women" (EK, 26). They keep "life from its impacts" (EK, 27), and causing "[j]ealousy. Hatred of each other. Defeat. To hedge life. To hold it in bounds. Guard your wife. Guard your money. Learn, but do not touch." (EK, 27). Such a fog has "gradually come to be more and more [a] subtle film catching us all" until "DEMOCRACY—has come, which is a thin, scientifically, philosophically perfect film, we can just see through enough" (EK, 27). Democracy here seems to be the culmination of the process of obscurity, an all-encompassing ideology that is so pervasive as to seem natural. It is "[f]lexible as collodian, as invisible as an electric sheet. Tough, universal—a magic lining between men everywhere and their desire. Even into the laws. That is why money is desired more than ever. To buy off. And they do not even know that it exists" (EK, 27). Democracy as Williams describes it here is not a relation or process but a thing that lays heavily over society. This is democracy used to regulate and control, to ensure that "[c]ourage is being managed so that it leads not where it will hit" (EK, 27). The way of thinking that makes science and philosophy into Science and Philosophy also makes democracy into DEMOCRACY, a rigid structure that encloses experience within its limits. However, as Williams admits, it is possible to "just see through" the "perfect film," the possibility of clarity opening up space for change, for the "unscummed impact of the sense and mind" (EK, 26). The apparent seamlessness of ideology might, in fact, admit the opportunity for subversive and transformational activity in the form of individual human agency. To realize that such opportunities exist is to see beyond the sheen of system and alienation and to get to real "understanding": "Because the knife is polished they think it's sharp" (EK, 27).

Science and Philosophy, then, present themselves as knowledge, just as Democracy presents itself as freedom. This is the "inhuman phase" of knowledge

(EK, 41), which reifies thinking, presenting education in terms of a dualism of inner and outer: the scholar or professor and the student, the specialist and the layperson, the refined and the vulgar. The notion that knowledge can lie behind "the bounds of the understanding," in some ideal location accessible only to the priestly few, means that "it does not exist for us, much less for our imagination" (EK, 42). To place the attainment of knowledge within the bounds of the understanding, to place it in the world, in context, "precedes all further progress. To conceive clearly the materials of our thought" (EK, 42). The difficulty in achieving this is immense for the nonspecialist and unqualified, however, and here Williams exposes the problem of access to a forum of debate that is blocked by the intimidation felt by the outsider wishing to speak on a subject dominated by expertise. Without the correct language, the danger is silence—"Conversation has come to be impossible save among specialists in a certain pen, between the lists no language reaches" (EK, 46)—yet Williams enables himself to speak by overturning the hierarchy and revealing the scholar as a minority interest:

> So far, all serious discussions of knowledge have been from the viewpoint or view of scholarship. And at once I am in difficulty. For how can I know this to be so? I have neither the time, money, nor the ability—perhaps—to spend in an exhaustive search to make such a statement authoritative. I might be Shakespeare for all the help I could give.
>
> Thus there is nothing to do, it seems, but accept the unproven statements as of equal weight with those of a life spent in research—or to acknowledge that there can never be a worthwhile discussion of knowledge save from the scholar's eminence—where he is so far above the vulgus that by his very scholarship he himself has become a curious species. (EK, 43)

The key phrase here is "of equal weight," Williams balancing specialist knowledge with life experience, and judging that while the latter might be "unproven" in terms of the dominant paradigm, when looked at from an alternative viewpoint, that of the "vulgus," authority may be as "curious" and alien as the "outside world" may seem to the specialist. Narrowness of focus, Williams concludes, excludes "everything in the wide realm of life," and "in the process a view of life, the embodied or actual view, is lost" (EK, 43). Far from taking an anti-intellectual viewpoint, however, Williams is calling for a democracy of knowledge, a recognition of difference without hierarchy. "We can't do without proof. We can't do without knowledge. What then? We have to acknowledge first besides degrees and conditions of scholarship, that there is a division between those who know (some certain thing) and those who do not know it. We have to acknowledge then, that the scholar, not being ignorant, has not the knowledge which the ignorant man possesses. All that the wise man knows is colored by his wisdom. And all that the ignorant man knows is colored by his ignorance. Both are parts of the whole" (EK, 44).

Education, if it is to succeed in a democracy, must work for everyone. This involves the recognition of knowledge as a part of the life process of each citizen and of the commonwealth. "We must advance a proof," says Williams, that scholarship has "perhaps slighted," and that is that "in every man there is a certain knowledge which by his life he proves, wise or fool. He has in his own way proven it. An example of it being that the ignorant man finds the scholar's knowledge often disembodied. As the scholar finds himself, by his own knowledge, inhumanly cut off from his kind" (EK, 44). Scholarship can only hold its conclusions as valid when proven "upon humanity" (EK, 44).

To reach a position where there can be "conversation or communication between farmers and engineers," a language must be spoken that is understood by all. "Strange to say I have found a very general language," Williams declares, a language that makes the "wider knowledge" accessible to "men in general" and the basis upon which all separations are united: "Together, meanwhile, on equal grounds we have art" (EK, 45–46). Aesthetic knowledge "has power to envision—it has to do with time—and the test of time, with color, diverse forms, contact of the senses—with style, invention—the creations of genius and of animals and flowers" (EK, 44). Art, then, is an understanding of experience, a form of knowledge that is inhabited and lived and which can be universally accessible. It is also, importantly, a means of communication, and therefore of culture building and identity formation. It is "[a] very simple, easily worded abstract design: a clarity as gracefully put as I am able of putting it with respect to the meaning" (EK, 46). It is "[a] steady development of what I understand . . . as well as I am able to think, and pretend no more," a process: "Then another design and so on to others to embody America and myself in it" (EK, 46–47).

Education, then, is a process of becoming that transforms the self as the self works outwardly to transform the environment. The teleological world view of a school system based "on the principle of a confused mass striving for the unseen summit of a topless cone," does nothing but "perpetuate confusion and despair," because it is focused on an end that can never be reached (EK, 50). Williams's contextualism favors a reorientation of learning that emphasizes the importance of means over ends, a union of knowing and doing characterized in the acquisition of craft skills: "In the apprentice system knowledge was a means, not an end—and it was consequently humane, logically based on a clarity as the culmination of understanding. . . . [A] pride in a craft is logically sound" (EK, 50–51). Williams's stress on process here is distinctly Deweyen: "[L]ife is development, [and] developing, growing is life. Translated into its educational equivalents, that means (i) that the educational process has no end beyond itself; it is its own end; and that (ii) the educational process is one of continual reorganizing, reconstruction, transforming" (DE, 49–50).

Knowledge is not, writes Williams, "at the end of the deduction but in each phase of it and everywhere" (EK, 71). This relational and interactive field is well demonstrated, he goes on, in poetry, which is the use of words with "all the contours best defined." Poetry is Williams's example because "it is a field which I know," and, "since education is accomplished almost entirely by the use of words[,] . . . knowledge started with the 'word,' it might do far worse than to go right back to the beginning—with the addition of the cleansing of the 'word,'which is the work poets have in hand" (EK, 6). A writer, like any craftsperson, learns in the making; there is no foreseeable result until the work is done: "[H]e writes and the best of him, in spite even of his thought, will appear on the page even to his surprise, unrecognized or even sometimes against his will, by proper use of words" (EK, 7). What exactly is this proper use of words? The proper use is to see words *as* words, as real things and not as symbols for "ideas, facts, movements which they may under other circumstances be asked to signify" (EK, 17). This knowledge of the materiality of language is "the knowledge that the others mirror," the others being philosophy, science, and history (EK, 72). "All other presentation uses writing to speak about something else. . . . But poetry is all of a piece, knowledge presented in the form of pure writing which is made of the writing itself" (EK, 72–73).

Williams's attack on the conception of language as separate from the objects it names, and his call for the "proper use of words," indicates his belief in the potential for social transformation through a reconstruction of what words are taken to mean. If education is about empowering, and education is also about words— communication—then to focus on the making of words is the first step toward lifting the blanket of alienation—"cleansing the word"—and encouraging the community-building practice of conversation. The "proper use of words" is to unite thinking and doing as praxis. Paulo Freire offers a perspective that both Williams and Dewey would endorse when he argues that "[t]here is no true word that is not at the same time a praxis. Thus, to speak a true word is to transform the world. . . . An inauthentic word, one which is unable to transform reality, results when dichotomy is imposed upon its constitutive elements [i.e., reflection and action]."[44] The act of speaking a true word is a democratic and communal act, since it "is not the privilege of some few men, but the right of every man. Consequently, no one can say a true word alone."[45] Words are thus dependent on their context, and each person's words are dependent on every other person. For true words to be spoken in a dialogue, equality is essential because "dialogue cannot occur between those who want to name the world and those who do not wish the naming—between those who deny other men the right to speak their word and those whose right to speak has been denied them."[46] Whether Williams or Dewey are writing about art, education, or science, their purpose is the same: to liberate or open up channels of communication they perceive to be closed down by forces of incorporation. These forces — institutions of culture that seek to maintain a museum conception of art, business interests that prefer a pacified and inarticulate workforce, national interests fearful of an uncontrollable and impure multicultural society—are at root antidemocratic and potentially totalitarian in their tendency to divide and conquer that which should be be brought together. An education that functions to integrate ideas and practices, which challenges precedent rather than following it, and that constructs new meanings rather than conforms to established ones, must begin with the generation of dialogue as a process of creation. Such a dialogue, as Freire argues, "cannot be reduced to the act of one person's 'depositing' ideas in another, nor can it become a simple exchange of ideas to be 'consumed' by the discussants."[47]

Dialogue requires contact. Williams was far less convinced of the school's ability to break down conventional patterns of thinking than Dewey, despite his continued interest in education. For Williams it is the primary impact of the text that offers the surest means of contact, an embodied demonstration of linguistic agency unmediated by institutional structures, however benign they might appear to be. While Dewey sought to pierce the traditional educational process by introducing experimental pedagogic methods into the classroom, Williams's emphasis on the richness of the local environment, with the text as part of that environment, perhaps more properly describes his own notion of the space in which learning takes place. For Williams, America really was one vast classroom.

FOUR

Tactus Eruditus

a reply with the bare hands

Let Facts be submitted to a candid world.
— The Declaration of Independence.

What Dewey calls consummatory experience Williams describes as contact. The extent to which contact can be made becomes a measure of the value of art, and of the limitations of America as the site for creative activity. Making contact, for Williams, is an act of ontological affirmation and also of social responsibility inasmuch as successful contact transforms the world as it transforms the self. It is, or should be, according to Williams, a way of making changes, of initiating a growth of understanding through improved communication. Contact is immanent, active and transactional, a giving and receiving of stimuli that pulls the world into the self as the self extends outward, a version of Emerson's search for an "original relation to the universe." In *Nature,* Emerson suggests that "In proportion to the energy of his thought and will, [every rational creature] takes up the world into himself,"[1] and there is more than an echo of this sentiment in *Spring and All:* "The inevitable flux of the seeing eye toward measuring itself by the world it inhabits can only result in himself crushing humiliation unless the individual raise to some approximate co-extension with the universe" *(sic)* (SA, 105).

This sort of Romantic communion of the self with the universe is not easily achieved, however, because of what Dewey calls "resistance" from other forces which may be "indifferent and even hostile to life" (AE, 20). Encountering resistance prevents contact, and to overcome the "prohibitions" Williams must take them on and break them down. Achieving contact becomes a negotiation of all the forces around him, calling for a thoroughgoing critique of contemporary American life. Indeed, the need for contact is so strong in Williams because of the very absence of such engagement in American culture as he sees it. The idea of contact develops into much more than an aesthetic ideal; it evolves, through the magazine *Contact* (co-edited with Robert McAlmon), *Spring and All*, and *In the American Grain*, into a theoretical critical framework that we might call the political economy of contact, concerned with problems of individualism, capitalism, American identity and historical development, and their relation and relevance to aesthetic production.

Williams's critique of American culture develops within the context of a wider reevaluation of American identity taking place in the years following World War I. The war had thrown America into world affairs and demonstrated the extent of the nation's global influence. America emerged from the war as the wealthiest nation in the world, and with a recognition of this strength came a heightened self-consciousness and self-scrutiny. For many intellectuals, the recognition of economic prowess as the major defining characteristic of modern American life was seen as deeply threatening, thwarting the development of a culture commensurate to the nation's new world position and reducing the promise of the New World to an arena for exploitation, misplaced self-confidence, and reactionary know-nothingism. Critics saw America as culturally immature and economically musclebound, the nation's potential diminished by an adolescent lack of coherence and direction. America had, perhaps, come of age with the war, but adulthood is more than physical strength, and the disjunction between cultural and commercial authority was read by many as a sign of an impending crisis of purpose.

The form this cultural criticism took was substantially shaped by the critics and writers centered around the *Seven Arts* magazine, founded in 1916 and including James Oppenheim, Waldo Frank, Randolph Bourne, Van Wyck Brooks, Paul Rosenfeld, Louis Untermeyer, and Sherwood Anderson. The magazine's motto, "An Expression of Artists for the Community," might also have served for Williams and for Dewey, since both men, like the *Seven Arts* group, were concerned with the development of a shared culture derived from local conditions and integrated into the fabric of communal life. They all recognized the necessity of creative work as a form of community building. Often couched in modish Freudian terminology, the energies of the nation were seen to have been severely repressed, engendering a neurotic sensibility. The critic is thus engaged in a process of liberation through therapeutic analysis, freeing the "true nature" of America from its domination by a petrified superego, often characterized as Puritanism and/or as the business interests. The successful release of energy is considered a triumph of youth—of springtime, in Williams's lexicon—and of primitive impulses, corresponding in social terms with the growth of interest in Native American and African American cultures, especially jazz, and the cult of youth during the 1920s, with its slackening of attitudes toward sex, in particular, and accepted codes of conduct in general. Liberals such as Williams and Dewey saw the pressing need for such impulses to be guided and encouraged toward a healthy democratic maturity. As we have already seen, their concern with aesthetic and educational issues is bound up with the serious business of generating an

American culture from local materials, a culture that is capable of transforming the youthful energy of the nation into new forms of democratic life.

BLOUAUGH!

Spring and All, In the American Grain, and the five issues of *Contact,* map out Williams's poetics and politics of contact. These works are determinedly individualistic, Williams seeking to fulfill the promise of American democratic freedom within the framing limitations of a highly regulated modern capitalist economy. The drive for creative freedom—freedom from an imported European gentility and from a mass culture of consumption—is a political struggle, Williams's romanticism informed by a belief in free yet responsible citizenship, the conditions for the existence of which he considers are yet to be realized. Modernity's erosion of individual autonomy is, for Williams, a denial of diversity and difference in favor of a leveling homogeneity. The struggle for creative freedom is also a struggle for civic freedom, and Williams's attempt to articulate his liberation from corrupting habits and traditions is a declaration of independence, a re-enactment of the revolutionary origins of the nation itself.

The covers of the first two issues of *Contact* spell out what is lacking and what is needed in American culture, the epiphanic force of actual contact graphically stated by the word's large typeface, which swells out of the sentences, otherwise adrift with ellipses, solidifying thought into the form of that one word, the concept actualized in the magazine:

> . . . . art may be the supreme hypocrisy of an
> information-cultured people . . . . without
> ## Contact
> . . . . . justifiable perhaps if it becomes at last actually
> the way sensitive people live . . . .
> (Issue 1, December 1920).

The second issue (June 1921) continues the theme, emphasizing the need for "place" in a "loose world":

> . . . . adrift, finding a place in abstraction sensually
> realized through
> ## Contact
> with his loose world . . . . a vast discharge of energy
> forced by the impact of experience into form.

Art without contact is nothing but hypocrisy, merely "the beauty parlor of civilization," as Dewey remarks (AE, 346). These two statements are, in fact, full of

Deweyan resonances, no doubt in part due to Robert McAlmon's interest in Dewey's articles for *New Republic* and the *Dial,* which he and Williams had been following through 1920 and 1921 and which had influenced his own pieces for the boys' aviation magazine *The Ace*.[2] Most striking, perhaps, is the notion of an energy discharge honed into form by the impact of experience. What Williams and McAlmon are calling contact is clearly what Dewey would call *an* experience, stressing the creative combustion possible in the interaction between lived experience and location. The fusion of self and environment achieved in successful contact means that personal identity folds into national identity, the individual and his or her surroundings becoming forces within a single field of action. Dewey's article in the *Dial* of June 1920, entitled "Americanism and Localism," became an important touchstone in Williams's concern with contact and locality, and he adopted Dewey's phrase "the locality is the only universal,"[3] reprinting it without explanation in the second issue of *Contact,* along with a related remark by Maurice Vlaminck also culled from the *Dial:* "Intelligence is international, stupidity is national, art is local."[4]

Dewey's essay is a response to James Oppenheim's "Poetry—Our First National Art," from the February 1920 issue of the *Dial.* For Oppenheim, national identity can be discovered through literary form: in Russia, prose fiction, in Germany and England, the poetic play, in Greece, Rome, and Italy, the epic. The very name, the United States, claims Oppenheim, "reveals our dilemma in art," because America "is not a nation in the Old World sense," being not an "organic fusion" but a "collection in which the differences are more marked than the likenesses." However, Oppenheim believes that America is "finding herself through a rather loosened-up lyric poetry." This is so because in the lyric, according to Oppenheim, the unconscious of the poet is directly revealed, free from the surface uniformity of American life yet strained "through the sieve of the American environment, the American ideals, manners, scenery, and chaos, [so that] he gets a product which is universal on the one hand but on the other with what might be called the American flavor."[5] The American novel, by contrast, never rises beyond the "depiction of manners to a revealing of character."

In "Americanism and Localism," Dewey reverses Oppenheim's statement, claiming that in America there is a wealth of individual characters but no manners, because "manners are a product of the interaction of characters and social environment, a social environment of which the background, the tradition, the descent of forces, is a part" (AL, 687). To understand the American scene, it is pointless, Dewey continues, to take "all the localities . . . and extract their greatest common divisor" because the result will be nothing but "a crackling surface. The bigger and more diversified the country, the thinner the net product" (AL, 687). Dewey agrees that America is a collection of diverse units, but stresses the need to resist the drive toward some kind of abstract uniformity of identity. Instead, difference should be celebrated, the richness of local life in all its idiosyncrasies being the bedrock of what it means to be American. Dewey differentiates between the country, a spread of localities, and the nation, which is "something that exists in Washington and other seats of government" (AL, 684). Thus, Dewey considers the local newspaper to be "the only genuinely popular form of literature" America has achieved, while magazines such as the *Saturday Evening Post*, in trying to be national, speak of nowhere.[6]

There is a contradiction even within the local press, however, between the interests of the local and the desire for national standardization and uniformity. The same papers that "fairly shriek with localisms devote a discrete amount of space to the activities of various Americanization agencies" (AL, 684). Dewey thinks that those who are attacked as refusing or unable to be Americanized are perhaps more typically American than those who would eradicate difference, because the former are more concerned with their immediate situation, "their tenement house, their alley, their factory, their street," than with abstract notions of nationhood. Being American, for Dewey, is simply about being in America and working with it, about making an identity rather than measuring assimilation against an absolute standard. In a passage that no doubt appealed to Williams, Dewey observes that "Americanization consists in learning a language strangely known as English. But perhaps they [immigrants] are too busy making the American language to devote much time to studying the English" (AL, 684). Language is a primary force in identity formation and community building for Williams also, American words gathering meaning as they are turned in the soil of usage. For Williams, American was by no means English in any accepted sense, and had to be recognized as a distinctly new invention if the American language was to be the carrier of a new culture.

The first edition of H. L. Mencken's study *The American Language* was published a year before Dewey's *Dial* article, its popularity soon leading to second (1921) and third (1923) editions. The 1920s, in fact, proved to be a period of massive growth of interest in the character of the American language, with the establishment of the Linguistic Society of America, of *American Speech*, the *International Journal of American Linguistics,* and the publication of the *Dictionary of American English,* Leonard Bloomfield's *Language,* and George Philip Krapp's *The English Language in America.* This was also notably a period which, across the Atlantic, saw the publication of the Newbolt Report and George Samson's *English for the English* (both in 1921) which called for the need to defend standard English in England against the encroachment of regional dialects and class variations.[7] The need to maintain standards in England contrasts sharply with the celebration of diversity in Mencken's book, (although, of course, calls for standardization were far from limited to England), suggestive perhaps of the shift of power and confidence from England to America in the post-war years.

Mencken continued to gather fresh material throughout the 1920s and 1930s, and a radically reorganized and expanded fourth edition appeared in 1936. Williams reviewed the book for the *North American Review,* and while he is disappointed that the exuberance of the earlier editions has been lost in favor of a more scholarly tone, it is still "to me one of the most fascinating books in the world . . . bred to the bone of the country itself, nurtured from its plains and streams" (SE, 172-173). The ongoing nature of Mencken's project emphasizes the view of American as a language in a state of flux, continually being added to and transformed by new social and ethnic groups. Mencken claims that the American "likes to make his language as he goes along,"[8] just as Dewey had said that Americans are busy "making" their language. Williams, too, reminds us that "a man makes a poem, makes it, mind you" (SE, 257). This stress on making recognizes language as plastic and contextually derived, that there is no standard, no mother tongue. Mencken lists literally thousands of etymological and phonetic transformations in all aspects of language handled by Americans, words and even proper names shaped by and for the environment, manipulated and renewed as new situations emerge.

Despite the growing body of work proclaiming the emergence of a distinctive American culture, Williams found the ground hard and the free flow of interactive experience restricted at every turn by forces that denied contact and threatened to undermine cultural independence. "There is a constant barrier between the reader and his consciousness of immediate contact with the world," he complains in *Spring and All* (SA, 88). Because of this barrier, "the reader never knows and never dares to know . . . what he is at the exact moment that he is" (SA, 89). To initiate contact, everything that stands between the artist and his or her direct experience of the world must be swept aside. As Williams and McAlmon explain in *Contact* 1: "Our only insistances [sic] are upon standards which reality as the artist senses it creates, in contradistinction to standards of social, moral and scholastic value -hangovers from past generations no better equipped to ascertain value than we are." They will be American simply "because we are of America; racial or international as the contactual realizations of those whose work we publish have been these." Nationality is seen as fact of location, not a code of behavior and style. Indeed, Williams makes sure to point out at the end of *Contact* 1 that there is to be no privileging of American writing: "[N]o one need expect us to publish his things simply because they happen to have been written in the United States." The point of contact is to recognize the inseparability of creativity and locality: "[C]ontact with experience is essential to good writing or, let us say, literature. We have said this in the conviction that contact always implies a local definition of effort with a consequent taking on of certain colors from the locality by the experience."[9]

The emphasis made by Williams, and by Mencken and Dewey, on language as it is actually used and informed by local conditions, can be seen as a direct challenge to the genteel "Amerenglish" encouraged, according to Malcolm Cowley, at Ivy League colleges at the time. "If we tried," says Cowley, "to write about more immediate subjects, we were forced to use a language not properly our own. A definite effort was being made to destroy all trace of local idiom or pronunciation and have us speak 'correctly'.[10] Bearing in mind Dewey's distinction between country and nation and his attack on agencies of Americanization, the rejection of a uniform language becomes a tactic for evading the homogenizing process of national consolidation and bureaucratic rationalization. Language, as a means of exchange that accrues value, and therefore power, to the extent that it is acquired by different social groups in different forms and in different quantities—certain groups, such as scholars, politicians, and other officials, having "more" language than others—will need the notion of a standard if this power is to be maintained.[11]

As national consolidation moves toward a single, unified language, regional differences can become marginalized and their exchange value reduced. The establishment of a standard, the resources of that standard deposited in the dictionary, creates a nationwide currency enabling efficient transactions. But like a bank, the dictionary can only authorize withdrawals to those with an account—that is, those who already belong to the bank as customers. Once language is recognized as a verifiable system that contains specific rules for usage and grammar, it can act as a way of blocking access to those who either do not or cannot belong to its system. Standard language becomes worth more than nonstandard idioms and words attain different values in the exchange system. Cowley's "Amerenglish," as an elite standard, obtains power as a form of status and through the exclusion of difference. For Williams, the power of money and the power of an exclusivist culture work together to shrink the field of reference to within their own boundaries. Along with a copying of Europe, he writes, came "a snobbism from which or from the effects of which very few escaped. The secondary split-off from what, but for fear, had been a single impetus, finally focused itself as personal wealth in America, important since it is wealth that controls the mobility of a nation. But dangerous since by its control it can isolate and so render real values, in effect, impotent" (SE, 146).

As aspirational standards, the English language and the money wage served as the major media of Americanization for immigrants, and effective ways of ensuring a modicum of social cohesion. Yet both standards are reductive, and make alternative modes of communication and transaction redundant. As Stuart and Elizabeth Ewen have suggested, the abstract and symbolic system of money was necessary to life, yet it "seemingly operated by an autonomous and lifeless physics" which "rendered much of the way in which non-industrial peoples understood themselves, and the reproduction of their daily lives, useless." As a widely disseminated mass medium, the money system "ripped the structure of people's *needs* from their customary roots, and by necessity transplanted their needs in a soil nourished by the 'rationality' of corporate industry and the retail marketplace."[12]

Every fresh wave of immigrants stretched the capacity of America as a nation to maintain what it considered its distinctive identity as well as the authority of its institutions. Many saw immigrants as a threat to the basic principles of the nation, bringing with them radical politics and lax moral standards. The Yale social scientist Edgar Furniss, in his book *Labor Problems* (1925), voiced a common anxiety when he urged that "Americanization is the paramount need, not only for the immigrant, but for the very existence of the Republic. Unless the millions of immigrants present and future are made an integral part of the population, understanding our institutions, sharing the standards and ideals of the democracy, the Nation itself is imperiled."[13] Twenty years earlier, speaking to the graduating class of 1905 at Bryn Mawr College, Henry James had berated the "unprecedented" and "uncontrolled assault" on the English language by "the American Dutchman and Dago, as the voice of the people describes them."[14] "The forces of looseness are in possession of the field" (J, 47), argues James, and a standard is needed to restore coherence and order: "a common language, with its modes of employment, its usage, its authority, its beauty," would lead to the authority of a "coherent culture" (J, 6), embodying "our admirable English tradition" (J, 20).

James's standard of usage, authority, and beauty is precisely the sort of linguistic capital that Williams was so suspicious of, a form of capital that produces, in Pierre Bourdieu's words, a "profit of distinction" in relation to those without equal funds. "Speakers lacking the legitimate competence," Bourdieu suggests, "are *de facto* excluded from the social domains in which this competence is required, or are condemned to silence."[15] When Dewey, Mencken, and Williams (who grew up in a predominantly Spanish speaking household perforated with French and English) heard the making of the American language, James heard only noise: "the grimaces, the shouts, shrieks and yells, ranging over the whole gamut of ugliness, irrelevance, dissonance, of a mighty maniac who has broken loose and is running amuck through the spheres alike of sense and sound" (J, 43). This is the "Blouaugh!" of Williams's sea elephant, which has "Trundled from / the strangeness of the sea," this bellowing, exotic, primal creature with a ravenous appetite which those of "practical voice" may gawk at for entertainment but would prefer that "They / [. . .] put it back where / it came from" (CP1, 341–343).

Williams's relentless call for the recognition of the American idiom, the "Blouaugh!" of the improvised tongue, "which is heard from the lips of those to whom we are talking in our day's affairs" and "mingles with what we see in the streets and everywhere about us as it mingles also with our imaginations" (KH, 59), challenges the centralization and standardization of everyday life. The kind of culture-as-containment being built by advocates of Americanization is not culture at all if its role is to restrict communication and sever community ties. The words *common, community,* and *communication* are related around the same root word, *munis,* meaning a gift exchanged. Imposing abstract standards of value on language and other goods to obtain profits of distinction and material gain undermines the free exchange that fosters the growth of community and communication: the common good. This kind of culture is one of separation and removal, a refusal to engage with the world as it is, "to be blind or deaf," as Williams says of those who will not tune their imaginations to "the language of the day" (KH, 59). A pecuniary culture recognizes only status, and bears little relation to the idea of culture as human practice, as the "tending of natural growth."[16] It is something to be possessed rather than inhabited, an object rather than a process: "America has sought to surround itself with the appurtenances of a finished culture which is of no direct significance in the new sphere. But by this emphasis such a culture of purchase, a culture in effigy, has become predominant" (SE, 147). A culture that is "finished," closed, bought, and used as a standard for value judgments prohibits, renders "impotent" culture as cultivation (the original etymological and historical meaning of culture): an active, procreative process of engagement and growth, the "real values." By "real," Williams is looking for a substance for value, an organic and physical presence of actual activity, of contact. He is after a prelapsarian, predualistic state where culture and nature, words and things, individuals and society, interact and evolve together; that is, grow. It is a desire to go back in order to go forward. This is what *In the American Grain* sets out to do, to plough (Fr. *cultiver*) the soil of a native American culture, an act of education and fertilization. Before Williams can do this, however, before his transactional economy of contact can work, the standards of America's alienated, reified pecuniary economy must be exposed and exploded. The barrier between the citizen and his or her consciousness of immediate contact must be lifted.

How, exactly, does Williams propose that contact can be achieved? Rather enigmatically, his short answer is through the imagination. The long answer, carried through the pages of *Spring and All,* is less easily figured, and as Williams reaches out to commune with modern America, he finds that the power of an entrenched business culture endangers his freedom. To make contact is to risk engulfment.

SPRING IS ICUMMEN IN

Many of the poems in *Spring and All* deal with the complexities of modernity, with the city and its battered inhabitants, the challenge to traditional values posed by mass spectacles such as baseball and the movies, and new cultural phenomena such as the automobile, all shadowed by the regulating and abstracting fact of money. In these urban poems, Williams's belief in contact is put under great pressure and often thwarted, his individualism dented by, for example, the latent aggression felt at the ball game, where the crowd could at any time turn into a mob. Faced with the often overwhelming power and pervasiveness of a mass culture fueled by the interests of capital, Williams's desire for contact becomes nostalgic, his prowess as a poet seeking the more conventional pastoral solace of communion enjoyed by "the farmer and the fisherman who read their own lives" in the sky (SA, 100), retreating from the city crowd "with the closeness and / universality of sand" (SA, 128). Contact with modernity threatens engulfment in the mass and Williams struggles to control his material against odds severely weighted against him. The poems become a battle for the preservation of individual autonomy in the face of modernity's tendency to reduce individuality to commodified surfaces of managed information.

In poem VII ("At the Faucet of June"), a meditation on the solid presence of objects infused with summer sunlight is interrupted by "J.P.M." leaping "from among / the steel rocks" (SA, 109). J. P. Morgan is a usurper with "extraordinary privileges / among virginity," corrupting the fertile American cultural soil with imported European art, paid for with money made at home selling products that speak more for America—"about / the finest on / the market today"—than any number of Veronese or Rubens. J. P. Morgan Jr., as representative of modern America,—the "son / leaving off the g"—breaks into the song of June, disrupts the song "of sunlight and grass." The effect is "Impossible / to say, impossible / to underestimate." The power of business cannot be held by the poem, it cannot be articulated or controlled, only felt as a disruption. Nonetheless, it cannot be ignored either. This is the challenge of Williams's poetics of contact: he must negotiate in his writing the dialectic of creative control and domination by reality in all its dangerous forms. He must get to the point where he can "break through to the fifty words / necessary" (SA, 99), take control of the language and, through the language, his position in the world.

This movement between control and its loss is played out in poem IX ("Young Love" [SA, 113–115]) through a scenario with a "Miss Margaret Jarvis" (a nurse Williams knew as an intern at Child's Hospital). The attraction is there: "Once / anything might have happened," but it did not. The poet is close but distant: "I was your nightgown / I watched!" In the prose following the poem, Williams writes that "I think often of my earlier work and what it has cost me not to have been clear." As the poem wonders at one point, "what to want?" To achieve the experience of contact is to know, to be clear, or as Williams writes, clean: "Clean is he alone / after whom stream / the broken pieces of the city— / flying apart at his approaches" (SA, 115). This is the kind of creative control the poet seeks, where the world follows the path of the poet, breaking up and reassembling according to his design. But reality is resistant and hungry, and there is always the danger of losing control and being swallowed: "in my life the furniture eats me." Contact is never a meeting of equals; it is a struggle between unequal forces. Williams wants to be in the world, but not made indistinguishable by its inclusiveness. He wants to keep the edges on things, not to erase differences. The self is in and of the world, but must be distinguished from everything else in the world. Williams's democratic individualism is about the poet working to hold off the threat of the subsumation of each unique object and person into an undifferentiated mass, yet wishing to bind these things and people together in a mutually respectful form: the poem, composition, or community; that is, the environment, or field of action within which discrete elements combine and interact.

The threat posed to individual autonomy is most clearly stated in two poems concerned with mass entertainment: poems XV and XXVI ("Light Becomes Darkness" and "At the Ball Game"). In poem XV (SA, 127–128), the movies are seen as the modern substitute for religion, manipulating the emotions and jumbling perception, translating woe into joy, changing light into darkness, darkness into light. Movies divert attention from the actuality of things and situations by "simply rotating the object"—that is, the referent and the film itself—"cleaving away the root of / disaster which it / seems to foster . . ." (SA, 128). Film is seen as homogenizing perception and meaning, just as religion once abstracted morality into Law. The crowds, with the "universality of sand," witness secular "passion plays." They are a "dynamic mob," devoid of individuality. This is not solidarity, the crowd does not cohere into shared purpose; it is simply a cluster of particles defined only by proximity. Thus, the possible nobility of the Russian peasant woman on screen goes unnoticed—there is no class consciousness, no possibility of identification. The kind of peasant traditions Williams bemoans the lack of in the poem "To Elsie" do not inhere in the consciousness of the people, but are reified as flickering images on the screen. This is not contact but withdrawal.

In poem XXVI (SA, 147–149, doubts about the possibility of a truly democratic culture come to the fore again. "In detail" the crowd is "beautiful," that is, individually. But as a mass "It is alive, venomous / it smiles grimly / its words cut . . . / It is the Inquisition, the / Revolution." The game is enjoyed "all to no end / save beauty," but the beauty is directionless, imbued with "a spirit of uselessness" that, worryingly, "delights them." Beauty resides in the individuals, but it lives "day by day in them / idly"; they laugh "in detail" but are "without thought." Like the movies, organized sport reduces participation to little more than passive spectatorship, the potentiality of the watching self severed from any tangible engagement with events. Williams's fear of the mob, of citizens stripped of individuality and agency, is clearly linked in these poems with the emergence of mass culture. As manifestations of the burgeoning entertainment industries, the generation of spectacle for profit represents for Williams the insidious leveling tendency inherent in a democracy becoming corporate. Indeed, as far as Williams can see, the logical outcome of such an incorporated democracy is its conversion into terror.

The ballpark and the movie house were recent phenomena and both served well as means of assimilating immigrants into urban American life. While the initial popularity of baseball was due to its informality, the emergence of professional teams and leagues meant that by the 1880s the game had become big business. Professional baseball, converting impromptu recreation into an exhibition of expertise within defined limits, demonstrated the efficacy of following rules and channelling the drive for success into an ordered, regulated frame.[17] Baseball, like the movies, is a social leveler at the point of consumption, but solidly hierarchical at the point of production. Movie stars and ballplayers are cultural signifiers of an aspirational society, yet access to that sphere of participation is minimal, leaving the majority as onlookers, presented with largely unattainable goals. This is Dewey's "spectator theory of knowledge," and what Williams means by lack of contact, or divorce.

Williams's most scathing indictment of modern America in *Spring and All* is poem XVIII ("To Elsie" [SA, 131–133]). This poem encompasses his concern with the value of the local, the undermining of this value by the prohibition of any firm connection with the land and with community caused by the gospel of wealth, and the desolate yet often paradoxically beautiful results thrown up by the violence of this prohibition. The poem is a descent from the general to the particular, from the nation to the individual, gathering strength as it moves down from its state-of-the-nation address ("The pure products of America / go crazy"), past region-wide differences ("mountain folk from Kentucky / or the ribbed north end of / Jersey), and through the population of dispossessed "deaf-mutes, thieves" and promiscuous "devil-may-care men," until it reaches perhaps the most vulnerable group of all, the young, rootless working women whose lives are fraught with the continuous threat of exploitation. They have "no / peasant traditions to give them / character,"

> but flutter and flaunt

> sheer rags—succumbing without
> emotion
> save numbed terror
> under some hedge of choke-cherry
> or viburnum—
> which they cannot express [. . .]

Here, the brutality of a life structured only by the necessity of menial labor, and consoled merely by a kind of dime store glamor, contains a logic which is equivalent to, and also results in, the helpless surrender of rape. Like the rampant J. P. Morgan leaping from behind the steel rocks, the power of those sanctioned by a culture of rugged individualism to take to "railroading / out of sheer lust of adventure" has the effect of silencing opposition—"Impossible / to say, impossible / to underestimate"—for those like Elsie, nothing but "numbed terror . . . which they cannot express." Williams's response as a poet and as a citizen is limited at best. There is the consolation that one of these girls may be rescued by the state and employed by a suburban professional—Dr. Williams himself, in the case of Elsie—but other than this, all the poet can do is idealize the girl with an awkwardness similar to his ambivalent portrayal of Ma Duncan in *The Great American Novel*. Elsie is the genuine article, with even "a dash of Indian blood," so she can conform to Williams's model of blood contact. She brings home, literally, to Williams, "the truth about us" when, perhaps, he would prefer a more pastoral mood, with the imagination straining "after deer / going by fields of goldenrod." He has taken on the burden of Elsie in his life and in his poem, as one who must assume some sort of control, to witness, to adjust, and even to drive the car of American civic responsibility. "To Elsie" poses difficult questions, because the system that saves her is the same system that created her and almost destroyed her. And what good is contact, the "dash of Indian blood," to Elsie and the thousands like her? By taking in the girl, Williams saves the destruction of one life, but can this nostalgia for "peasant traditions" and local communities do more than provide temporary succor for the urban liberal? The portentousness of the poem's last line begs a response which Williams attempts to provide in other poems in the series.

VRUMMMMMMMMMMMMM

By the early 1920s, the automobile was perhaps the most obvious symbol of America's modernity. The car represented, at the same time, the slackening of community ties in favor of individual freedom, and also the extent of America's corporate power and wealth.[18] The question Williams leaves us with at the end of "To Elsie" is an urgent one: who will take responsibility for the effects of modern life? If contact is dangerous, it is also necessary if the energy created by modern capitalism is not to swell to such proportions that it cannot be controlled. The constellation of issues centered around the trope of auto-transportation in poems XI ("The Right of Way" [SA, 119–20]) and XXV ("Rapid Transit" [SA, 146–47]) pulls Williams back and forth between celebration and despair, contact and divorce. Each poem is a negotiation of opportunity and danger, and as in "To Elsie," Williams is snared by an economy of values that provides and then withdraws from contact, offers a vocabulary only to restrict usage.

What made the car such a massive force for change in America was the way that design and manufacture appealed to so many of the bedrock ideals shared by most Americans, even if the finished product did serve to explode those ideals by the force of its impact. Low priced, mass produced, and designed for the average driver, the American car was lighter, more powerful, more capable of withstanding rough use and easier to repair than European models. It also sat higher on the road in order to negotiate the undeveloped American roads. As a rough working description of how Williams saw his own poetry, this is quite an accurate analogy: built for the territory, no extraneous features, a deceptive simplicity achieved through precision design.[19]

Williams, of course, was fond of the machine analogy, claiming that "[a] poem is a small (or large) machine made of words . . . there can be no part, as in a machine, that is redundant . . . Prose may carry a load of ill-defined matter like a ship. But poetry is the machine that drives it, pruned to a perfect economy. As in all machines its movement is intrinsic, undulant, a physical more than a literary character" (SE, 256). This passage reads as a response to the challenge to the validity of art in an age of mass production, an assurance that poetry can be functional, efficient, and charged with energy. Dewey was to point out in 1929 that if America "is to achieve and manifest a characteristic culture, it must develop, not on top of an industrial and political substructure, but out of our material civilization itself. It will come by turning a machine age into a significantly new habit of mind and sentiment, or it will not come at all" (ION, 100). "Can a material, industrial civilization," Dewey asks, "be converted into a distinctive agency for liberating the minds and refining the emotions of all who take part in it?" (ION, 100). Judging by Williams's notion of the poem as machine, it would seem that his reply to Dewey's question would be in the affirmative. It is not so simple, however, for Williams's advocacy of the small community, its independence and its contact with the soil of its own locality conflicts with his fascination with the transformative power of technology. It is the machine, after all, that breaks down community life: "More and more alone as time goes on, shut off from each other in spite of facile means of communication, we shrink within ourselves the more, the more the others strike against our privacy" (SE, 232).

The car, as a literary device, provides space for writing—"I am alone only when I am in the car"—enabling the writer to slip the ties of place even as he inscribes his movements within that space as he drives. Driving and writing become versions of the same activity, the formal demands of the former embedding themselves into the shape of the latter. Movement accelerates and brakes, often unexpectedly; perception turns corners, vision becomes obscured and then clears, things appear and are gone. There is no time for "ill-defined matter" in a poem written on the road, and the coordination of mind and body demanded of the driver is necessarily "intrinsic, undulant, a physical more than a literary character." This kind of organic union of physical and linguistic action does seem to answer to Williams's description of the poem as machine. It does not, however, resolve the larger question of the effects of the control of technology by a business elite. Is the freedom that Williams enjoys while driving a kind of micro-freedom within a larger network of control? Does driving, in other words, provide an illusion of freedom which itself serves to maintain a broader fixity? [20]

"To drive the streets at all seasons is . . . my delight," writes Williams in his autobiography, "alone in my car, though it is only to return home at the end of an hour. It is not unexciting, either. It is a formal game" (A, 307). Here, the field of action is boundaried by the limits of an actual time and space—the distance he can travel from home and still return within an hour. The form of the drive is transactionally derived from local conditions—the road system, the necessity of returning home. Returning home is the point of closure, the acknowledgment of limits, of responsibility. The freedom experienced while driving is not achieved by lighting out for some unstructured territory; rather, it is a freedom to play with the shape of limitation, to find new combinations within the local scene. As Williams observes elsewhere, "We live in one place at a time but far from being bound by it, only through it do we recognize our freedom."[21] The kind of existential freedom Williams is referring to here does not, of course, extend to freedom from ideological and political conditions. We have already seen that Williams saw the power of wealth and privilege as a force that restricts freedom of movement, so how free is free? The formal permutations of the roads excite Williams, but he always returns home, just as Thoreau admits that "[o]ur expeditions are but tours, and come round again at evening to the old hearthside from which we set out." This kind of domestic restriction, with its acceptance of limitations, undercuts for Thoreau the liberation offered by the journey, which should be undertaken "in the spirit of undying adventure, never to return."[22]

If the local area is the field of action, the structure of which home is the center and the radiating roads are the patterns of possibility, the prospect of mobility is always determined by a more basic fixity.[23] Williams as avant-garde writer is always grounded by Williams the suburban professional. Driving is a way of drifting between the two roles, a form of temporary escape from definition. Williams is always passing through.

Henry Ford's dream of universal individual mobility was itself realized on the basis of a fundamental immobility. The introduction of the assembly line necessitated, in Ford's words, "the reduction of the necessity for thought on the part of the worker and the reduction of his movements to a minimum."[24] Materials were delivered to the worker at a waist-high level so that "wasted motion" was not expended in walking, reaching, stooping, or bending. Skills, qualifications, and initiative were unnecessary for factory work, dissolving the American ideal of social mobility—all jobs were the same, there was no ladder to climb—and the Protestant Ethic of meaningful work. Freedom is shifted to the realm of leisure and consumption, and driving, by the 1920s, had become the paradigmatic form of leisure, or escapist, activity.

In "The Right of Way," the car forms and frames perception, which is further regulated by the rules and direction of the road. The poem is not critical of these restrictions, however, and celebrates the liberation of aimless driving enjoyed "by / virtue of the law." With the car, the individual is enfranchised to inhabit the modern world of speed. The freedom of the road becomes analogous to the freedom of the imagination, where quotidian reality is charged with energy to become of "supreme importance," and where necessity is overruled in favor of experimentation—"Why bother where I went?" Driving, as a semiautomatic activity, empties the mind of everyday tensions, enabling the driver to "pass with my mind / on nothing in the world" except the sense of freedom itself. The people passed along the roadside appear and disappear; only details are noticed. Movement removes time for careful study, allowing only for immediate perception. The broken lines sequence information; only one thing is seen at a time—a house, a woman, a man, a child, a watchchain. These are glimpses from a moving vehicle—a car or a poem—and the meaning resides in the movement itself rather than in the particularity of the images. They just happen to be what is in the frame at that moment : "[I]t is a nameless spectacle." We might say, as Roland Barthes observed of the Citröen, that the poem "excites interest less by its substance than by the junction of components."[25]

The kind of freedom achieved in "The Right of Way" is basically passive—the generated speed has its own intrinsic logic, which leaves the driver "spinning on the / four wheels of my car / along the wet road." The only contact promised by this poem is the possibility of a collision. Williams's excursions may be a modernized form of Thoreauvian "sauntering," but the sense of freedom is reduced to the extent that the path is externally managed by the vested interests of the companies providing the facilities being used. From the road you can only see what is by the roadside.[26] The impetus behind road development in America derived less from a general demand for access to, in Ford's words, "God's great open spaces," than from a coalition of private pressure groups, including oil companies, tire manufacturers, and land developers lobbying for new streets. Roads were built out of public money obtained through taxation at the request of private interests. The street changed from an open communal space to a danger zone serving as an artery for motor vehicles. Recreation moved off the street and into the car, as carefully landscaped automobile-only parkways sprang up around the outskirts of cities, providing a scenic but distanced view for day trippers as the road guided them toward purpose-built leisure centers.[27]

It was not absolutely necessary to have a car to enjoy the "open country" of Pelham Bay Park, mentioned in Williams's "Rapid Transit." With the advent of roads such as Robert Moses's Northern and Southern Parkways out of New York City, however, personal transport was essential since the underpasses were purposely built too low for buses to clear.[28] As the environment becomes increasingly managed by corporate interests, the idea of personal freedom must negotiate a progressively restrictive dialectic between movement and fixity. Is such freedom as the automotive industry offers an enabler of individual autonomy or a more congested version of the rugged capitalist's freedom of opportunity? Certainly, Henry Ford could speak of the individual freedom provided by his cars while restricting freedom in the factory. Williams can enjoy his own private freedom of the road while obeying the restrictions of the law and his public responsibilities. As a political question concerning the nature of democracy, the language of individualism suggests how an ideologically overdetermined discourse can restrict at the level of actual social administration while continuing to function as a code for freedom at the level of popular understanding. This is most apparent in the advertising language and "axioms" used in "Rapid Transit," a poem much less at ease with the contradictions of a mass transportation culture than "The Right of Way."

Tocqueville believed that language inevitably degenerated in a democracy, because "the majority lays down the law in language as well as in other respects." Since the majority is more preoccupied with business, politics, and commerce than with philosophical speculation or literary pursuits, it is not surprising that "Most of the words coined or adopted for its use will . . . bear the mark of these habits; they will mainly serve to express the wants of business, the passions of party, or the details of the public administration."[29] Tocqueville's sentiment is not dissimilar to James's: without a standard, language will sink into the gutter of base preoccupations. Williams is as opposed to the tyranny of the majority as Tocqueville or James, but he understands that an aristocracy of letters is no solution, since any hierarchical system is based on an imbalance of power, and to use language as a force of domination is no different than using any other form of wealth.

Williams told John Thirlwall in the 1950s that in "Rapid Transit" he was "studying a presentation of the language as it is actually used" (CP1, 505). In the poem, we find that such a language does mainly express the wants of business and the details of the public administration. It is rudimentary information, reducing the complexity of human life and death to empty statistics—"someone dies every four minutes / in New York State"—and banal axioms such as "Do not get killed." This is the language of advertising which translates the "open country" into a commodified leisure park. If this is the language "as it is actually used" in a democracy, what is the democratic poet to do except to repeat it? As the challenging voice says, what the hell does the poet know about it, what can the poet offer that does not undermine democracy by constructing a privileged "poetic language"? Here, Williams may benefit from another aspect of democratic language criticized by Tocqueville:

> The most common expedient employed by democratic nations to make an innovation in language consists in giving an unwanted meaning to an expression already in use. This method is very simple, prompt, and convenient; no learning is required to use it correctly and ignorance itself rather facilitates the practice; but that practice is most dangerous to the language. When a democratic people double the meaning of a word in this way, they sometimes render the meaning which it retains as ambiguous as that which it acquires.[30]

The absence in a democratic culture of a fixed social structure maintaining consistent values means that language can slip the ties that bind words to things and be appropriated freely by anyone for his or her own purposes. For Williams it is this very unsettled quality that allows him to splice the language "as it is actually used" into a poem and to make it say things it is not expected to say, achieving an uneasiness through chafing the worldliness of the word against the skin of the aesthetic.

Williams follows the axioms of the road safety campaign with one of his own. It is disruptive and confusing in contrast to the linear and repetitive "Careful Crossing Campaign / Cross Crossings Cautiously." There is no correct way to read Williams's axiom: "HORSES / PRANCED / black & white"; or perhaps "HORSES black & PRANCED white"? These are only possibilities; we must register the words as things on the page, as physical shapes, not necessarily as information. The alliteration of the road safety slogans might suggest a smooth flow, a logic, a neat progression of the line, but the *C*s collide too quickly into a linguistic pileup. Williams's axiom is more of a field than a road, the words finding their own place, as unpredictable as horses. The open form of the phrase seems to hint at a nostalgia for a kind of "natural" freedom no longer possible. This is borne out by three lines from an earlier version of the poem and later cut by Williams, where the horses are followed by an exasperated voice which asks: "What's the use of sweating over / this sort of thing, Carl; here / it is all set up—" (CPI, 505).

The rest of the poem is taken over by the language of advertising, a mode that supposedly tells things as they are—language and landscape as commodities. It is indeed all set up; all the poet can do is place the words in a poetic environment for ironic effect. By taking language "as it is actually used," has Williams appropriated it or has he in fact become restrained by it, forced to merely repeat its message?[31]

Williams can claim found language for his poems because he believes in the artist as seer, empowered by his creative prowess to transform the mundane into objects of aesthetic beauty. The artist "uses the banal to escape the banal" (SE, 236). The problem here is that this assumes that the artist can somehow neutralize, or scrub clean, as Williams would put it, the ideological conditions of language. He does believe in limits—for example, his constant dismissal of the notion of free verse—but he thinks that these limits must be made by the individual in interaction with the environment, linguistic or otherwise. This position takes for granted that the artist can somehow step outside ideology, brush off by force of the imagination unwanted meanings from words and make something that runs off its own steam. The appeal of the machine analogy for Williams lies in the belief that science is method rather than doctrine and uninformed by the corruptions of business, that it gives birth to technological innovations which can also be kept clean. Of course, a machine does function by its own intrinsic logic, but the use to which it is put is always geared to some extrinsic end. The problems Williams faces in *Spring and All,* in attempting to sieve through modernity and use its resources, contorts his drive for contact into a battle against restricting and reductive forces, resulting at times in a tactical withdrawal from the chaos of the big picture to a contemplation of units small enough to retain coherence and definition: the local, the individual person, thing or word. Having brushed with the present and struggled with the extent of its otherness, Williams descends, in *In the American Grain*, into the past to locate an original ground upon which to rebuild a contactual relationship with America.

THE GIFT

In the article "Yours, O Youth," from *Contact* 3, Williams attacks those American writers who have gone to Europe to find a cultural sophistication not available at home. This, for Williams, is an abdication of responsibility, which ignores the immediate in favor of the very traditions that are stifling the growth of an indigenous culture: by running off "to London and Paris . . . they have forgotten or not known that the experience of native local contacts, which they have taken with them, is the only thing that can give that differentiated quality of presentation to their work . . . " (SE, 35). The culture that expatriates seek will only materialize when the artists themselves provide it by working with their localities. In "Americanism and Localism," Dewey wrote that "we have been too anxious to get away from home. . . . When we explore our neighborhood, its forces and not just its character and color, we shall find what we sought" (AL, 668). Williams is unequivocal on this point: "It has been by paying naked attention first to the thing itself that American plumbing, American shoes, American bridges, index systems, locomotives, printing presses, city buildings, farm implements and a thousand other things have become notable in the world." American artists must learn to "have the inventive intelligence of our engineers and cobblers" (SE, 35).

Robert McAlmon's commitment to a specifically American writing grounded in an American locality waned after he left for Europe in December 1921.[32] In *Contact* 4, he writes that "the contact is first with topnotch comprehension rather than with locality or race or mere environment" (*Contact 4,* 16). The locale may have become irrelevant for McAlmon, the force of individual "genius" being of primary importance, but for Williams this genius was itself integrally bound up with a sense of place. Despite his advocacy of individual freedom, Williams could not separate this freedom from the demands of the environment which provided it. This becomes the main theme of *In the American Grain*, where Williams insists that "there is a source in America for everything we do" (IAG, 109). At other times, however, Williams sounds more like McAlmon, as in the 1915 essay "Vortex" where he writes, "I will express my emotions in the appearances . . . of the place in which I happen to be [but] . . . I will not make an effort to leave that place for I deny that I am dependent on any place" (RI, 58). Williams needs the environment to sustain the artist, yet he also wants to be free from the necessity of that sustenance. He wants to avoid environmental determinism in favor of autonomous individual freedom while continuing to stress the crucial role of locality. This relationship between individuality and the demands of place is perhaps not as oppositional as it first appears. It is possible to be shaped by environment without relinquishing freedom of choice, so long as the power of environmental forces are recognized, respected, and engaged with rather than submitted to. When the local scene is acknowledged as crucial—Dewey believes that "sympathy will come as soon as we stay at home for a while"—the artist will choose it as the site for creative action (AL, 668). To perceive the self as an extension of the world is not to relinquish the autonomy of the individual, but to increase the scope of what it means to be individual. Individuality becomes the site for social and artistic responsibility rather than self-centeredness and self-delusion.

In *Spring and All*, Williams attempted to remove, or at least come to terms with, modern "prohibitions" preventing contact. By the time of *In the American Grain* he had decided to search for the very roots of such "blockages," the initial fracturing of unity between self and place. To get to the American soil the ground must be cleared. In the later essay "Against the Weather" (1939), Williams detailed the process he began with *In the American Grain:* "If, as writers, we are stuck somewhere, along with others, we must go back to the place, if we can, where a blockage may have occurred. We must go back in established writing, as far as necessary, searching out the elements that occur there. We must go to the bottom" (SE, 202). This involves the "obligation" of unraveling "archaic forms" that might give "past writing" a "false cast." "We have to dig. For by repeating an early misconception it gains acceptance and may be found running through many, or even all, later work. It has to be rooted out at the site of its first occurrence."(SE, 202)

Although, in some respects, *In the American Grain* conforms with and contributes to the prevailing trend in American cultural criticism during the early part of the century in reading American history through a Freudian framework of repression and liberation, posing the Puritan as the heavy-handed superego against the "naturalness" of the Indian as id, Williams's book is also an excellent example of that favored form of Puritan address, the jeremiad.[33] In many ways, *In the American Grain* shares the same ambitions as a book such as Cotton Mather's *Magnalia Christi Americana:* it is a state-of-the-covenant address. Like earlier jeremiads, it sets out precedents for desired behavior through a roll call of exemplary figures, saints or heroes; it details the falling from grace of the community, and seeks to transform the present through its invocation of the past. In a passage situated right at the center of the book, Williams's exhortation is clearly directed to the nation, developing from accusation to challenge and then to warning. He insists that Americans must learn from the past, must reclaim their history by beginning at the root and building up from the base. As exemplary text, *In the American Grain* demonstrates a process of culture building in a future-oriented project of national rejuvenation, grounded in a working knowledge of the past:

> Americans have lost the sense, being made up as we are, that what we are has its origin in what *the nation* in the past has been; that there is a source in AMER-ICA for everything we think or do; . . . we have no conception at all of what is meant by moral, since we recognize no ground our own—and that this rudeness rests all upon the unstudied character of our beginnings; and that if we will not pay heed to our own affairs, we are nothing but an unconscious porkyard and oilhole for those, more able, who will fasten themselves upon us. (IAG, 109)

Understanding history is essential for survival; indeed, "aesthetically, morally we are deformed unless we read" (IAG, 109).

The failure of Americans to recognize any ground as their own is bound up with an adherence to categories of experience and history that derive from elsewhere. In Dewey's powerful position paper of 1917, "The Need for A Recovery of Philosophy," he argues that philosophy has become a scholastic discipline that "magnifies the history of past thought" and forces subject matter into "received systems,"[34] effectively shutting down any possiblility of philosophy becoming engaged with the world outside its own disciplinary parameters. Just as Williams warns that without understanding that the source of thought and action is contextually derived—American—there can be no conception of the moral that makes any sense locally, Dewey is equally concerned that slavish following of imported precedents will cramp and distort America's democratic project. This certainly does not mean ignoring the past—"Imaginative recovery of the bygone is indispensable to sucessful invasion of the future"—but the status of that recovery should be, as it is for Williams in *In the American Grain*, "that of an instrument." To isolate the past, "dwelling upon it for its own sake and giving it the eulogistic name of knowledge, is to substitute the reminiscence of old-age for effective knowledge."[35]

The purpose of philosophy for Dewey is to be instrumental in bringing "to consciousness America's own needs and its own implicit principle of successful action."[36] This is a broad and open-ended conception of philosophy not as a scholarly discipline but as a form of applied intelligence. Williams, likewise, sees no division between history and writing, between past and present. It is the action of the present writer upon the materials of the past that energizes those materials and gives them future-oriented valency. The source of what is meant by moral is in "AMERICA" itself, in the history of its peoples. Such "unstudied character" must be brought to consciousness, made available as a living source of power, as, in Dewey's words, "an intelligence which is not the faculty of intellect honored in text-books and neglected elsewhere, but which is the sum-total of impulses, habits, emotions, records, and discoveries which forecast what is undesirable and undesirable in future possibilities, and which contrive ingeniously in behalf of imagined good."[37]

The releasing of America's creative energies is couched by both Williams and Dewey in terms that suggest that political liberty must be accompanied by cultural liberty if there is to be any meaning to American democratic freedom. Conforming to "received systems" of knowledge is dangerously close to, and may be a prelude to, bowing in the presence of another feudal overlord. As Williams writes, if Americans are not careful they will become a mere resource for those "more able" to seize the potential and who will "fasten themselves upon us" (IAG, 109). Dewey acknowledges that "[o]ur life has no background of sanctified categories upon which we may fall back." This may foster insecurity and a hankering for a stable framework of values but, he warns, "we rely upon precedent as authority only to our own undoing—for with us there is such a continuously novel situation that final reliance upon precedent entails some class interest guiding us by the nose whither it will."[38]

Williams and Dewey are both clear that American cultural independence is a condition of democracy and a protection against domination. The full realization of cultural resources, not gathered into museums and archived out of existence but put to creative use in the present, is an important measure of the liveliness of democracy and an equally important guard against the consolidation of power, cultural and political, by anti-democratic forces. Williams's *In the American Grain* is designed as an embodiment of this pragmatic conception of democratically instrumental knowledge as cultural electricity.

The mixture of verbatim transcription of historical documents and subjective, deliberate distortion of materials that comprises *In the American Grain* fuses past and present, compressing time into the figure of the present author, or, more accurately, the present text. The book becomes an incarnation of American history, a selective and usable, immanent past, with Williams as the medium, the embodiment of a transtemporal tradition. This strategy places Williams deeply in the American literary grain, alongside Mather, Thoreau, and Emerson, among others, in a tradition that emphasizes interpretation as a means of personal and social regeneration. As Thoreau observes, "[a] written word is the choicest of relics. . . . It is the work of art nearest to life itself. It may be translated into any language, and not only read but actually breathed from all human lips;—not be presented on canvas and in marble only, but be carved out of the breath of life itself. The symbol of an ancient man's thought becomes a modern man's speech."[39]

Williams's re-articulation of an American written tradition deliberately belies, in the sheer multiplicity of voices, the common European argument that America had no past and no literature. Furthermore, as Williams selects, edits, arranges, and rewrites, he is inscribing himself into that tradition as an active force. Writing to Horace Greeley in 1939, Williams explained that the book was "a study in styles of writing," and that he had "tried to write each chapter in the style most germane to its sources or at least the style which seemed to me appropriate to the material." Where possible, he had "copied and used the original writings" (SL, 187).

In the American Grain is as notable for what it leaves out as for what it includes. Like Bourne, Brooks, Frank et al., Williams is certainly in search of a "usable past," but he has little interest in establishing a Eurocentric teleological tradition of American literature. Thus, despite using strategies of reading and writing markedly similar to Emerson and Thoreau, neither are mentioned in the book. Nor are those other staples of the "American Renaissance": Irving, Cooper, Melville, or Hawthorne. Instead, Williams concentrates on "nonliterary" figures such as Eric the Red, Père Sebastian Rasles, and Daniel Boone. For Williams the ground of American literature does not depend upon the establishment of a canon of nineteenth-century writers that will measure up to European standards of excellence. It is necessary for the poet to reach farther back, "through a dead layer" (IAG, 213), to get "the feet of his understanding on the ground, his ground, *the* ground, the only ground that he knows, that which *is* under his feet" (IAG, 213). The canon of classic American texts put forward by critics such as Brooks is just another example of reductive scholastic thinking for Williams, another quest for acceptable standards which functions to bleach out variation and contradiction, pulling some kind of familiar signal out of the noise. Williams wants no part of it:

> The predominant picture of America is a land aesthetically satisfied by temporary fillgaps . . . We crave filling and eagerly grab for what is there. The next step is, floating upon cash, we wish to be *like* others. Now come into the Universities, the conformists of all colors . . . It is imperative that we *sink*. But from a low position it is impossible to answer those who know all the Latin and some of the Sanscrit names, much French and perhaps one or two other literatures . . . We cannot answer in the smart language, certainly it would be a bastardization of our own talents to waste time to learn the language they use. I would rather sneak off and die like a sick dog than be a well known literary person in America . . . (IAG, 214–215)

The "styles of writing" Williams deploys in In the American Grain defy reduction to a single common language, his definition of American expanding to include Icelandic, Spanish, French, and Indian sources. Vera Kutzinski, in her discussion of the book, makes the pertinent distinction between American literature and New World writing, the latter category based on the simple ontological fact of work deriving from the American continent rather than a more limited body of texts chosen by some prearranged agenda.[40] Williams further loosens the grip of Europe as, to use Edmundo O'Gorman's phrase, "history's paradigm,"[41] by dismantling the logic that strings American development along an unbroken chain from Columbus to the present, supplanting Columbus with Red Eric as his starting point, destabilizing the accepted point of origin. Throughout the book,

Williams persists in jumbling chronologies, points of view, factual and fictional discourse, until the distinctions between past and present, archival evidence and authorial polemic disintegrate. Williams's history is a history charged with the force of what Dewey would call "creative intelligence," a history intertwined with the writer, a strategy that led the few critics that actually reviewed the book to dismiss it as "subjective history," with a "maximum of 'interpretation' and a minimum of research," as "poetry, not history."[42] D. H. Lawrence proved the exception, grasping the fact that although Williams's history was not "ordinary history, which is a complacent record of the civilization and Europizing (if you can allow the word) of the American continent," it was a "sensuous record of Americanization of the white man in America." Picking up the distinction between locality and nationality, Lawrence sees how Williams reverses the idea of man claiming the land to stress the need for the land to claim the man. Environment becomes a protagonist, a historical agent itself in the formation of an identity that is not abstractly conjured from nowhere but derives from "a specific soil." Making Dewey's point —"the only universal is in the local"—Lawrence writes that "The local in America is America itself," that is, not a narrow parochialism—"the parish-pump stuff"—but in the very "subsoil which spouts up . . . into the lives of men." Lawrence also sees the relevance of *In the American Grain* as social criticism, noting the aggressive but hopeless nationalism of the "100%ers." Impossible, says Lawrence, because the only one hundred percent American is the Indian, and "not even the most American American can transmogrify into an Indian." Like Dewey, Lawrence sees that "most of the 100%ism is national, and therefore not American at all." National America "is a gruesome sort of fantasy. But the unravished *local* America still waits vast and virgin as ever, though in process of being murdered."[43]

Williams refuses to allow the voices in *In the American Grain* cohere into *an* identity, into *a* national language, reducible to a given number of recognizable characteristics. The specificity of times, places, and individuals defy reduction, held together only by their embodiment in Williams's text. To this extent the book is subjective history, but not in the dismissive sense suggested by Burke. Being subjective does not make the texts less "real," less "factual." In fact, the texts become more pertinent because they have been energized by the present writer. History is an abstraction until it is localized in the historian.

Williams seeks, in *In the American Grain,* to conjure an interpenetration of past and present, with the individual/writer as the embodiment of transtemporal liberation. The process of transcription is central to this.[44] In "Quotation and Originality," Emerson writes that we are "fed and formed" by the past. "The old forest is decomposed for the composition of the new forest. The old animals have given their bodies to the earth to furnish through chemistry the forming race, and every individual is only a momentary fixation of what was yesterday another's, is today his, and will belong to a third tomorrow. So it is with thought."[45] Everything is inherited, "we but quote them," but this does not reduce the individual to merely a vessel into which history is poured: "[T]here remains the indefensible

persistency of the individual to be himself." The obverse of inheritance and quotation is creative individuality, the power of transformative assimilation, the ability to see that "a state of mind is the ancestor of everything." The capacity to absorb history into the self and to transform the present with this knowledge
Emerson calls Genius or, as with Williams, imagination, the connective force that
is the measure of capacity for contact. The blame for the atrophy of imagination
in America, Williams lays, rather predictably, at the feet of the Puritans.

The attack on Puritanism in *In the American Grain* is fierce and thorough
because, like Mencken, Brooks, and others, Williams considers the Puritan legacy
to have been the most dominating and destructive element in the formation of
American identity. The Mayflower Pilgrims were, he claims, the residue of "Tudor
England's lusty blossoming," the hard and "little pips . . . in which lay the character of beginnings in North America" (IAG, 63). If they were pure, "it was more
since they had nothing in them of fulfillment than because of positive virtues."
The Puritans are like fairy-tale curiosities, children, dwarves, and elves (IAG, 64),
their endless bleating of "the jargon of God" as alien as their beliefs and habits.
This peculiar and intense emptiness, Williams believes, is due to the Puritan
emphasis on the spirit, which denied the material and bodily in favor of abstraction. They were always elsewhere, never noticing the earth upon which they
stood. The land itself "was not favorable," being geographically sympathetic in its
harshness to the "doggedness of a northern race, cold, close, and slow to that"
(IAG, 67). What should have been the beginning of a new world, Williams sees
as a failure from the start, "the whole weight of the wild continent" making "their
condition of mind advantageous, forcing it to reproduce its own likeness, and
no more" (IAG, 68), resulting in an America that is "a panorama of murders,
perversions, a terrific ungoverned strength," of "gross know-nothingism, of black-
ened churches" and a generation interested solely in "opportunist material advantages' (IAG, 68).

The chapter on Cotton Mather is comprised solely of excerpts from *Wonders
of the Invisible World* concerning the witchcraft trials. The following chapter acts
as a response to Mather's world view as we find Williams in Paris meeting the
French historian Valery Larbaud, with whom he discusses American history, particularly the Puritans and then the Jesuit Sebastian Rasles. Rasles is the real counterpoint to Mather, the chapter sitting at the heart of the book, suggesting the
pivotal role Rasles plays in Williams's thesis. But before we get to Rasles we get
Williams and Larbaud. By feeding himself into the text, Williams foregrounds his
own participation as a historical agent, a voice among voices, a direct challenger
to the authority of dead letters. Williams's presence as a character pulls the text
into the present, undermining the distancing effect of reading history and also
making us aware of how much he controls and shapes the information presented.
His own self-inscription de-authorizes the sense of objectivity that verbatim
extracts provide; Williams gives us the democracy of styles and then directs us
back to the individual, the controlling writer in the present. Thus, he manages to
maintain a sense of plurality while embodying this plurality in himself. Through

this device Williams reminds us that history is not about authenticity but about interpretation, an active process of understanding, not a passive observation of data.

Williams visited Larbaud during his stay in Paris in 1924, but as Bryce Conrad suggests, Williams's account of the meeting is far from accurate, Williams using the scenario as a device through which he can air his views on Mather, Rasles, and the study of history.[46] The meeting is also a convenient way for Williams to parody the difference between European and American characters, Williams playing the untutored hayseed to Larbaud's urbane, scholarly intellectual. Like a farmer in a suit of city clothes, Williams portrays himself as constrained by Paris, longing to bust out: "I felt myself with ardors not released but beaten back, in this center of old-world culture" (IAG, 105). In the presence of Larbaud, Williams becomes "unexpectedly confused. He is a student, I am a block, I thought. I could see it at once: he knows far more of what is written of my world than I." Pulling himself together, however, Williams makes the distinction between observation and participation: "But he is a student while I am—the brutal thing itself" (IAG, 107). By differentiating himself from the European intellectual, Williams is not advocating a "gross knownothingism," but by being "the brute thing himself" he is able to give a primary force to his part of the discussion as the carrier of American history, an authority that learning alone cannot give. What begins as defensiveness becomes an recognition of agency. Again, the individual—Williams—is the locus of forces.

Williams's critique of America's Puritan heritage, and his demonstration of a road not taken in Rasles's approach to the nation and its native inhabitants, is structured around contending economies of contact and withdrawal, spending and saving. These are political economies that involve different conceptions of relatedness. The questions raised by Williams are concerned with crucial democratic issues: how does individuality relate to freedom? What rights do individuals have, and by what authority? What is the relationship between individual responses to environment and the creation of national character? How might alternatives to ingrained antidemocratic habits be discovered and utilized?

The fecundity of America was an invitation to opportunists of all shades to lay claim to the land. Van Wyck Brooks suggests that the pioneering age never had a "living, active culture, releasing the creative energies of men. Its function was rather to divert these energies, to prevent the anarchical, skeptical, extravagant, dynamic forces of the spirit from taking the wind out of the myth of 'progress', that myth imposed by destiny upon the imagination of our forbears in order that a great uncharted continent might be subdued to the service of the race."[47] Williams cannot but agree when, in *The Great American Novel,* he notes with disgust that "Progress is to get" (GAN,159). The Puritan privileging of otherworldly abstraction as a defense against the profanity of the world has developed, in Williams's view, into an obsession with that other abstraction, money. The pursuit of wealth is also a form of withdrawal, epitomized by Ben Franklin whose "mighty answer to the New World's offer of a great embrace was THRIFT.

Work night and day, build up, penny by penny, a wall against that which is threatening, the terror of life, poverty. Make a fort to be secure in" (IAG,156).

America was dominated in the name of abstractions having no tangible relationship with the actual land: religion and wealth, forms of delay, of distancing
from the exigencies of place. Ownership, Williams points out, should not be mistaken for belonging: "The American character is acquisitive, but mediate, like the
Morgan interests, Mr. Franklin at the helm, the International Mercantile Marine
that owns, as mortgager, the White Star, the Red Star, the Atlantic Transport lines,
etc. American lines but English ships. We own them. But who HAS them?"
(IAG,175). Physical existence is displaced into exchange value, and the transaction is always between abstract quantities. Waldo Frank reads American history
the same way in *Our America,* seeing the Constitution as nothing but a transfer of
financial power from the king to the republic. The Revolutionary fathers freed
themselves "from English creditors, and then bound down as their own debtors
an increasing amount of the American population. The Constitution . . . se-
cured the commercial oligarchy which persists today." Liberty, Frank concludes,
meant nothing more than their wanting to make money for themselves.[48]

In the figure of Sebastian Rasles Williams sets up an alternative to the abstract
money economy of the dominant American tradition, an alternative that challenges to the very root the founding principles of America. The French Jesuit
Rasles lived with the Abnaki Indians for thirty-four years, "TOUCHING them
every day," "a spirit, rich, blossoming, generous, able to give and to receive" (IAG,
120). He is able to make contact with the New World because he becomes part of
it. His transactions are based on a gift economy of donation and acceptance, as opposed to the Puritans' and pioneers' abstract economy of spiritual and financial
gain. In a gift economy, according to Marcel Mauss, reciprocity functions as an obligation and self-interest becomes subsumed into the system of "total services"
where "everything . . . is there for passing on, and for balancing accounts. Everything passes to and fro as if there were a constant exchange of a spiritual matter, including things and men, between clans and individuals, distributed between social
ranks, the sexes, and the generations."[49] This kind of exchange is of a spiritual nature and enables social bonding, the circulation of gifts, each one containing something of the giver's soul, weaving an intricate tissue of personal interrelatedness.
The thing given, importantly, is not inactive, it is part of the giver and animated by
the spiritual force "of its forest, of its native heath and soil. It is truly 'native': the
[spiritual force] follows after anyone possessing the thing."[50] Possession infers an
obligation to pass on, wealth is to be expended as a demonstration of nobility. In
his embrace of native things, Williams writes, Rasles demonstrates what it is

> to be *moral*: to be *positive*, to be peculiar, to be sure, generous, brave—TO
> MARRY, to *touch*—to *give* because one HAS, not because one has nothing. And
> to give to one who HAS, who will join, who will make, who will fertilize, who
> will be like you yourself: to create, to hybridize, to crosspollenize,—not to steril-
> ize, to draw back, to fear, to dry up, to rot. (IAG,121)

The crucial point of Rasles's transactional contact is, for Williams, in the sense of obligation and responsibility. Part of the self is given over to the community to which it belongs, to the land it inhabits. This is presented in great contrast to the Protestant approach to living in America, where value is converted into money terms, removing any sense of personal relationship and used to justify exploitation through an abstract economy of accumulation. Buying land from the Indians justifies the settlers' legal right as they see it to "cut the ground from under the Indian's feet" and set up palisades to divide their property from the natives (IAG, 114). This acquisitive drive, this "tremendous force" which increases "the gap between touch and thing" (IAG, 177), stamps out alternative forms of transaction, making contact more and more difficult as the power of wealth increases. In "The American Background" Williams describes wealth as a squatter usurping the ground of the small-scale, related communities, "irresponsible because unrelated to the territory it overran" (SE, 149).

This was the dilemma of Daniel Boone, another of Williams's exemplary men, who carried the seed of destruction into the wilderness despite himself and could thus never rest as the conquering spirit of the settlers moved into the territory he had opened up. Boone, like Rasles, is situated by Williams in a position of openness toward the New World, an openness that allows the "beauty of a lavish, primitive embrace in savage, wild beast and forest" to rise "above the cramped life about him" and possess him wholly (IAG,136). Boone, claims Williams, saw the Indian "as a natural expression of the place" (IAG, 138). From this Boone learns to fuse his individuality with the land, "to be *himself* in a new world, Indianlike" (IAG, 137). While this is conceived as a embrace of difference, a fusion of horizons, an original relation to the universe, Boone is still, of course, the carrier of civilization and its evils. Individually he may represent for Williams an alternative to ownership as domination but he is still the facilitator of that domination, even if, like Cooper's Leatherstocking, this makes him a tragic outsider doomed to disappear. Nevertheless, for Williams, Boone's "genius" is to recognize that the difficulty of relating to the New World is "neither material nor political but one purely moral and aesthetic" (IAG, 136). Boone "offered himself to his world" where the Puritans pulled off "pieces to themselves from the fat of the new bounty" (IAG, 136–137).

While Williams does not look too deeply into Boone's role in the settlement of Kentucky, this is because he wants to stress the possibility of a "moral and aesthetic" stance toward place that embraces with passion rather than simply takes. Ownership is not the issue here in the sense of property acquired. Instead, dwelling is seen as coterminous with offering oneself up to place in a kind of wedding of self and world. When Kentucky is bought by white settlers an old Indian articulates the crucial difference between the two economies Williams has set in opposition: "You have bought the land . . . but you will have trouble to settle it" (IAG, 138).

The concern for a "moral and aesthetic" stance toward place Williams developed during the 1920s was intended to provide a counterweight to the encroachment of capitalist incorporation and the dilution of individuality and cultural specificity threatened by it. The boom years of the 1920s certainly heightened Williams's awareness of the danger to democracy posed by a culture that seemed to celebrate only greed and the power of wealth. The increasing consolidation of wealth in the hands of the few appeared to confirm economically what was happening socially through the restrictive and homogenizing nativist nationalism evident in immigration quotas, Prohibition (that preferred Williams term for the restriction of energies), and the rise of the Klan. America in the 1920s appeared to liberals such as Williams and Dewey as a travesty of democracy. Economic and industrial power had not liberated the people but had turned them into a mass dangerously close to becoming a mob. As the prosperity of the 1920s fell into Depression, the menace both Williams and Dewey saw in the entwined interests of party politics and big business could not be understated. With an entrenched oligarchy seemingly bent on destroying democracy at home and the rise of political extremism in Europe, the optimism of Dewey's and Williams's individualistic cultural politics came, during the 1930s, under increased pressure to find a workable third way through the collectivist ideologies of both Right and Left. While the temptations of the Right could obviously offer no attraction to advocates of freedom and plurality such as Dewey and Williams, the willingness of many American intellectuals and writers to move toward some form of alliance with Soviet Communism presented a more complex challenge, particularly when conditions appeared to demand a rigorous socialistic response to the now apparently proven evils of capitalism.

FIVE

WHY I AM NOT A COMMUNIST

Poetry is a rival government always in opposition to its cruder replicas.

— William Carlos Williams

For many critics of American culture, the stock market crash of 1929 merely confirmed what they had long suspected: the nation's relentless pursuit of material wealth was a shortsighted scramble for ascendancy that courted anarchy. Such moral bankruptcy had, indeed, inevitably been followed by economic disaster. During the early 1930s, before the policies of the New Deal began to take effect and before the Popular Front took the sting out of the communist critique of capitalism, many American liberal intellectuals considered the Soviet Union as a possible model for an alternative economic and social system. Dewey, in *Impressions of Soviet Russia* (1929), saw Russian society as a vast experiment, "the most interesting one going on upon our globe," which sought to create a new "collective mentality" whereby individuals became, through "constructive tasks," "organic members of an organic movement" free from the "competitive struggle for personal profit."[1] As the Depression began to bite, the vigor and progressive spirit of the Soviet enterprise, particularly the economic strategy of the Five Year Plans, brought home the need for a radical revaluation of American capitalism.

Interest in the Soviet system was to be short-lived, as evidence of indoctrination and persecution revealed the reality of Stalinism. Nonetheless, what liberals like Dewey perceived was the value and potential of social and economic planning. What they also picked up was, perhaps more significantly, a vocabulary of revolution, which they sought to apply to American conditions and within an American historical context. Liberalism, Dewey was sure, had to distance itself from its nineteenth-century laissez-faire roots (which served only as an "intellectual justification of the *status quo*" [LSA, 26]) and work to "socialize the forces of production, now at hand, so that the liberty of individuals will be supported by the very structure of economic organization" (LSA, 62).

The attraction of the Russian example of cultural revolution was shared by Williams. Reviewing the poetry of the Missouri dirt farmer H. H. Lewis in 1937, Williams claims that when Lewis "speaks of Russia, it is precisely then that he is most American, most solidly in the tradition, not out of it, not borrowing a 'foreign' solution." Russia here seems to represent the notion of revolution rather than an actual country, Williams reading "Russia" as a trope for something indigenously American. Lewis is "the American patriot of our revolutionary tradition," fighting, as did the "persecuted colonist," "to free himself from a class enslavement which torments his body with lice and cow dung."[2] Lewis is a good example for Williams because his work is rooted in his daily experience, "speaking his own language as he hears it spoken in his own place and day."[3] While Russia might be an inspiration for America in a rhetorical sense, however, this emphasis on being "rooted in daily experience" made any possibility of communism itself finding a place in America absurd. Dewey's brisk dismissal of Communism as a political ideology, in fact, uses the very terms Williams chooses to celebrate Lewis. The fact that the party was run from Moscow was reason enough for Dewey not joining—"simply out of the question." The Communist Party "does not speak the American idiom or think in terms relevant to the American situation." Worst of all, the party is "identified with a fanatical and doctrinaire inflexibility."[4] Soviet Russia might be an interesting phenomenon and even serve as inspiration for American experiments in social revolution, but to think that communism could take root in the United States was a possibility neither Williams nor Dewey ever seriously entertained.

In "Against the Weather" (1939), Williams writes that to have liberty one must be "cultured by circumstances to maintain oneself under adverse weather conditions as still part of the whole. Discipline is implied" (SE, 209). Liberty, then, entails a responsibility to be engaged in the affairs of the world, to be part of, rather than free from, the workings of history: "liberty to partake of, to be included in and to conserve. Liberty, in this sense, has the significance of inclusion rather than a breaking away" (SE, 208). If liberty involves revolution, it will come from within conditions, out of its own ground with its own idiom, not in the form of some imported ideology nor by being cut off from the roots of experience and taking refuge in dogma.

Dewey knows that liberty is contingent upon historically specific conditions, and that to strive for liberty first demands an understanding of these conditions (the "discipline" that Williams mentions): "the conception of liberty is always relative to forces that at a given time and place are increasingly felt to be oppressive" (LSA, 35). To understand one's place in history is to understand what needs to be done. The necessity of recognizing adaptability and historical contingency as requisites for the maintenance of liberty is as pertinent in poetry for Williams as it is in life: "Jefferson said it. We should have a revolution every ten years. The truth has to be redressed, re-examined, re-affirmed in a new mode. There has to be new poetry. But the thing is that the change, the greater material, the altered structure of the inevitable revolution must be *in* the poem, in it. Made of it. It must shine in the structural body of it" (SE, 217). The quest for form is a kind of radical political action; it is through creative action that new forms are realized. "There is a bookish quality too patent in Communism today, taken from a book that appears not to have been properly related to its object—man" (SE, 217).

While the experimental aspects of Soviet communism and its celebration of local conditions as coterminous with the revolutionary spirit reminded liberals such as Dewey and Williams of the vigor of America's own revolutionary optimism, the doctrinaire and teleological theoretical underpinning of communism could never be accommodated within their pragmatic contextualism. What both Williams and Dewey are after is a democratic politics which can revolutionize the American socioeconomic system with the equivalent force of Communism, a locally derived revolution of everyday life commensurate with the promise of American individualism. Dewey is adamant that "[i]n one word, democracy means that *personality* is the first and final reality."[5] Williams and Dewey certainly veered leftward during the 1930s, but their socialism remained more rooted in Jeffersonian virtue than Marxian dialectics. Indeed, even though Dewey spent much of the decade campaigning for the establishment of a third political party, both he and Williams shared a deep suspicion of organized political parties and their ideological underpinnings.

After Herbert Hoover's election in 1928, economist Paul H. Douglas organized the League for Independent Political Action (LIPA) with the aim of establishing a progressive third political party free from ties with business interests. Douglas was inspired by Dewey's *The Public and its Problems* (1927) and Dewey himself became LIPA chairman, working for the organization until its demise in 1936.[6] During this time, the LIPA, with Dewey as its figurehead, attempted to forge an alliance between liberal Republicans, socialists, farm laborers, and intellectuals; in fact, to gather together anyone willing to resist the bankruptcy of traditional politics and to chart an independent third path that would lead to true liberty. The hostility Dewey felt toward the entwined interests of politics and business is clearly evident in an address he delivered before the New History Society in New York City in December 1930, where he compared the urgency for political change to the fight against slavery: "[J]ust as the Republican Party was born in the irrepressible conflict against the extension of chattel slavery, so the new party will be born to liberate us from the enslavement of governmental agencies to selfish and predatory interest."[7] The choice of analogy is interesting here, for while Dewey clearly places current politics as a struggle for liberation out of slavery, he does not use the rhetoric of class war and workers' enslavement but draws upon an American precedent that, while it had the effect of liberating slaves, was motivated also, if not more so, by a desire to preserve the Union. Dewey's vocabulary of struggle is righteous and potentially revolutionary, but his revolution is an American rather than a Russian one, designed, as Williams's conception of liberty suggests, "to conserve" rather than destroy.

The policies the LIPA urged the new party to implement hinged on whole-sale economic planning, including the socialization of utilities, banking, and credit, alongside heavy tax increases for high earners to pay for relief programs. By 1932, the LIPA platform extended beyond the proposals of the New Deal, which Dewey viewed as a mere tinkering with capitalism, calling for three to five million dollars for public works, two hundred and fifty million dollars for annual direct relief, worker's insurance, an old age pension, the abolition of child labor, and a six-hour day.[8] This platform is clearly similar to that of the British Labour Party, which was certainly a model for many LIPA officials during 1932, when the or-ganization began working closely with the Socialist Party though not, notably, with communists, whose beliefs were already seen as alien to the American way of life. A residual Soviet influence might perhaps be detected, however, in the plat-form's title: the Four-Year Presidential Plan.

The poor showing of the Socialist Party in the 1932 election led to recrimi-nations from both the Socialists and the LIPA and the end of their collaboration. The Socialists blamed progressives for voting Democrat, fearing a Socialist vote would be a vote for Hoover, and attacked the LIPA for being ideologically weak. The LIPA accused the Socialists of dogmatism, of being unwilling to make them-selves more palatable to an American electorate. Dewey's view remained constant, which was that while the LIPA had socialist goals—the socialization of produc-tion and distribution—it did not have and did not need a socialist, or Marxist or communist for that matter, justification. The necessity for such goals was in re-sponse to concrete social conditions and needs: there was no need for an ideolog-ical system to explain what had to be done.

Dewey continued to campaign for a third party until 1936, becoming hon-orary chairman of the United Action Campaign Committee, which worked to gather support for the Farm Labor Political Federation (FLPF). The FLPF, it was envisaged, would go on to eventually form a new third party. While many LIPA members had moved over to either Roosevelt or the Socialist Party, Dewey con-tinued to hold out for an alternative. The FLPF constituency was certainly differ-ent to the middle-class intellectuals who made up the LIPA, being comprised of discontented farmers and laborers, and Dewey's language followed accordingly, writing that "We must get down into the dirt and dust of the arena and fight for human rights in a practical, aggressive, realistic manner."[9] Growth of third party activities, particularly among farm and labor organizations in, for example, Wisconsin and Minnesota, led to the creation of the American Commonwealth Political Federation (ACPF) in 1935, with, initially, a view to running a third party candidate in the presidential election of 1936. Again, however, fears of a poor showing, concerns over a divided liberal vote favoring the Republicans, and factional conflict meant the ACPF's efforts came to nothing, the LIPA also col-lapsing with most of the leaders moving over to Roosevelt. Dewey voted for Socialist candidate Norman Thomas in 1936 just as he had four years earlier.

Dewey's involvement with the various campaigns for a third party reveals both his skepticism toward partisan politics and at the same time his acceptance that organization and social planning is necessary for the overthrow of entrenched economic and political interests detrimental to participatory democracy. His belief in forging alliances between disparate groups is well in keeping with a pragmatic response to events, yet the failure of such alliances exposes the extent to which ideological differences tend to supersede cooperation even when necessity demands a united front. If Dewey believes in organized political action, even if adherence to such organization is temporary and dissolved when situations change, why does he refuse to align himself with, for example, the Socialist Party, when his program of social action is so close to theirs? Why does he not, as his fellow members of the LIPA did, back Roosevelt's New Deal more enthusiastically, especially when he saw so much of value in its policies?

In brief, Dewey's answers to these questions are, firstly, that the Socialist Party is no solution because its ideological position predetermines its response to conditions, whatever those conditions are. Second, the New Deal is inadequate because it is primarily designed to save capitalism rather than transform it. These are reasonable and consistent arguments, but do they resolve the issue of how Dewey reconciles his resistance to organized politics with the need for a planned economy, which, of necessity, entails organized political action to get started? Furthermore, how does the extensive social planning Dewey has in mind for America square with his celebration of American individualism?

PLANNED LIBERTY FOR THE CORPORATE INDIVIDUAL

The articles Dewey wrote for *The New Republic,* appearing on the cusp of the Depression between April 1929 and April 1930 and published as *Individualism Old and New,* seek to define the problems faced by American capitalism and attempt, through a mapping of the historical moment, to draw up a plan of action based on actual conditions. The articles are also a strident defense of American individualism in the face of powerful forces of incorporation. For Dewey, business mergers, the "massification" of society caused by industrial capitalism, and the collectivism of Soviet Marxism were all versions of the same threat to democracy: they all served to reduce individual agency and participation in everyday affairs. While Dewey had little time for what he saw as orthodox Marxism's distortion of scientific method by extrapolating a universal law (dialectical materialism) from local analysis (feudal and industrial Europe), he did accept that Marx was perceptive enough to understand the direction of forces. Marx, Dewey observes, can justly be seen as the prophet of current economic consolidation, and if "his ghost hovers above the American scene, it must find legitimate satisfaction in our fulfilment of his predictions" (ION, 90). Furthermore, "the issue which he raised—the relation of the economic structure to political operation—is one that actively persists" (ION, 91). This basic Marxian observation is at the core of *Individualism Old and New.* The function of Dewey's text, however, is not to incite class war but to offer a response to the problem of a democracy losing itself in economic and political inequality: "One sure way in which the individual who is politically

lost . . . could recover a composed mind, would be by apprehension of the realities of industry and finance as they function in public and political life" (ION,
96). What Dewey develops is an argument for a kind of democratic socialism
grounded in the realities of American industrial life and commensurate with the
claims of American individualism. It is a socialism grounded in Dewey's insistence
that the individual is inseparable from society, and designed to destroy the popular American myth of socialism as "arithmetically derived individualism" that uses
political means to divide up and distribute wealth equally among all. Such a
myth, Dewey dismissively observes, can only be entertained by those who believe
the individual to be "an isolated and independent unit" (ION, 90).

Dewey begins *Individualism Old and New* by conceding that traditional
American values have failed to stand up to the strain and pace of modern industrial life, and sees the problem as one of cultural lag: "[P]hysically and externally
we belong to the twentieth century" while "in thought and feeling, or at least in
the language in which they are expressed, we are living in some bygone century,
anywhere from the thirteenth to the eighteenth" (ION, 45). The resulting state of
mind is understandably, writes Dewey, one of bewilderment and confusion. The
"money culture" to which everyone belongs, with its emphasis on free competition and upward mobility, has been taken for granted and "treated as an inevitable
part of our social system" (ION, 46). Yet this very system, calling as it does for a
philosophy of complete economic determinism, is contradicted by the beliefs
actually held by Americans, beliefs formed from an idealism that "is probably the
loudest and most frequently professed philosophy the world has ever heard"
(ION, 47). Successful men are praised not for their energy but because of their
"love of flowers, children, and dogs, or their kindness to aged relatives." Despite
the erosion of family life and a rapid increase in the divorce rate, there is the "most
sentimental glorification of the sacredness of home and the beauties of constant
love that history can record" (ION, 47). Increasing secularization has not diminished respect for the church, and regardless of improvements in education and
science, "one-half of the pupils in the last years of the high school think that the
first chapters of the Hebrew Scriptures give a more accurate account of the origin
and early history of man than does science" (ION, 47). What, asks Dewey, is the
cause of this bizarre contradiction between the outward aspects of life and the
sentiments of the people? To some extent it is, he considers, due to the rapidity of
industrialization, which has caused people to turn in fear to the "magic formulae"
of older creeds in order to "ward off the evils of the new situation" (ION, 48). Yet,
considering the potential made available by new forms of knowledge and technology, it is "our great abdication" to glorify the past instead of "seriously asking how
we are to employ the means at our disposal so as to form an equitable and stable
society" (ION, 48).

The American tradition itself, admits Dewey, is a double one, promoting
both equality of opportunity and freedom for all on the one hand, and the pursuit
of material gain on the other. Thanks in part to the machine, the latter has
emerged in the ascendancy, widening the split between public and private
interests. The "development of individualities," which the tradition "prophetically

set forth," has therefore not occurred. Instead, there is "a perversion of the whole ideal of individualism, to conform to the practices of a pecuniary culture," which has become "the source and justification of inequalities and oppressions" (ION, 49).

The war revealed for Europeans, perhaps for the first time, the power of America as a nation and as a culture. In America itself, Dewey suggests, this consciousness of "Americanism" as a "distinctive mode of civilization" may not exist, but it does in Europe and "as a menace," causing a defensive reaction whereby "[a]cute hostility to a powerful alien influence is taking the place of complacent ignoring of what was felt to be negligible" (ION, 50). Dewey thinks there is much to learn from the European perspective, citing Mueller Freienfels's *Mysteries of the Soul* (1929) as a good example of the trend in European views of America. Freienfels sees the American mind as a type that subordinates the subconscious to conscious rationality and attunes mind to the conditions of action upon matter; emotional life is quick, excitable, undiscriminating, lacking in individuality and mental direction; there is no inner unity and thus no personality. Quantity overrules quality, technique is an end rather than a means, and differences are ignored in favor of standardization (ION, 52). The criticism is familiar, Dewey admits, voiced by critics at home as well as abroad, and he does not deny that such national traits exist, yet "their import is another thing than their existence" (ION, 53). Dewey is pleased that Freienfels regards these traits as probably transitional, because this stresses development and change, rather than defining a categorical identity. Many of the defects of the present, Dewey suggests, may well be inherited: "Transitions are out of something as well as into something; they reveal a past as well as project a future" (ION, 53). Are present evils, he wonders, "revelations of what the older type of culture covered up"? Recalling the criticism of America's Puritan origins so prevalent during the 1920s, as we have seen in works such as Williams's *In the American Grain,* Dewey suggests that "[a] culture whose tradition rests on depreciation of the flesh and on making a sharp difference between body and mind, instinct and reason, practice and theory, may have wrought corruption of flesh and degeneration of spirit" (ION, 54).

If America is flawed, Dewey counters by drawing attention to the deeply entrenched class systems of Europe, which restrict individual freedom at least as much as so-called American uniformity. And, he asks, what is wrong with technique?

> The world has not suffered from absence of ideals and spiritual aims anywhere near as much as it has suffered from absence of means for realizing the ends which it has prized in a literary and sentimental ways. . . . In the end, technique can only signify emancipation of individuality, and emancipation on a broader scale than has been obtained in the past. (ION, 55)

Returning to Freienfels, Dewey notes his observation that the impoverishment of the individual is accompanied by an enrichment of community resources. The question Freienfels does not ask, Dewey observes, is why it is that collective enrichment does not operate to elevate the life of individuals. Failure to ask this question constitutes for Dewey "the chief failure of critics whether foreign or native" (ION, 55), critics who deal with symptoms and effects but ignore the basic economic fact that technique and technology are controlled by interest in money profit. Traditional individuality, he admits, cannot hold up against the revolutionary effects of machine technology, but to claim that the submergence of individuality is an American phenomenon only avoids the problem of constructing a new individuality "consonant with the objective conditions under which we live" (ION, 56). The first step toward understanding the problem is to recognize the collective age in which we live, argues Dewey. Only then will the issue "define itself as utilization of the realities of a corporate civilization to validate and embody the distinctive moral element in the American version of individualism: equality and freedom expressed not merely externally and politically but through personal participation in the development of a shared culture" (ION, 57).

Rugged individualism may still be seen as a national characteristic, but for Dewey it has little relation to life as it is lived, and is more often than not used simply as a justification for defeating "government regulation of any form of industry previously exempt from legal control" (ION, 58). A more appropriate way of describing America would be as a culture of corporateness: "Not only are big mergers the order of the day, but popular sentiment now looks upon them with pride rather than with fear. Size is our current metaphor of greatness in this as in other matters" (ION, 59). Mass production and mass distribution "have created a common market, the parts of which are held together by inter-communication and inter-dependence; distance is eliminated and the tempo of action enormously accelerated" (ION, 59). Reactions to growing corporateness are "psychological, professional, political; they affect the working ideas, beliefs and conduct of us all" (ION, 60). "Mass production causes a kind of mass education in which individual capacity and skill are submerged." As far as the artist is concerned, those "who are still called artists either put themselves, as writers and designers, at the disposal of organized business, or are pushed out to the edge as eccentric bohemians." The artist may remain as a "surviving individual force, but the esteem in which the calling is socially held in this country measures the degree of his force. The status of the artist in any form of social life affords a fair measure of the state of its culture. The inorganic position of the artist in American life to-day is convincing evidence of what happens to the isolated individual who lives in a society growing corporate" (ION, 60–61).

Modern capitalism removes individual initiative and undermines community needs, Dewey points out, striking an atypically pessimistic note in his assessment of the burgeoning mass media: "We live exposed to the greatest flood of mass suggestion that any people has ever experienced. The need for unified action, and the supposed need of integrated opinion and sentiment, are met by organized propaganda and advertising. The publicity agent is perhaps the most significant symbol of our present social life" (ION, 61). Such all-pervasiveness makes resistance all but impossible, since "sentiment can be manufactured by mass methods for almost any person or any cause" (ION, 62).

One of the most striking changes brought about by the shift from production to consumption capitalism is the abandonment of thrift in favor of buying as "an economic 'duty.'" Consumption becomes a social virtue and a responsibility because it turns the wheels of industry (ION, 63). Economic depression, under such conditions, is used as evidence of a falling off of virtue, of general social failure. Of course, in a corporate society, when economic disaster does strike, no one escapes. Such a fragile environment inevitably breeds fear and anxiety, and "where fears abound, courageous and robust individuality is undermined." Mechanization, mergers, and combinations have multiplied these fears, destabilizing the belief in "honest and industrious pursuit of a calling or business," and stirring many to gamble on the stock market (ION, 68).

A split between public and private interests exists in the "business-mind" itself, according to Dewey, and will remain so "as long as the results of industry as the determining forces in life are corporate and collective while its animating motives and compensations are so unmitigatedly private" (ION, 69). While there is "much planning of future development with a view to dividends within large business corporations, there is no corresponding coordinated planning of social development" (ION, 69). A unified mind will only exist when "conscious intent and consummation are in harmony with consequences actually effected," yet the arena within which planned social development might be shaped—politics—is as confused and tainted with economic opportunism as business itself (ION, 69–70). The consequent social drift reveals itself in "our excited and rapacious nationalism," because "corporateness has gone so far as to detach individuals from their old local ties and allegiances but not far enough to give them a new center and order of life." If the "daily community" cannot provide social connection "the romantic imagination pictures a grandiose nation in which all are one" (ION, 70–71).

Individualism, for Dewey, should not have a fixed meaning. Old definitions of individualism are defunct because conditions have changed. Old forms cannot solve new problems. The question to be asked should not be: how shall the individual oppose him or herself to the corporate world? It should be: "what qualities will the new individualism exhibit?" Ideological structures cannot be superimposed onto an existing situation, creating "a seeming consensus" by "artificial and mechanical means" (ION, 81). The very way we think about ourselves and about society must be re-formed by close scrutiny of actual conditions. This involves a fundamental intellectual change, utilizing "the controlled use of all the resources of the science and technology that have mastered the physical forces of nature." What is needed is an "imagination large enough to encompass their potential uses" (ION, 86). Blaming the machine for the troubles of the modern world is nothing but a sign of the "paralysis of the imagination" (ION, 87); technology must be seen as an extension of "our natural organs of approach to nature," not as a barrier (ION, 88). Used with "Discriminative sensitivity . . . [and] selection," science and technology can be used to create a new culture and a new individuality (ION, 89).

Economic planning and management are essential, writes Dewey, and politicians and business leaders must recognize their social responsibility. "We are in for some kind of socialism," Dewey claims, and "associated thought" should be entered into "constructively and voluntarily" in order to avoid the "destruction and coercion" so catastrophically wrought by Soviet Russia (ION, 98). What is needed is a public, participatory socialism rather than the kind of capitalist socialism already evident in the entwined interests of industry, finance, and politics. Calling for an "assumption of responsibility," Dewey insists that "The over-lords will have to do something to make good" (ION, 93). He proposes a council made up of captains of industry and finance, labor representatives and public officials, which would supervise "the public control of industry and finance for the sake of social values." Such a project would have "vast intellectual and emotional reverberations" from which no aspect of "our culture would remain unaffected." Thinking of politics as a means rather than an end "will lead to thought of the ends it should serve" and "induce consideration of the ways in which a worthy and rich life for all may be achieved." In this way "directive aims" will be restored, marking "a significant step forward in the recovery of a unified individuality" (ION, 98).

This participatory vision of collective interaction and planning is designed to preserve and cultivate a socially based individuality: "[I]ndividuals will always be the center and consummation of experience, but what the individual actually *is* in his life experience depends upon the nature and movement of associated life."[10] A democracy of this kind recognizes "the necessity for the participation of every mature human being in the formation of the values that regulate the living of men together."[11] Limits placed on full participation in social life suppress individuality. Such limits may serve the interests of power brokers but in no way can this be described as democracy. "Others who are supposed to be wiser and who in any case have more power" claim to know what is best for everyone else, which is a "form of coercion and suppression . . . more subtle and more effective than is overt intimidation and restraint. When it is habitual and embodied in social institutions, it seems the normal and natural state of affairs." The experience of the masses is, indeed, "so restricted that they are not conscious of restriction." For Dewey, however, this is not a specific issue of class discrimination, because in a democracy, when one suffers, all suffer: "It is part of the democratic conception that they as individuals are not the only sufferers, but that the whole social body is deprived of the potential resources that should be at its services."[12] While Dewey recognizes "the existence of class-conflicts as one of the fundamental social facts of social life to-day," he remains "profoundly skeptical" of class war as a means by which conflict can be eliminated.[13] Any revolution effected by violence can, in a modernized society such as America, "result only in chaos" and the destruction of the country itself.[14]

The corruption of democracy by business interests has nevertheless made a mockery of its principles, argues Dewey. "Today there is no word more bandied about than liberty," he complains. "Every effort at planned control of economic forces is resisted and attacked, by a certain group, in the name of liberty." This group is made up of those concerned with "the preservation of the status quo; that is to say, in the maintenance of the customary privileges and legal rights they already possess."[15] Liberty is not just an idea, "[i]t is a power, effective power to do specific things," and any demand for liberty is thus a demand for power. When "the managers and beneficiaries of the existing economic system" defend their right to liberty, it is merely "a demand for preservation of the powers they already possess. Since it is the existing system that gives them these powers, liberty is thus inevitably identified with the perpetuation of that system."[16] The possession of power is always a matter of distribution, the retention of power already possessed by one group made possible only by reining in the capacities of others, so "wherever there is liberty at one place there is restraint at some other place." What is needed, argues Dewey, is "a more equal and equitable balance of powers that will enhance and multiply the effective liberties of the mass of individuals." It is nonsense, he goes on, to suppose that there is no social control at work in the present system; "The trouble is that it is exercised by the few who have economic power, at the expense of the liberties of the many and at the cost of increasing disorder."[17] Social control is needed to distribute liberties equally, thus, "the tragic breakdown of democracy is due to the fact that the identification of liberty with the maximum of unrestrained individualistic action in the economic sphere, under the institutions of capitalistic finance, is as fatal to the realization of liberty for all as it is to the realization of equality,"[18]

Such a redistribution of liberty returns Dewey to the need for a transformation of education in order to provide everyone with the knowledge and skills necessary for maximum participation in society. That the average person would not be able to grasp such knowledge and skills, is a fallacy Dewey blames upon current inequality and class prejudice: "The indictments that are drawn against the intelligence of individuals are in truth indictments of a social order that does not permit the average individual to have access to the rich store of the accumulated wealth of knowledge, ideas and purposes." Not only will the present social order not permit the "average human being" to share in the "potentially available social intelligence," it refuses to do anything that might widen access to this store.

> Back of the appropriation by the few of the material resources of society lies the appropriation by the few in behalf of their own ends of the cultural, the spiritual, resources that are the product not of the individuals who have taken possession but of the cooperative work of humanity. It is useless to talk about the failure of democracy until the source of its failure has been grasped and steps are taken to bring about that type of social organization that will encourage the socialized extension of intelligence. (LSA, 38–39)

Liberalism as it should be, says Dewey, is committed to "the liberation of individuals so that realization of their capacities may be the law of their life," and to the creation of a "social organization that will make possible effective liberty and opportunity for personal growth in mind and spirit in all individuals" (LSA, 41). Such a liberation "must now become radical, meaning by 'radical' perception of the necessity of thoroughgoing changes in the set-up of institutions and corresponding activity to bring them to pass. For the gulf between what the actual situation makes possible and the actual state itself is so great that it cannot be bridged by piecemeal policies taken *ad hoc*" (LSA, 45).

The difficulty is in creating the necessary democratic forms that could control the forces of a strong industrialized economy. The danger, Dewey admits, is that in attempting to get away from the "evils of private economic collectivism," it is all too easy to "plunge into political economic collectivism," since "[r]ecent events have shown that state socialism or public collectivism leads to suppression of everything individuality stands for."[19] Dewey is looking for a socialism that is not state socialism, but this proves to be a difficult position to envisage. By the early 1930s, Dewey's hope, as envisioned in *Individualism Old and New,* that state capitalism might be a transitional phase on the way to democratic collectivism driven by a representative, co-ordinating and directive economic council, seemed farther away than ever. It became clear to Dewey that corporate America was not about to endanger its position by remedying the breakdown it had created: "As long as politics is the shadow cast on society by big business, the attenuation of the shadow will not change the substance."[20]

This increased pessimism is due, in part, to Dewey's disappointment with the way New Deal policies had done nothing to change the basic principles of capitalist production, and were more concerned with stabilizing business than helping workers. The National Recovery Administration (NRA), for example, "had a glimpse of self-governing industrial groups, but, quite apart from its conflict with the existing legal system . . . loaded the dice in favor of the existing system of control of industry—with a few sops thrown in to 'labor'. At best it could not have worked out in the direction of freely functioning occupational groups."[21] The New Deal was concerned with overproduction, not underconsumption, and as such it placed itself on the side of business and agricultural interests, and against the needs of the community. While many New Deal supporters touted the Roosevelt administration as pragmatism in action, experimentalism in public affairs, Dewey was firm in his rejection of ad hoc measures: "Experimental method is not just messing around nor doing a little of this and a little of that in the hope that things will improve. Just as in the physical sciences, it implies a coherent body of ideas, a theory, that gives direction to effort."[22]

In contrast to the piecemeal actions of the New Deal, Dewey's diagnosis is a call for wholesale economic restructuring along socialist lines: "[L]abor has prior claims upon production which take precedence of current return upon property, even when property ownership is due to investment of savings from labor income. . . . We cannot achieve a decent standard of living for more than a fraction of the American people by any other method than that to which the British Labour Party and the Social Democratic Parties of Europe are committed—the socialization of all natural resources and natural monopolies, of ground rents, and of basic industries."[23] The first step toward this socialization should be a massive program of public works, especially housing, redistribution of wealth through taxation, and the nationalization of banking, public utilities, natural resources, transport, and communications. "In order to restore democracy, one thing and one thing only is essential. The people will rule when they have power, and they will have power in the degree they own and control the land, the banks, the producing and distributing agencies of the nation. Ravings about Bolshevism, Communism, Socialism are irrelevant to the axiomatic truth of this statement."[24] By combining an analysis of power with his educational theory, Dewey lifted his philosophy during the 1930s to the level of socialist radicalism. True education is not a withdrawal from action, it becomes action, because "there is no education when ideas and knowledge are not translated into emotion, interest, and volition. There must be constant accompanying organization and direction of organized and practical work. 'Ideas' must be linked to the practical situation, however hurly-burly that is."[25]

The "practical situation," however bad it got, could never accept a version of Soviet communism. Dewey, unlike many liberals, may have refused to embrace the New Deal Democrats but neither did he ever take seriously the American left's flirtation with communism, even though he admitted that he could not "blind myself . . . to the perceptible difference between communism with a small *c*, and Communism, official Communism, spelt with a capital letter."[26] Dewey was faced during the 1930s with fighting the excesses of corporatism on two fronts: what he called capitalistic socialism and Soviet communism. His contextualism demanded a solution to social crisis from within American industrial society, and as such it could not brook either preservation of the status quo (New Deal tinkering) or the imposition of "foreign" solutions (communism). Dewey was wary of condemnation, which he sees as "too often a way of displaying superiority; it speaks from outside the scene; it discloses symptoms but not causes." But if condemnation is "impotent to produce" and "can only reproduce its own kind," how is Dewey's own analysis of conditions more useful than, for example, the Communist criticism he is so evidently swiping at? The difference is resolutely one of attitude rather than efficacy. Dewey's acceptance of flux allows that "[m]any outcomes may be projected" (ION, 112). Since communists can only accept one outcome, their diagnosis is not only scientifically corrupt but politically and socially totalitarian. In practice this sounds like: things may get worse or they may get better. Given the way state socialism worked out under Stalin and Hitler, Dewey's ostensibly soft response to the Depression fares infinitely better. When Dewey writes that "[i]f dogmas and institutions tremble when a new idea appears, this shiver is nothing to what would happen if the idea were armed with the means for the continuous discovery of new truth and the criticism of old belief," it is hard not to gasp in anticipation (ION, 116). How to arm the idea with the means and what these means are exactly are two questions, unfortunately, Dewey does not answer. His faith in creative intelligence as a bulwark against ideology, however, was shared during the 1930s by Williams, himself under siege from Right and Left and equally resistant to imported formulae. Dewey's call in *Individualism Old and New* for the reconceptualization of "work itself" as "an instrument of culture" (ION, 101; see chapter 2) is the kind of cultural politics Williams was seeking to enact in through a poetics grounded in technique.

WEDGE, LEVER AND FULCRUM, PULLEY AND INCLINED PLANE

Williams, like Dewey, was appalled by the suffering brought on by the Depression and equally vocal in his condemnation of the system that caused and failed to remedy it. Yet Williams's socialistic views, again like Dewey, never led him, as such views led so many writers of the 1930s, toward any partisan political position. Indeed, in many ways, Williams's position on writing and politics stands as a counterpart to Dewey's ideas on the individual and social planning. Just as Dewey saw planning as a nonpartisan, instrumental means for the generation of individual liberty, Williams viewed technique and craftsmanship in writing as the instruments of radical creativity. Dewey's argument for planning is grounded in a belief in the objectivity of scientific method: ongoing observation and experimentation leading to possible solutions. Williams's belief in technique is likewise understood as a nonideological means of accurately constructing a response to, and out of, historical contingency. Both strategies are undoubtedly inflected with socialistic connotations; indeed, Williams drew extensively on Louis Zukofsky's and George Oppen's Marxist-influenced creative uses of Pound in articulating his own views on technique, while Dewey's socialism is, as we have seen, indebted to the British Labour Party. Nevertheless, Williams and Dewey, while often appealing to the rhetoric of revolution, are both consistent in their rejection of Marxist or communist dogma. Their revolution remains a Jeffersonian one, an individual revolution of consciousness, a response to local events driven by experience and without supporting doctrine.

Dewey argues in *Individualism Old and New* for a new kind of individual equal to the challenge of the technological age. Once there is an "imagination large enough" to encompass the "potential uses" of science and technology, then it will be apparent that technology is not the tool of the oppressor but the facilitator of liberty (ION, 86). Williams shares this faith in technology as the instrument of liberation, both literally in terms of improving social conditions and with regard to the discipline of writing as the technology of composition. Reflecting on the state of America in a letter to Ford Madox Ford in September 1932, Williams refers to "the actual blasphemy which has overtaken my own New Jersey," the "chaos of factory towns and their squalid suburbs" which "breed blindness, arrested minds and a furious desperation of the spirit." One of these days, he goes on, "all necessary factory work will be done in one twentieth of the mutual cancelling machine menageries we have today—these will be decently arranged in reasonably healthful localities with properly appointed cottages around them and the horror of a past age will become apparent."[27]

Bringing about such a transformation can be achieved, Williams believes, not through ideologically sanctioned political activity, but rather through restructuring and reintegrating creative thought along communal lines: "unless a people is cultured enough to express themselves fully, in all colors and shapes of their living moods," they will be "unfit to have intercourse with their neighbors and unable to make head or tail of their own lives."[28] This is, of course, a political position, but like Dewey's view that blaming the machine for the troubles of the modern world is a "paralysis of the imagination" (ION, 87), Williams avoids discussing the actual political struggles that would be necessary to effect such a revolution in thinking, insisting that the transformation of thought must be individually achieved. How exactly the machine is liberated from the hands that make it the cause of trouble is not clear. At the local level—the self—there is a good chance that changes can be made for the better, but Williams considers the abstract theorizing of the American communists ridiculously futile: "They are only thinking in 'big terms' whereas the history of the country and the local dynamite that is embedded in it will blast them to hell and one before they have had time to wipe their asses after the first shit."[29]

Williams's argument against communism conforms to Dewey's rejection of ideology as antithetical to the American spirit of experimentation and improvisation. For Williams, the communists have no real understanding of American life as it is lived, relying instead on an imported formula of class struggle and revolution. Instead of useless debating, Williams writes, dismissively, they ought to study "anatomy or physiology, not to speak of psychology, for a year or two. Or even cooking." The objection is to the tyranny of theory over practice—you did not "make a cake by reading a book (Marx) either."[30]—and the suspicion that Marxism is just another totalizing system.

Williams's faith in American democracy is most plainly stated in his response to a questionnaire sent out by *Partisan Review,* and published in April 1936 under the title "What is Americanism?: A Symposium on Marxism and the American Tradition."[31] "My opinion," writes Williams categorically, "is that the American tradition is completely opposed to Marxism." America, he admits, "is progressing through difficult mechanistic adjustments" which it is, nevertheless, "confident it can take care of." Unlike "the democratic spirit," Marxism, "a static philosophy of a hundred years ago," has not been able to keep up "through the stresses of an actual trial. Marxism to the American spirit is only another phase of force opposed to liberalism. It takes a tough theory to survive America, and America thinks it has that theory."[32] Throughout its history, Williams continues, democracy has been "the essential shaft about which all the other movements and trends of thought have evolved—without changing it in any way." The fact is, he claims, that more radical thought (he cites Paine, Debs, and Haywood) seems "foreign to the environment. It is the same democracy of feeling which will defeat Marxism in America and all other attempts at regimentation of thought and action. It will also defeat fascism—though it may have to pass through that."[33] Summing up with a comment on the growing body of "proletarian" writing, Williams suggests that "the very premises of the revolutionary writers prevent an organic integration with the democratic principles upon which the American spirit is founded." This final Deweyan touch takes Williams back to the need for contact, a fusing of form and content in writing and, by extension, in life. The vast majority of so-called revolutionary writing in America in the 1930s was little more than blunt sloganeering strung along the pentameter, and there were prolonged debates in the *New Masses* and *Partisan Review* over the form and content question. The swing to Socialist Realism in 1932 as Communist party policy did much to alienate many fellow-travelling writers, laying down as it did a ground plan that left little scope for experimentation and idiosyncrasy and confirming the totalitarian tendencies Williams had suspected all along. Eliot's example of new formal strategies was supported by some critics, such as William Phillips and Philip Rahv, as a potential direction for radical poetry, but others viewed Eliot's work as nothing more than decadent bourgeois subjectivism. This kind of formulaic imposition of doctrine could never appeal to liberals such as Williams or Dewey, who found absurd the idea that traits such as "[f]air-play, elementary honesty in the representation of facts and especially of the opinions of others" could be described as "bourgeois virtues" when they were in fact the consequences of hard-won democracy."[34]

Williams knew that dogma was not, nor would it ever be, poetry. Any attempt to formulate a radical social position in writing must come through a transformation of the very structure of that writing. Without formal innovation, without technique, poetry will remain, regardless of its "message", fundamentally conservative in function. As Dewey observes, "[t]echnique can only signify emancipation of individuality, and emancipation on a broader scale than has been obtained in the past" (ION, 55). Williams's position is plain in his review of George Oppen's first book, *Discrete Series:* "If the poems in the book constitute necessary corrections of or emendations to human conduct in their day, both as to thought and manner, then they are good. But if these changes originated in the poems, causing thereby a direct liberation of the intelligence, then the book becomes of importance to the highest degree." This importance is not in the content since then "the fact that it is a poem would be a redundancy. What is important is "what the poem *is.*" This is "a technical matter, as with all facts, compelling the recognition of a mechanical structure. A poem which does not arouse respect for the technical requirements of its own mechanics may have anything you please painted all over it or on it in the way of meaning but it will for all that be as empty as a man made of wax or straw."[35]

Just as Dewey sees that social change is dependent upon new ways of thinking about social relations, Williams's belief in actual transformation can only come through a careful reshaping of the way meaning is constructed. This is the artist's job, to build a poem "on the bedrock of a craftsmanlike economy of means." "An imaginative new social order" requires "a skeleton of severe discipline for its realization and maintenance." By a "sharp restriction to essentials, the seriousness of a new order is brought to realization." Only by being "an object sharply defined and without redundancy will [the poem's] form project whatever meaning is required of it. It could well be, at the same time, first and last a poem facing as it must the dialectic necessities of its day. Oppen has carried this social necessity, so far as poetry may be concerned, over to an extreme," by presenting "a clear outline for an understanding of what a new construction would require." His poems "seek an irreducible minimum in the means for the achievement of their objective, no loose bolts or beams sticking out unattached at one end or put there to hold up a rococo cupid or a concrete saint, nor either to be a frame for a portrait of mother or a deceased wife."[36]

Pound had insisted that "I believe in technique as the test of a man's sincerity,"[37] the integrity of craftsmanship being a measure of certainty, a certainty that the work is what it says it is and not something else. Technique is a form of knowledge and a form of action; it is sincere, or honest, because of this integration of knowing and doing: "technique is itself substance," as Williams put it (SE, 104). Utilizing a technique realizes in the physical world a human intention. Pound's emphasis on technique and sincerity powerfully informs the poetics of Williams and "Objectivist" writers such as Louis Zukofsky and George Oppen, whose left-leaning interpretation of Pound's ideas deeply impinged on Williams's thought during the 1930s. What unites these poets is their commitment to rigor in perception and writing that responds to the complexity of social relations and political issues. The influence of Zukofsky, in particular, on Williams is considerable, and the Objectivist aesthetic, outlined principally by Zukofsky in the early 1930s, offers a clarity of political focus to Williams's work. As a response to the dilemma of a socially committed poetry Williams faced during the Depression, the Objectivist stance offered a sophistication conspicuously absent from the many American communist or proletarian writers Williams was so skeptical of.[38]

In "Program: 'Objectivists' 1931," Zukofsky draws his definition of an "objective" from optics: "The lens bringing the rays from an object into focus." Extended to poetry, this focusing is driven by a "[d]esire for what is objectively perfect, inextricably the direction of historic and contemporary particulars."[39] The stress here is on the accuracy of knowing and placing: "to place everything— everything aptly, perfectly, belonging within, one with, a context." This is a form of mapping, of grasping the dimensions of a thing amongst things, that Williams had always insisted was the ground of a democratically motivated poetry of place. It is the responsibility of the poet, in Zukofsky's words, to be "objectively perfect," that is, not to re-present reality, but to embody it. This is "sincerity," in which "shapes appear concomitants of word combinations. . . . Writing occurs which is the detail, not mirage, of seeing, of thinking with things as they exist, and of directing them along a line of melody."[40] Each word forms, and is formed by, its context. The poet's job is to work with the "historic and contemporary particulars," to shape the form. To shape the poem, which is "things as they exist," is to shape reality, to direct and not just to follow. Thus, poetry is a form of social engagement, because words are not removed from social reality but are elements of that reality. Oppen says, echoing Williams's own remarks on *Discrete Series,* that "one cannot make a poem by sticking words into it, it is the poem which makes the words and contains their meaning."[41] The poem is in history, it has a time and a place, and the meaning of the poem derives from that time and place, "a moment when you believe something to be true, and you construct a meaning from those moments of conviction."[42] The construction of this meaning is "bound up with events and contingencies," and because of this, whatever direction the poet may lead the poem is part of his or her social existence: any deviation from "particulars" is an abdication of "sincerity" and an evasion of engagement.[43]

The Objectivists' yoking of aesthetic and political concerns clearly drew upon the contextualist position Williams already had well worked out. Yet in offering a more explicitly leftist slant to Williams's ideas, they helped reinforce the strength of Williams's own stance toward the dilemma of what function writing might perform during the Depression. Williams did not give up writing for political activism, as Oppen did, but he was only too well aware of the necessary limits of poetry as a revolutionary act. If Williams does not make big instrumental revolutionary claims for his work it is because he cannot. Writing poetry is not class war. The power of art, rather, lies in its ability to transform experience, not the ownership of the means of production. In the first issue of the reactivated *Contact* magazine, edited by Williams with Robert McAlmon and Nathanael West, Williams puts bad writing on a par with bad social policy, suggesting that no amount of theorizing or propagandizing will cure either. Like Oppen, Williams believes that poetry and politics might require separate and specific responses:

> You might say: People are in distress the world over, writing will not relieve them (or make them worse off). Why not take the money there is for a magazine like this and give it away—as food—to the bums, for instance, living in packing cases over near the East River these winter nights?[44]

Redistribution of existing resources is no answer for Williams while "there's food enough rotting now in the world, even within sight of the place where these men are hanging out, to feed them every day in the year." If writing is a resource, it is because it is not convertible to any instrumental cause. Writing that attempts to "plead a social cause, to split a theory, to cry out at the evil which we all partake of" is, Williams argues, bad writing, a version of "the same sort of stupidity" that blames money for greed or puts ideology before experience. In contrast to the polemicist, the writer "has no use for theories or propaganda, he has no use for but one thing, the word that is possessing him at the moment he writes. Into that focus he must pour all he feels and has to say, as a writer, regardless of anything that may come of it. By word after word his meaning will then have been made clear."[45]

Williams's belief in the writer's focus on the materials at hand is not an avoidance of politics but a recognition that action must derive from circumstances and not rely on theoretical underpinning. If this action is to be revolutionary, it will be because of its originality, certainly not because it conforms to any kind of party orthodoxy. Williams told John Thirlwall in the 1950s that "I felt that the revolution was coming. I was never in favor of the [Communist] Party, but I did think that some revolution [would come] which would bring down the socialites and give the poor people a chance."[46] What Williams had always known was that revolution meant first and foremost a revolution of the imagination. Until the imagination is free to make contact and transform the way things are made and understood, no amount of money, theory, or propaganda will make a difference. Williams's poetics influenced, and was influenced by, Zukofsky and Oppen, their combined input resulting in an analysis of American culture and society that is recognizably pragmatic and democratic—in the American grain—and probably more revolutionary in intent than anything the Communist Party's literary wing came up with during the 1930s.

The emphasis Williams puts on craftsmanship and technique—"technique is itself substance" (SE, 104)—is in opposition to the erosion of skill-based work taking place in an increasingly automated culture. As such, the craftsman stands in resistance to any form of capitalist alienation. It was hardly necessary to be a Marxist to recognize the symptoms of this alienation. Dewey explains that

> [T]he subordination of the enterprises to pecuniary profit reacts to make the workers "hands" only. Their hearts and brains are not engaged. They execute plans which they do not form, and of whose meaning and intent they are ignorant—beyond the fact that these plans make a profit for others and secure a wage for themselves . . . The philosopher's idea of a complete separation of mind and body is realized in thousands of industrial workers, and the result is a depressed body and an empty and distorted mind. (ION,104)

Manifested in poetry, such an alienated and reified condition might show itself in what Williams describes as "crude symbolism[,] . . . strained associations, complicated ritualistic forms designed to separate the work from 'reality'—such as rhyme, meter as meter and not as the essential of the work, one of its words" (SA, 102). In this kind of writing the form has an "apparently altogether closed and rational autonomy" which bears no relationship to "reality"; indeed, such forms are "designed to separate" language from the world and keep them separate, their relationship obscured.

An exploration of what Oppen referred to as "categories of realness" might serve as a description of what Williams is attempting in his collection of poems from 1935, *An Early Martyr and Other Poems*. Presented with the "realness" of human suffering, Williams shuffles between objective description and allegory in search of a formal language adequate to the social situation. *An Early Martyr* is characterized by a number of poems dealing with the poor. The book is dedicated

"To John Coffee [Coffey]," the early martyr of the title and of the first poem. Coffey was "a young radical who wanted to help the poor, was convinced that they should be helped, and decided to do something about it" (IWWP, 56). Coffey's unorthodox tactic was to steal expensive furs from department stores and then contact the police and confess, hoping that the publicity would enable him to make his plea for the poor in court. The police, however, denied him the opportunity by placing Coffey in an insane asylum in 1920. He was eventually released and by the mid-thirties was back in New York "being thrown out of basement bars when he began to prate his social sermons there" (A, 299).

It is an indication of the strange mix of Village bohemianism and proletarian posturing that constituted the radical literary scene at the time that Coffey was not dismissed as a naive exhibitionist but seen as a romantic hero.[47] In "An Early Martyr," Coffey is still the "factory whistle / That keeps blaring—/ Sense, sense, sense!" (CP 1, 378), but his disruptive acts have been ineffective:

> [...] the set-up
> he fought against
> Remains—
> and his youthful deed
> Signalizing
> the romantic period
> of a revolt
> he served well
> Is still good—

The revolt is still good, it seems, but the romantic period is over. Indeed, the suffering of the 1930s demanded more than dadaist gestures, and much of the glamor attributed to the workers in the post-World War I years—one thinks, for example, of Mike Gold in his dirty shirts and Stetson, smoking Italian three-cent cigars and spitting frequently on the floor—was clearly inappropriate.[48] It is the spirit of revolt that Williams wants to hold on to, the dissenting voice, notably the voice of the lone individual against the impenetrable force of the institutions of the state. Even in polemical moments such as this, Williams cannot bring himself to think of political action in terms of a class struggle, but as a defense of individual liberty.

In other poems in *An Early Martyr* concerned with the poor, Williams refuses the general and focuses on specific individuals, presenting the characteristic rather than attempting the representative. The poems are objective, not metaphors for poverty. The subjects are usually women: a woman "with a face / like a mashed blood orange"; the "Poor Old Woman" "munching on a plum"; "A big young bareheaded woman / in an apron"; the victim of the raper of Passenack. These are distinct individuals, unconnected to each other and respected in their uniqueness.

Yet the poems are connected by their inclusion in the book, they are separate but related, a collection of true statements. One thinks of Oppen's explanation of his own book's title: "A discrete series is a series of terms each of which is empirically derived, each one of which is empirically true."[49]

As with Oppen's work, however, the empirically true serves as social criticism through its arrangement—its formation—by the poet. The presentation of the empirically true ought to be clear enough politically as well as formally, yet particularly during the thirties the pressure to drive home the point could cause tension between, as Robert von Hallberg points out in his discussion of Williams's thirties poetry, "two poles of discourse, explanation and description."[50] It is Williams's belief, along with the Objectivists, that accurate description of the facts, as a form of knowledge, is a way of concretizing experience and making it accessible to change. The apparent political neutrality of this position, with its reservation of judgment in favor of presentation, opened Williams to criticism from the Left during a decade when explanations seemed more in order than description. The poets included along with Williams in An 'Objectivists' Anthology were accused of just such an abdication of political responsibility by a Poetry reviewer in 1933. Zukofsky responded by quoting Lenin's claim that the revolutionary proletariat "rejected Marxism, stubbornly refused to understand (it would be more correct to say that they could not understand) the necessity of a strictly objective estimate of all the class forces and their interrelation in every political action."[51] This "strictly objective estimate of all the class forces" is exactly what Zukofsky believed the Objectivists were attempting to achieve. Williams may not have known his Lenin but he would agree that the poet should have a precise knowledge of what is around him, taking a measure of his context. This knowledge is ascertained by a clarity of perception that eschews any technique that might divert attention away from the immediate. Williams's knowledge is essentially nonpartisan because there are no preconditions, no agenda outside the poem. Political alignment must come after the "strict objective estimate." Writing a poem is thus analogous to Dewey's notion of scientific method: it is dependent on its materials and its immediate conditions, and the results cannot be externally manipulated. What materializes from this process is a clear view of the terrain, a prospect of what may be possible within the limits of the facts. In "A Poem for Norman MacLeod," Williams points out that "The revolution / is accomplished" when "noble has been / changed to no bull," and that "You can do lots / if you know / what's around you / No bull" (CP1, 401). We might be reminded here of Williams's point that in "the word that is possessing him at the moment he writes" he pours "all he feels and has to say." In this case the pun on "noble" offers a compressed argument for integrity made out of "what's around you": the revolution is in seeing the possibilities words will yield up.

It would be inaccurate to describe all the poems in An Early Martyr as elements in a discrete series, since Williams utilizes a variety of styles and often strays from the definition. One such poem, which attempts something very different from the objective studies and is far more strident, is "The Yachts" (CP1,

388–389). Dealing with the America's Cup yacht races Williams had seen in Newport, Rhode Island, and recalling the scene from the *Inferno* where Dante and Virgil must cut through the limbs of the damned in order to prevent their boat from sinking, "The Yachts" is an indictment of the untouchable brilliance of American capitalism. The poem also suggests a criticism of the equally untouchable process of two-party politics, the endless vying for position preventing any policy from making a difference. In a letter to Pound of August 1934, Williams refers to the party political struggle for power as a race, "the organized opposition by the wealthy Republicans" threatening "everything Roosevelt is trying to do. It's a race: he'll do it his way, putting over the rudiments of an idea, or they'll get the whip hand back and kill the idea."[52] As the parties battle amongst themselves, the people remain separate and indistinct, "an ungoverned ocean"—a mass through which the yachts, "with broad bellying sails," "glide to the wind tossing green water / from their sharp prows." The grace of the yachts, of course, is supplied by the medium through which they move, "the sea which holds them." The sea is "moody, lapping their glossy sides, as if feeling / for some slightest flaw but fails completely." While the parties fight in the name of the people, the people themselves are excluded from what is little more than a spectacle of shimmering power. As the wind picks up, the boats gain speed and the scene becomes a terrible struggle for survival: "Now the waves strike at them but they are too / well made, they slip through, though they take in canvas."

The machinery of government has become impervious and indifferent to the element that holds it afloat, and the poem moves to a bitter conclusion as the people, clammering to get aboard, are "cut aside":

> It is a sea of faces about them in agony, in despair
>
> until the horror of the race dawns staggering the mind,
> the whole sea become an entanglement of watery bodies
> lost to the world bearing what they cannot hold. Broken
>
> beaten, desolate, reaching from the dead to be taken up
> they cry out, failing, failing! their cries rising
> in waves still as the skillful; yachts pass over. (CP1, 388–389)

From the perspective of the yachts, the people are simply an "ungoverned ocean" struggling to get on board for safety. From within *An Early Martyr*, with its collection of portraits of discrete individuals, the homogeneity presented in "The Yachts" is a striking glimpse of the view from the deck of government where people such as the "Poor Old Woman" are no more than part of an undifferentiated mass.

In another poem, "The Catholic Bells" (CP1, 397–398), Williams offers a response to the failure of representative democracy described in "The Yachts."

"Tho' I'm no Catholic," the poem begins, "I listen hard" as the bells name, or testify to, the plurality of things and people: the leaves, frost, flowers, and sky, the young and old, sick and well. The people in this poem are not submerged in a desperate sea, they are individuals with names, characteristics, customs, and beliefs: "Mr and Mrs Kranz" and their new baby, the "lame / young man in black with / gaunt cheeks and wearing a / Derby hat, who is hurrying / to 11 o'clock Mass." It is not so much the church that unifies this community as the pervasive sound of the bells, the life-affirming saturation of the ring. The poem risks a nostalgic sentimentality, and perhaps outside the context of the other poems in *An Early Martyr* it would seem so, but as a counterpoint to "The Yachts" it is an act of defiance against the brutality of privilege and a demonstration of faith in the resilience of a local community in a time of great hardship. It is this kind of faith, in the poem and in its subject, that enables Williams to believe that a work of art can be evidence "of a new world which it has been created to affirm." The artist, by dealing directly with "the sensuality of his materials," might, "and finally must be expanded—holds the power of expansion at any time—into new conceptions of government" (SE, 196–197). This conception is, in "The Catholic Bells," again for Williams a local one, a Jeffersonian and Deweyan vision of self-regulated and self-sustaining community, continuous and indifferent to the sleek power of the yachts of so-called representative government. The particularity of Williams's citizens defies incorporation by the interests of business. The poem also, as a retort to the polemics of proletarian poetry (of which "The Yachts" might be seen, perhaps, as something of a parody), resists what Dewey calls the communists' "absurd attempt to make a single and uniform entity out of the 'proletariat.'"[53]

POEMS TO LIVE IN

Dewey recognized the corporate nature of modern America and saw corporateness as not necessarily a bad thing in itself. While he saw incorporation as favoring the excesses of capitalism as well as being intrinsic to the pernicious collectivism of communism, it had also created a "common market" held together by "intercommunication and inter-dependence" (ION, 59). Corporateness, then, might be conducive to community building if its strengths can be harnessed and its dangers avoided. The marginalized position of the artist in contemporary life is offered by Dewey as an index of individual isolation in a society "growing corporate." The imaginative power needed to turn corporateness into community is also best embodied in the artist. As Williams knew, this power is blocked by a culture where value is only measured in terms of pecuniary profit . It is also blocked where ideology replaces creativity. Organized politics of right or left therefore amounted to much the same thing. For Dewey and Williams the middle way is the creative path taken by the imagination. In the face of mass production they both stress the importance of technical skill and craftsmanship as qualities that enhance and preserve individuality. Alongside the experimental method of science, technique and craft provide a measure of an individual autonomy wedded to the materials and experience of everyday life. This is their answer to communism and their response to the alienation and suffering brought about by capitalist power. Even Dewey's argument for social planning is a call for a social process of perpetual renewal as opposed to a planned society. It is an argument for collective social engagement, not government by committee. Williams may not have had much of an interest in the nuts and bolts of social organization but he believed, as Dewey did, that it was the artist who held the key to the power of creating "new conceptions of government." The revolutionary social responsibility of art is to be individual and to build relationships out of this individuality. This responsibility does not need logical or theoretical proof, though it does require the less doctrinaire but equally committed attitude of faith.

Such a view of art's responsibility is far from programatically worked out by Williams—it is, after all, an experimental process and not a theory—and is constantly put under question in many of his essays. In "The Basis of a Faith in Art," probably written in 1937, but not published until 1954, Williams uses the dialogue between a poet and an architect (representing Williams and his brother) to pose a series of questions about the social function of art. Framed as a debate between brothers, the essay offers a model of community building that begins at home, the bond of intimacy between interlocutors in the text reaching out to connect text and reader. Furthermore, the explicitly social and practical functions of the architect offer a useful counterpoint to the notionally less utilitarian pursuits of the poet through which Williams can develop an argument for writing as a form of construction and habitation.

Writing for Williams is an exploratory act, "more a matter of how I could cling to what I had and not relinquish it in the face of tradition than anything else" (SE, 177). Tradition, or existing culture, is seen as outside the self, something the creative self must push against. Placing oneself is difficult when the positions available are the legitimated "safe stereotype" of convention, or "chaos." Faced with these choices, it is necessary to make a position that conforms to the individual's needs; it is necessary to "begin to invent—or try to invent" (SE, 177). The creation of a sustaining place of being is firstly, then, a recognition of what one is not:

> I always knew that I was I, precisely where I stood and that nothing could make me accept anything that had no counterpart in myself by which to recognize it. I always said to myself that I did not speak English, for one thing, and that that should be the basis for a beginning, that I spoke a language that was my own and that I would govern it according to my necessities and not according to unrelated traditions the necessity of whose being had long since passed away. English is full of such compunctions which are wholly irrelevant for a man living as I am today—but custom makes it profitable for us to be bound by them. Not me. (SE, 177)

Writing is here inseparable from identity creation and, in another of Williams's invocations of the Declaration of Independence, a refusal to be assimilated into the dominant ideology. The writer shakes off compunctions and refuses to profit from custom, which is, after all, a form of bondage to conformity. To write, how-ever, is not simply an act of self-emancipation, it is a social act, a form of build-ing for habitation by society: "You build houses for people. Poems are the same" (SE, 178). Individual liberty through creativity facilitates cultural freedom and social bonding: people are "the origin of every bit of life that can possibly inhabit any structure, house, poem or novel of conceivable human interest. . . . If we don't cling to the warmth which breathes into a house or a poem alike from human need[,] . . . the whole matter has nothing to hold it together and be-comes structurally weak so that it falls to pieces" (SE, 178). Like building a house, a poem must consider the materials out of which it is made and from where they have come; it must be responsive to its environment, because its exis-tence is due to the sustenance it receives from its context: "[T]he minute you let yourself be carried away by purely 'architectural' or 'literary' reasoning without consulting the thing from which it grew, you've cut the life giving artery and nothing ensues but rot" (SE, 178). Creativity is not free from the world, "all the arts have to come back to something," and that thing is "human need" (SE, 178). Williams insists that "the purpose of art IS to be useful" (SE, 179). What might this use be?

In part, the use is in creating a shared culture in "defiance" of the "destroying horror of an oppressive existence," an act of construction and connection "in the hope that he [the writer] may gather to himself others with whom he would like to see the world better populated" (SE, 180). The art must be precise, so that communication is as direct as possible, "CLEAN of the destroying, falsifying, be-smurching agencies with which [the writer] is surrounded. Everything he does is an explanation. He is always trying his very best to refine his work until it is noth-ing else but 'useful knowledge'"(SE, 180). The clarity of poetry functions as a critique of inadequate government, because it is pure liberty "in opposition to its cruder replicas" (SE, 180). Poetry is thus the fierce testimony to, in Dewey's terms, realized capacities as the law of life (LSA, 41).

Art, then, cannot become the propaganda wing of party interests, because this would subordinate individual liberty and undermine the direct energy of transmission between artist and work, work and audience. The artist "is a pitiful liar if he allows himself to be used that way" because, despite political allegiances, the artist alone knows how he or she "can work most effectively" (SE, 183). The kind of "useful knowledge" Williams speaks of is not, then, vulgarly instrumen-talist, but if it is not a tool for organized political activity, even when such activ-ity is needed, then how does an artist work socially and at the same time main-tain his or her individual liberty? This is the problem of being an artist in a democracy, and Williams has moved so far along his line of argument as to reach the difficult position of someone who is, as stated, dependent on the people for his material and for his communal audience, yet determined to stay separate from them as an independent creative individual. The problem is not lost on Williams, and the architect spots the inconsistency: "You still want to maintain your independence as an artist. You don't want to be told what to do . . . Yet from the people, you say, the artist derives all that he has. Aren't theses two viewpoints mutually contradictory? I think they are and I think you're not half the people's man you think you are" (SE, 185). The artist proceeds to clarify his position, perforated by objections, the text in effect becoming disruptive of its own production:

> He [the artist] must maintain his independence—
> Which amounts to a divorce from society.
> —in order to be able to perceive their needs and to act upon the
>   imperative necessities of his perceptions.
> Independent and dependent! You make me laugh.
> Independent of opinion, dependent of body. The artist had better
>   be a poor man. (SE, 186)

The architect's skepticism is well founded, since the dependence on society, even as body, presumably enfolds the artist within the habits and customs of the people. His opinions must, it seems, to stay independent, be somehow of a different order to theirs, which marks the artist as an outsider. Being a poor man might not save the artist from cultural elitism and divorce from the society he claims to be part of. The architect, sensing a weakness in the argument, suggests that the artist is, in fact, "a rudderless nonentity furiously laboring at random whims, from among whose works, with time, a public takes the initiative to select its equally haphazard choices?" Instead of dismissing this as an insult, however, the artist agrees with the description. The democratic artist has no rudder other than context, and since the significance of art cannot be legislated for and must be discovered, the artist's work may well be ignored. In such a flux, the architect wonders, "whose is the government?" To which the artist responds: "The one who most needs" (SE, 186).

The independence of the artist as an individual, then, is paramount, yet he or she is connected to society by membership and by a shared responsibility toward those in need. This independence enables the artist to be somehow inside and outside simultaneously, able to get "a sense of totality; the whole; humanity as a whole" (SE, 192) while remaining capable of responding empathically, since, "How can a man be satisfied when he sees another man lacking [?]" (SE, 192). Williams concludes that "There is no conflict between the individual and society—unless the individual offend" (SE, 193). To suggest that it is society's function to "generate surpassing individuals" is "antiquated reasoning." Rather, "society, *to be served*, must generate individuals to serve it, and cannot do otherwise than to give such individuals full play—*until* or unless their activities prove antisocial" (SE, 193). Because the individual is intrinsically of society, to be against it would be to be against oneself. The self-interest of the individual cannot be separated from the social interest. Individual freedom can thus be read as a function of social service.

The value of an artist's contribution to society "is to be judged in the end not by the purchasers of his work," who may be "corrupt or tyrannical fools or institutions," but "inexorably *by society*—by society as a whole, the great being great only as society accepts and enthrones them" (SE, 193–194). The strength of work made in a state of freedom, Williams believes, can survive being co-opted by the power brokers of the culture industry because "in those very works of art are likely to lie the disruptive seeds which will destroy the very hosts who have taken them in—and preserved them for society even against their will" (SE, 193). The subversive potential Williams bestows upon art here is at the very least indeterminately delayed to some future moment when the latent power might be released. This might suggest that Williams is not quite sure when art becomes subversive. If it is bought and stored by fools and tyrants, how can he be sure that the disruptive seeds latent within it are precisely what they are buying, for the very purpose of keeping them away from society? The idea of the artist "in the end" being judged by the whole of society suggests further uncertainty over the time it might take for art to be released into the world.

Williams's main concern, however, is not so much with what happens to the work after the fact of its creation, but with the point that "[i]t is essential to good government that the poet, as an individual, remain at liberty to possess his talent, answerable to no one *before the act* but to his own conception of truth" (SE, 197). Williams has faith enough in work produced under these conditions to believe that it is incapable of dissolution and will find or be sought out by its audience. After all, the point of an experimental aesthetic working without precedent or standard is that outcomes cannot be predicted. What seems like the weakness of uncertainty in Williams is thus the very strength of unpredictability. As answerable to no one before the act, the artist can be "the critic of government whether the party in power like it or not," because his freedom defies limitation from any agency outside himself. This principle is "constantly operative under all conditions. All the best has been maintained in spite of government as a limiting power. Not against government, *not* against government but against usurpation of government by a class, a group, a set of any sort, king, bureaucracy or sans-culotte—which would subvert the freedom of the individual for some temporary need." Thus, by being outside but responsive to society the artist is "a social regenerator" (SE, 194).

Government, then, is a limiting power. This Williams accepts and can remain optimistic about since the "best" has survived the limitations imposed by government. Like Dewey, Williams's scorn is reserved for the hijackers of democracy who seek to manipulate government for its own ends. The artist's job—and the category for Williams includes any "type of person who is creative, who has something to give society" (SE, 194)—is to break down "imposed tyrannies," to be in constant revolt against fixity, to keep the experiment going. Art stands as liberty as it should be. As such it exposes the shortcomings of any government, any system that functions to curtail liberty. In *Paterson* this resistance to any kind of systemization would take its most expansive form, the poem becoming a thoroughgoing demonstration of Williams's longheld pragmatic stance toward the political function of art in a democracy.

SIX

PATERSON

---

beautiful but expensive

Waken from a dream, this dream of / the whole poem.
—William Carlos Williams

Given Williams's desire to realize the radical imperatives of liberal democracy in poetry as an essential component of a renovated American modernity, it is not surprising that the epic poem becomes a central focus for his creative ambitions. In *Paterson*, all of Williams's major preoccupations are reiterated and amplified within the context of the epic's explicitly civic function, which is, in Hegel's words, "the objective manifestation of a national spirit presented in its self-objectifying shape as an actual event."[1] The conflict between the authority of the narrative voice as textual monarch and the demands of a democratic plurality; the question of a cultural conversation of equals; the ambivalent defense of institutionalized boundary concepts such as marriage and art; the need to dissolve barriers between artificially separated polarities without loss of individual identity; the prospect of an art that can function as an agent of progressive education and cultural liberation; the attempt to salvage from marginalized social groups an alternative model of linguistic and economic exchange: these issues, the staples of Deweyan Progressive pragmatism, find in *Paterson* their articulation as high modernism. Because preoccupations resurface, however, is not to suggest that they reach a higher level of resolution. As we shall see, *Paterson,* for all its ambitions, is not about laying debates to rest; rather, it is about the unquestionable desire for finality and the need to reach a point where the drive for such an overbearing, and potentially totalitarian, totalizing impulse can be dissolved.

The epic form offers Williams, as it offered Pound, a space within which to engage with the interface between art and history, and to work through an extended exploration of the function of poetry in the modern world. What becomes clear in *Paterson* is what is implicit in all Williams's work: his attempts to create an American aesthetics and idiom grounded in experience hope to stretch beyond revitalizing creativity through restructuring the forms of bourgeois autonomous art, toward an avant-garde critique of the institution of art itself. The epic provides for Williams the materials for a dismantling and reassembling of the institutional frame, as the poem discovers that its structure is a failure of structure, its language speaks only of a failure of language, its quest for totality is a futile and potentially self-destructive quest. The limitations of art are not, here, the consequence of a romantic sensibility unable to transcend earthly corruption, but the result of society's separation of art from the rest of life, a subsystem within the institutional matrix of corporate capitalist society. Economic, educational, and aesthetic discourses of valuation thus feature prominently in *Paterson* as Williams seeks to redefine artistic work as a form of social democratic praxis dependent on, responsive to, and responsible for historical contingency. As Alec Marsh has rightly pointed out, *Paterson* "stages its own contingency," reflects "on its own madeness."[2]

To write an epic is to deliberately engage in the affairs of society, to tell the tale of the tribe. In the epic poet, as Northrop Frye observes, "a poetic knowledge and expressive power which is latent or needed in his society comes to articulation."[3] In *Paterson,* Williams nominates himself as that poet, seeking to extract from America the knowledge and power he believes is latent there in order to demonstrate and embody the promise of the nation's origins. His job is, as Jeffrey Walker explains, "ethical persuasion, not a 'compromised' playing to the audience's uninstructed tastes (*ie,* mere entertainment), and not the induction of acolytes into an alienated, yet imperious 'rare world' of literature."[4] Unlike Pound, who, it might be argued, chose the latter course, Williams's liberalism guides his epic ambition toward a pluralistic aesthetic of inclusion and equality, overseen by the poet as civil servant: "The poet has to serve and the reader has to—be met and won—without compromise" (SE, 183).

The danger of writing an epic poem is clearly that it might fix the "national spirit" in its "self-objectifying shape." Williams deliberately avoids this danger through a pragmatic conception of writing as experiment, or, in Hegel's terms, as "an actual event." If *Paterson* reaches any kind of totality, it is a Deweyan totality that contains its own unraveling. Dewey's view of totality is an attempt to eradicate the kind of tragic failure critics such as Georg Lukács have attributed to the modern world. An imagined ideal totality, whether nostalgically memorialized or projected into an unattainable future, is for Dewey a case of privileging absence over presence which devalues the actual in favor of an imagined elsewhere. Such conceptions of a perfect goal, of completion, "possess significance only as movements *toward* something away from what is going on now. Since growth is just a movement toward a completed being, the final ideal is immobile. An abstract and indefinite future is in control with all which that connotes in depreciation of present power and opportunity" (DE, 61). Dewey reverses the emphasis of Hegelian idealism, foregrounding process—"growing is growth, developing is development" (DE, 63)—the achievement of an imagined or desired end serving a functional, motivational role, but subordinated to the concrete experience of the present. This is one of the ways Williams reconceptualizes the structure of the epic, by transvaluing the totality as a means of holding together contradiction without succumbing to the idealist goal of synthesis.

Paterson's ambitions are, in large part, the agonized and unfulfilled ambitions of American Progressivism, and Williams's belief in the potential for constructive change and growth that lies latent but undisclosed in the American continent, language, and political system, is articulated through a grammar of radical liberalism. Dewey's part in constructing and disseminating this grammar is, as we have seen, not inconsiderable. What Williams and Dewey see when they look at America is potential: unprecedented wealth and resources, unparalleled diversity of population, unforeseen developments in science and technology, a constellation of political principles virtually untarnished by the wear of too little use. This potentiality and optimism can be positively iridescent with promise, but faced with rapacious greed, ruthless prejudice, and ambitious economic and cultural imperialism, a political philosophy based on the freedom of the individual seeks but struggles to find a space through which to prize open the enclosed structures of domination it hopes to undermine. It is a measure of the power of Williams's distilled Deweyan progressivism that in *Paterson,* even failure becomes reconfigured as a sign of renewed vigor.[5]

THE IDEA OF HARMONY, NEGATIVELY

In a letter to Henry Wells of 1950, Williams clearly articulated the processual and provisional nature of his work and how, even in failure, the aspiration embodied within it remained a socially transformative aspiration:

> The poem . . . is an attempt, an experiment, a failing experiment, toward assertion with broken means but an assertion, always, of a new and total culture, the lifting of an environment to expression. Thus it is social, the poem is a social instrument—accepted or not accepted seems to be of no material importance. It embraces everything we are. (SL, 286)

Williams accepts that the material at hand, the social reality that provides the substance of poetry, the means, is "broken." Like Dewey, he understands that a failed experiment is not grounds for abandoning inquiry. In fact, the inability to control the outcome of an experiment is a recognition of forces that cannot be manipulated without undermining the integrity of the experimental procedure. Experimentation is, as always, a method, a way of learning about phenomena, and no experiment can yield total or absolute information even though the desired outcome may be to achieve just that. As Williams told Marianne Moore in 1951, "At times there is no other way to assert the truth than by stating our failure to achieve it" (SL, 304). In another letter to Moore, this failure is seen as the necessary objectivity "to say what we see and let the rest speak for itself" (SL, 305). In embodying "everything we are," then, the poem as a "social instrument," must accept fragmentation and indeterminacy as a structural principle. Thus, the failure of the poem as experiment might well be necessary to the continuation of the process of experimentation. Certainly, as Dewey observes, "[h]armony with conditions," which Williams sought in constructing a work which pulsed with the real, "is not a single and monotonous uniformity, but a diversified affair requiring individual attack" (ION, 120).

A successful work of art, argues Adorno, "is not one which resolves objective contradictions in a spurious harmony, but one which expresses the idea of harmony negatively, by embodying the contradictions, pure and uncompromised, in its innermost structure."[6] To impose an enforced unity on the poem would be an act of bad faith and in contravention of the scientific method of experimentation; it would be a lie, and in "the structure the artist . . . cannot lie. . . . Look at the structure if you will truly grasp the significance of a poem" (SE, 204, 207). Williams always insisted that "[n]o verse can be free, it must be governed by some measure, but not by the old measure" (SE, 339). The "abstract idea of freedom" is not liberty but an "idea lethal to all order, particularly to that order which has to do with the poem" (SE, 339). If the poem "embraces all that we are" and the significance of the poem lies in its structure, then the social and political world, as part of everthing we are, must somehow be revealed in the structure of the poem. The poem functions as a synecdoche for society, which must be "governed" by a new measure discovered in the poem/society itself, a measure immanent in the materials and not an abstraction brought in as external governance. Abstraction, for Williams, is the force that pulverizes local distinctions into vacuous planiformity and facilitates the imposition of oppressive structures of meaning. What is needed is "a measure consonant with our time," since "[w]ithout measure we are lost" (SE, 339–340). What does measure mean in the modern world? To measure is to ascertain dimensions, to count, to chart, to locate points in time and space. Measurement is concerned with relations, with contexts. Given the fragmentary nature of modern existence, fixed standards of measurement are insufficient. The context must provide the measure, a system of coordinates that responds to the conditions of the environment. Following from Williams's faith in the incorruptible objectivity of scientific methodology, it is not surprising that he finds a possible index to contemporary American life—a measure—in the theory of relativity.

"How," asks Williams in "The Poem as a Field of Action" (1948), "can we accept Einstein's theory of relativity, affecting our very conception of the heavens about us of which poets write so much, without incorporating its essential fact— the relativity of measurements—into our category of activity: the poem. Do we think we stand outside the universe?" (SE, 283). Indeed, Heisenberg's uncertainty principle had put paid to the notion of an omniscient, impartial observer, a breakthrough that went a long way to confirming Dewey's own contextualism. In *Logic: The Theory of Inquiry* (1938), Dewey writes that "[w]e never experience nor form judgments about objects and events in isolation but only in connection with a contextual whole. This latter is what is called a 'situation.'"[7] An object or event is "always a special part, phase, or aspect, of an environing experienced world—a situation. The singular object stands out conspicuously because of its especially local and crucial position at a given time in determination of some problem . . . which the *total* complex environment presents. There is always a *field* in which observation of *this* or *that* object or event occurs."[8] Dewey's use of "total" does not denote closure and containment but refers to the extent or range of an object's or event's scope of action:

> Wherever there is an event, there is interaction, and interaction entails the concept of a *field*. No "field" can be precisely delimited; it extends wherever the energies involved in the interaction operate and as far as any redistributions of energy are effected. The field can be limited *practically*, as can all matters of degree; it can not be existentially located with literal exactness.[9]

Einstein's theory of relativity was, as Dewey observes, a "genuine revolution," destabilizing the way phenomena are understood, and providing both Dewey and Williams with a conceptual apparatus and hard science legitimation for their social and aesthetic arguments (QC, 117).[10] For Dewey, Einstein eliminated the notion of absolute properties in favor of "*relations of events*" which "secure, in their generality, the possibility of linking together objects viewed as events in a general system of linkage and translation" (QC, 117). These relations "do the business that all thinking and objects of thought have to effect: they connect, through relevant operations, the discontinuities of individualized observations and experiences into continuity with one another. Their validity is a matter of their efficacy in performance of this function; it is tested by results and not by correspondence with antecedent properties of existence" (QC, 117).

"Relativity applies to everything," says Williams (SE, 283). From being fixed, "our prosodic values should rightly be seen as only relatively true. Einstein had the speed of light as a constant—his only constant—What have we? Perhaps our concept of musical time" (SE, 286). The constant is the unit of measurement, and, "How do we know reality? The only reality that we can know is MEASURE" (SE, 283). To measure, to relate phenomena to the conceptual constant, is to bring world and mind together through the act of measuring. A sequence of measurements maps the field and also defines the field, it is a making as well as a discovering. When Dewey says that relations "connect, through relevant operations, the discontinuities of individualized observations and experiences into continuity with one another," he could be describing the structure of *Paterson*. The poet, like the scientist, discovers connections through observation of individual, specific occurrences—the local—and compiles these specifics, relates each to the other, to extrapolate meaning. The observer is the organizing force, located within the field, and therefore all observations are relative, related, to him or herself. Dewey and Williams would undoubtedly concur with Heisenberg that "what we observe is not nature in itself but nature exposed to our questioning."[11]

The kind of totality Williams seeks to embody in his epic is not, then, an absolute unity, an undifferentiated whole without ambiguity or dissonance. This he accepts, yet to write an epic he must still "find an image large enough to embody the whole knowable world around me" (A, 391). The "knowable world" is that which is phenomenally available. To embody the "whole knowable world" is, then, to embody the sum of the individual's experiences in that world. The attainment of this kind of ontological totality is akin to Heidegger's notion of *Dasein,* of being there, which suggests a state of being at home in the world, of presence and of historical specificity. It is, indeed, the knowable world "about me" that Williams seeks to embody, his context, and from this context Williams must read himself and the history of his people.

The poet does not, says Williams, "permit himself to go beyond the thought to be discovered in the context of that with which he is dealing: no ideas but in things. The poet thinks with his poem, in that lies his thought, and that in itself is the profundity. The thought is *Paterson,* to be discovered there" (A, 390–391). Thoughts do not exist independently of the poem, they are developed and inherent in the poem, as the poem. The conventional thinker, the scholar, writes Williams, "tries to capture the poem for his purpose, using his 'thought' as the net to put his thoughts into" (A, 391). This is "absurd" because the thoughts and "thought", in themselves, have no ground, are not related to the world. For Williams, it is not the poet's business "to talk in vague categories but to write particularly, as a physician works, upon a patient, upon the thing before him, in the particular to discover the universal" (A, 391). The aspect of discovery, of exploration, emphasizes the process of writing, the development of form through the plotting of contextual coordinates. The comparison between writing and medicine stresses the fact that the poet administers some kind of treatment to the language, is active in its regeneration. This practice is his duty: *Paterson* "called for a poetry such as I did not know, it was my duty to discover or make such a context in the 'thought'." It is "in the very lay of the syllables Paterson as Paterson would be discovered, perfect, perfect in the special sense of the poem. . . ." (A, 392). Williams is fully aware of his responsibilities as an epic poet, of the structural imperatives of the form. "I knew the rules of poetry," he admits, "even though I knew nothing of the actual Greek; I respected the rules but I decided I must define the traditional in terms of my own world" (IWWP, 74). After all, he was "writing in a modern occidental world," and an appropriate form must be invented from the stuff of this world. The form of *Paterson* "wasn't a finished form, yet I knew it was not formless" (IWWP, 74).

AMERICAN MEIOSIS

Williams's need to discover the universal in the particular is especially pertinent to the epic, with its characteristic interplay between the specific and the general. In Dewey's phrase "the local is the only universal" Williams found in shorthand the logic of the epic.[12] How, exactly, is the meaning or substance of the particular and the factual made accessible by the epic poet? By what method is history made apparent as a living, ongoing demonstration of presence? In what way can the local be made to speak the universal? Williams had already experimented, in *In the American Grain,* with the possibility of incarnating a plurality of voices, and it is this issue of breathing the past into the present that he takes up again in *Paterson.* Eric A. Havelock points out that the Homeric epic "has to exist in a culture of oral communication, where if any useful statement, historical, technical, or moral, is to survive, in more or less standardized form, this can be done only in the living memories of the members who make up the culture group." The epic is thus not an act of creation as much as it is an act of "reminder and recall," and involves not merely memory as a "mental phenomenon," but as "the total act of reminding, recalling, memorialising, and memorising."[13] The "technology of memorialisation" used by the epic poet in an oral culture combines the transmission of sound, sense, and rhythm through the orator repeating the poem, producing "a series of bodily reflexes"—lungs, larynx, tongue, and teeth—in order to articulate or re–call the utterance.[14] The poem moves from linguistic to muscular embodiment as it is absorbed by the recipient. "Say it, no ideas but in things" Williams prompts (P, 14), calling for a spoken (i.e., bodily) repetition of the phrase. The poem is here prodding and didactic, seeking to push the written words out into the mouth and mind of the reader. Four pages on, the request is repeated, this time more forcefully: "Say it! No ideas but in things," (P, 18). This is a command, an urgent "act of reminding." The "redeeming language" Williams hoped to find in the writing of *Paterson* must begin with a lesson on how to speak, and in speaking, how to remember, how to feel the shape of words formed by the mouth and how to hear the articulation of those words. In such a way is the reading subject implicated in the embodiment of the ideas registered in the text (as things). By remembering and reenacting the muscular actions of articulation, the poetic utterance, as Havelock argues, is identified as "a thing in itself which flows like a river."[15]

Williams wrote in his *Autobiography* that "[t]he Falls let out a roar as it crashed upon the rocks at its base. In the imagination this roar is a speech or a voice, a speech in particular; it is the poem itself that is the answer" (A, 392). The river is the source of a natural language that contains the history of place. The crash of water on the rocks endlessly repeats, with endless variation, this history for anyone to hear. The language is not independent of action, it is not in an abstract realm; it is generated by a series of transactions between elemental forces—water and earth—and the sound created is interpreted ("discovered," Williams would say) as voice and meaning by the imagination of the auditor. As in the incantatory response of the listener to the epic poem, the speech of the river prompts the response of the poem *Paterson,* a repetition in written form of the language caught by the ear and transformed by the mind. The reenaction in writing of the river's "speech or a voice" becomes part of the epic process of remembrance, part of the communication of a shared history, yet also "a thing in itself," which, in its respect for the form of its source, "flows like a river."

This is at least the desired outcome of Williams's epic ambition. Since, however, the reality of the modern experience will not and should not cohere into some formal totality but must remain incomplete and relative to conditions, the transmission of nature's language is not necessarily direct. The reciprocity of communication between nature and poet, poet and polis, is impeded, fractured, and dispersed: the conversation does not produce harmony but infers it only in the failing. The energy generated by the flow of the river does not necessarily reach its mark and the potential power is lost:

> A false language. A true. A false language pouring—a
> language (misunderstood) pouring (misinterpreted) without
> dignity, without minister, crashing upon a stone ear. (P, 24)

This movement between false and true, the difficulty of catching the words correctly, does not abate as the poem continues but remains as a persistent block-age to communication: "he looks down, listens! / But discovers, still, no syllable in the confused / uproar: missing the scene (though he tries) / untaught but listen-ing, shakes with the intensity / of his listening" (P, 100).

For Williams, it becomes necessary for the poem to engage with this sense of disconnection and depletion of energies, which he describes variously in terms of blockage and divorce. *Paterson* becomes the site for an attempt to understand the nature of what it means to be broken in order to bring about a remarriage of frag-ments and to reconnect and reestablish relationships that will restore the flow— the flow of power created through the *frission* of tactile connectedness in social, linguistic, political, and ontological terms.

The poem is more about violence than harmony, more revealing of corrup-tion than of innocence, more concerned with broken promises than with estab-lished bonds. Yet in concerning itself with forms of institutionalized alienation, *Paterson* attempts to gather up, redirect, and let loose the dispersed energy lost or misspent through violence, corruption, and divorce, in order to piece together a shattered culture almost despite itself:

> . . . . a mass of detail
> to interrelate on a new ground, difficultly;
> an assonance, a homologue
> > triple piled
> pulling the disparate together to clarify
> and compress (P, 30)

Williams's "mass of detail," which must "interrelate on a new ground, difficultly," relates the creative task of the poet with the procreative in nature, the way genetic information is spread through a chain of successive unions. In biology, the word homologue refers to a pairing of chromosomes at meiosis (the process of cell divi-sion followed by combination at fertilization), resulting in a series with constant successive differences of composition. Things are thus related through a biological network of correspondences, producing diversity within a common familial structure. Williams's compositional practice bears this out, as certain words and phrases recur in different contexts, attempting to take root and multiply con-nections. As with nature, connection and fertility in the poem is not a given, however; there is always the question of whether the seeds will be able to take root, whether the environment will accept or destroy them. Language, likewise, is at the mercy of forces greater than its smallest units. In the following passages, phrases appear that at first seem unconnected, only to return a few pages later in more detail. The "new ground" is broken "difficultly," the emergence of Williams's critique of an institutionalized blockage of possible relationships between language, knowledge, and experience slow to take hold:

> Divorce is
> the sign of knowledge in our time,
> divorce! divorce! (P, 28)
>
> . . . .
>
> certainly NOT the university,
> a green bud fallen upon the pavement its
> sweet breath suppressed: Divorce (the
> language stutters). (P, 32)

The language stutters because there is a blockage preventing the flow of knowledge from one body to another. What should be a genetic relationship between thought, the mind, and the life-world has been thwarted. Williams's association of the university with this disruption of natural processes of communion and communication reiterates his longstanding suspicion of institutional education as a brake to understanding and experiential knowledge:

> We go on living, we permit ourselves
> to continue—but certainly
> not for the university, what they publish
>
> severally or as a group: clerks
> got out of hand forgetting for the most part
> to whom they are beholden. (P, 44)

The "we" here presumably refers to writers whose creative output provides an occupation for scholars arrogant enough to think their work is more than the scrivening Williams believes it truly is. While this reads in part as personal bitterness that Williams suspects his work has been passed over in favor of the more conventionally satisfying scholarly route offered by, say, Eliot's dense canon, the attack on the university is consistent with Williams's almost instinctive distrust of any institutionalized order that swallows diversity and reproduces "something else, something else the same" (P, 44). This manufacturing of sameness stands palely before the fecund diversity of natural processes, which, like the poet (that other natural force), are in danger of being crushed by the bracketing, cataloguing, and neutering carried out by the bureaucratizing institutions of the corporate state.

In another passage, flowers eagerly spread in the sun are missed by the "tongue of the bee," causing them to "sink back into the loam / crying out" as they "wilt and disappear" (P, 20). Marriage has come "to have a shuddering / implication," which is that without consummation and procreation there is nothing but death. Alienated consciousness, which leaves the individual "divorced / from its fellows" (P, 28), means that communal ties that should bind members together serve, in fact, to do nothing but confuse:

> The language, the language
>   fails them
> They do not know the words
>   or have not
> the courage to use them .
>   —girls from
> families that have decayed and
> taken to the hills: no words.
> They may look at the torrents in
>   their minds
> and it is foreign to them . (P, 20)

The hint of madness here, of people whose own minds are alien to them, recalls again the pure products of "To Elsie," with "no / peasant traditions to give them / character" (SA, 131). Such girls have "no words," there is no available language that is local to them; all is foreign. What causes such alienation? "Who restricts knowledge?" asks Williams rhetorically. Well, the university has already been named and found wanting. "Some say," the poem goes on,

> it is the decay of the middle class
> making an impossible moat between the high
> and the low where
> the life once nourished . . . knowledge
> of the avenues of information—
> So that we do not know (in time)
> where the stasis lodges. (P, 46)

The middle class is envisioned here as an important mediating channel between high and low which, the poem appears to suggest, once facilitated the flow of information and knowledge between the two but has now collapsed into a gulf that separates. How this "decay" has come about is unclear, but what is evident is an implicit suggestion that if what "some say" is correct, there has been an abdication of responsibility on the part of the middle class, that they have failed to fulfill their duty as the class most able to act as social adhesive and a point of convergence where discourses of upper and lower can convene. What is also clear is that the resultant "stasis" has become, over time, normalized to the point where it is hard to imagine an alternative or a solution.

At this point Williams's attack on the university begins to read less like a wholesale rejection of institutionalized knowledge and more of a frustrated plea for this haven of middle-class values—freedom of speech and thought, diversity of opinion, open debate, liberty to work outside the prerogatives of commerce— to remember its purpose, which should be the invention of new avenues of communication and communal life: the "green bud fallen upon the pavement."

> And if it is not
> the knowledgable idiots, the university,
> they at least are the non-purveyors
> should be devising means
> to leap the gap. Inlets? The outward
> masks of the special interests
> that perpetuate the stasis and make it
> profitable. (P, 46)

William's use of the word *non-purveyors* suggests both a positive and negative meaning of the idea of witholding, and the mercantile echo deliberately situates the university within a culture of trade and commercial values. These lines partly present the university as "at least" the non-purveyors, that is, an institution that does, or should not sell its wares, while this refusal also confirms Williams's argument that the university is holding back what it should be giving. The university is, at the very least, guilty of not devising the means to leap the divide between social classes. If it is not the university that has caused the "stasis," then it is doing very little to assuage the problem. This negative reading clearly becomes the dominant one, yet the possibility of clawing a latent optimism from those lines due to a slightly unstable syntactic construction gives a hint of what might have been lost. The possibility of finding new avenues out of the stasis is soon stymied in what follows, as the "inlets," apertures for the flow of knowledge, are presented as themselves the mere masks of the "special interests / that perpetuate" the present situation. What looks like freedom is but a masquerade that serves to bolster entrenched private interests.

> They block the release
> that should cleanse and assume
> prerogatives as a private recompense.
> Others are also at fault because
> they do nothing. (P, 46)

The universities have, as Williams sees it, become a front for a larger conspiracy of "special interests" whose only concern is the maintenance of the status quo. Cultural resources are beginning to emerge in the poem as a recognizably volatile source of power which is being deliberately contained, thereby causing it to atrophy and decay, while "special interests" profit from what has by now been established as an unnatural condition, stasis. What should be a consanguineous community—with institutions that "cleanse"—has been corrupted by an imposed transvaluation of values, which has replaced natural increase and interrelatedness with restriction and a channeling of energies into what is "profitable," that is, what conforms to a culture based on accumulation and containment rather than distribution. While individuals suffer, institutions—educational and religious—serve nothing but the greater cause, which is money, as the poem makes certain to convey early in Book 2, Section II:

> [. . .] those poor souls had nothing else in the world,
>
> save that church, between them and the eternal, stony, ungrateful
>
> and unpromising dirt they lived by . . . . .
>
> Cash is mulct of them that others may live
>
> secure
>
> .   .   and knowledge restricted.
>
> An orchestral dullness overlays their world (P, 78).

THE OPEN HAND

In a speech given at the Institute of Public Affairs in Charlottesville, Virginia, in July 1936, Williams attempts to create a valid position for the artist as "social regenerator" within a culture formed by corporate capitalism.[16] The speech rehearses an argument similar in substance to Dewey's analysis in *Individualism Old and New,* calling for a revaluation of America's tradition of individual freedom within a state-regulated economy. Williams realizes, as Dewey had done, that the old values of rugged individualism have led, paradoxically, to the curtailment of individual liberty: what was "pro-social" has become "anti-social" (RI, 101). Williams, influenced by Pound, advocates the adoption of Major Douglas's Social Credit system as a middle ground between the "Dictatorship of Labor" and Fascism, which would simply "strengthen the grip of the existent dictatorship of the banks" (RI, 100).

The American Social Credit Movement (ASCM), led by Gorham Munson and promoted by the Social Credit review *New Democracy,* was, according to its manifesto, dedicated to resolving "the sterile Left-Right conflict. It destroys the poverty-amidst-plenty paradox. It enables political democracy to work as it was intended. It brings peace and plenty, security and liberty, the rebirth of America."[17] Douglas's theory claimed that the root of society's problems lay not with the capitalist mode of production but with its accountants. The monopoly that the banks held on credit meant that they drained purchasing power, in turn leading to diminished demand for goods. Surplus goods, unable to be sold at home, are redirected toward foreign markets, this expansionism leading inevitably, according to Douglas, to war. The bankers' monopoly of credit deprived workers of the fruits of their labor, the modern state being, in Douglas's view, "an unlimited liability corporation, of which the citizens are the workers and guarantors, and the financial system, the beneficiary."[18] Douglas proposed that local authorities should remove the administering of credit from private interests and the state should generate purchasing power by paying the individual a dividend for surplus value created by increases in production. This freeing up of credit would place the individual in control of his or her own powers and enable a liberty of action unrestrained by the constrictions of the banks' abstracted system of domination.[19]

The appeal of the Social Credit movement among middle-class intellectuals is unsurprising, offering as it did social change without revolution, and increased social availability of wealth without undermining the principles of private property and enterprise. The assumption is, as with Dewey's calls for planning in *Individualism Old and New*, that the social and economic framework need not be dismantled, simply repaired. Initiative is thus removed from the political to the administrative sphere, with the emphasis placed on making changes without presenting a thoroughgoing analysis of class and power structures. Financial credit, as the dysfunctional element, becomes the enemy, rather than the capitalist system that creates the institution in the first place.

For Williams, as for Pound, the Populist Jeffersonianism of the Social Credit argument was appealing because, as Alec Marsh explains, it "prepared them to see money as another form of representation much like a limited form of language. If the solution to the economic crisis lay in the conundrum of money, it was therefore wrapped up with the problem of speech. The power of money was, in fact, money's power to utter the otherwise inchoate wishes of social, political, and economic power that far exceeded the traditional poet's linguistic and literary resources."[20]

The control of credit, for Williams, becomes the struggle for the autonomy of the citizen and the artist, credit being the energy produced by any activity or work, the creative substance or "radiant gist." "This gist *is* the control of power by credit. . . . The force of the Social Credit philosophy is a clear-sighted envisioning of this gist" (RI, 105) in the sense that it recognizes that power should reside in the hands of its generator, to be directed toward whatever means he or she may choose. What the banks have done by taking over the management of credit is to detach financial credit from real credit—the purchasing power created through labor—and make money from nothing: this destabilizes the value of "real" credit and enables value to be imposed arbitrarily by a self-interested minority. The relationship between work done and payment received is randomly implemented by the rate of exchange established by the invisible hand of the market. The resulting alienation means that, among other things, it is impossible to measure actions by their effects, to maintain a solid foothold in the world of things, and to feel that individual agency or communication can actually connect with anything concrete. When the standard of valuation is an object's commodity value, then any labor or product that does not conform to the criteria of such valuation becomes worthless. This leaves the artist, unless he or she can earn a living by other means, outside the system, considered extraneous to the workings of society. Williams knows this from experience, complaining that not once in thirty years has he been able to publish one poem in a commercial magazine or publish one volume without at least partly paying for it himself (RI, 107-108). Even when published, these books "did not sell, they were not bought, because the market for them did not exist." This is a "situation offensive to my good sense as a man and repulsive to my hard won craftsmanship as an artist. And it is always so under the compulsion of a government based upon false values" (RI, 108).

The alienation caused by corporate capitalism has blocked the free flow of individual energy that creates community and culture. The need for a reciprocal relationship between individual and social freedom has been lost in favor of a ruling elite that hordes rather than gives back resources. This is true for Williams in business and in culture and his attack on the pauperizing effects of acquisitiveness in financial and artistic affairs is long-running and unrelenting. Dewey made the connection in *Individualism Old and New* between intellectual and financial capital, bringing into sharp relief the kind of issues of cultural freedom so dominant in *Paterson:*

> Intellectual and literary folks who conceive themselves devoted to pursuit of pure truth and uncontaminated beauty too readily overlook the fact that a similar narrowing and hardening [to that which takes place where industry is pursued apart from social ends] takes place in them. Their goods are more refined, but they are also engaged in acquisition; unless they are concerned with use, with expansive interactions, they too become monopolists of capital. And the monopolization of spiritual capital may in the end be more harmful than that of material capital. (ION, 117).

Williams would no doubt endorse the sentiments of this salvo. He consistently embraces the notion of beauty in America as necessarily contaminated, riddled with the corruptions and hybridizations of the world of which it is a part. This is so whether Williams is thinking about the people (such as Elsie), the language (or idiom), or the poems (*Paterson*'s failed and broken experiment). Just as business wants to strip off social duty from the profit motive, the same drive seeks to divorce culture from the world of things, needs, and sufferings. Williams's counternotion of reciprocity, based on service and duty, is a form of moral, mutual responsibility that seeks to maintain social relations and strengthen communal well-being through what Dewey calls "expansive interactions." The individual must be given free rein in order to utilize his "social servicability" (RI, 102). Society, "*to be served,* must generate individuals to serve it, and cannot do so otherwise than to give such individuals full play—*until* or unless their activities prove anti-social" (RI, 103). The artist's function is to be "a servant to society" (RI, 106). He or she is "the type of person . . . who has something to give to society," yet this offering is negated under the "present system of government," which enforces "an exaggerated, and almost exclusive, emphasis on the getting of money" (RI, 108). To make the individual's contribution effective, and to establish a mutually supportive society, the government, "should, socially conscious, serve *me*, protect me by guaranteeing me liberty to exist because, as a writer, I do not write books like those in the Drug Store Circulating Library" (RI, 107). And without economic liberty there can be no liberty at all. While Dewey thought that the monopolization of spiritual (or cultural) capital might turn out to be even worse than that of material capital, Williams sees the two as so entwined as to be virtually indistinguishable.

In "Revolutions Revalued," Williams locates the corruption of American democracy at the same point as he does in *Paterson,* with Alexander Hamilton: "We started crooked, as a nation—under heavy stress, the weakness of the Confederation, the danger of new foreign wars giving Hamilton his chance." While the "democratic principle in economic affairs fought hard to preserve itself useful and intact," in the end it gave in "to Hamilton's successful drive for an industrial autocracy and consequent economic centralization under narrow control. From that time on economic freedom of the individual was a lost cause" (RI, 101). Hamilton's ambitions for America as a manufacturing nation, a producer of commodities facilitated by capital on credit, is seen by Williams as an original sin against the new democracy, a fall away from a primal oneness of fact and value. Hamilton, claims Williams in *Paterson,* "never trusted the people, 'a great beast', as he saw them" (P, 84), and this lack of social connectedness and sense of responsibility leads to the severing of ties between individual and social interests. The consolidation of resources needed to create an industrial state Hamilton accomplished in part through the "Assumption" by the Federal government of the postrevolutionary national debt, centralizing credit and debt control, and serving to benefit speculators who had bought up certificates originally paid to American soldiers and other patriots. The establishment of a national bank provided capital and credit for America's industrial development, yet profits were privately and not publicly enjoyed: "The Federal Reserve System is a private enterprise . . . a private monopoly," the power to regulate all money given to it by a "spineless" Congress. "They create money from nothing and lend it to private business (the same money over and over again at a high rate of interest), and also to the Government whenever it needs money in war and peace; for which we, the people, representing the Government (in this instance at any rate) must pay interest to the banks in the form of high taxes" (P, 90). In other words, "the Federal Reserve Banks constitute a Legalized National Usury System, whose Customer No. 1 is our Government, the richest country in the world. Every one of us is paying tribute to the money racketeers on every dollar we earn through hard work" (P, 91).

Williams contrasts the "open hand" of liberalism against the "clenched fist" of all totalizing abstract systems of domination, including communism, fascism, and corporate capitalism, suggesting the generosity of the former as opposed to the restrictive, withholding aggression of the latter. In both politics and aesthetics Williams promotes process over system, communication over restriction, transmission over accumulation. As in gift economies, Williams conceives of wealth as something that accrues, or at least maintains, value by passing it on, not by hoarding. Language would, under such a dispensation, acquire richness through transmission, creating communal ties as it moves from person to person. Service is an act of generosity that literally creates a community through acts of positive reciprocity. Where market forces dominate and gift property is converted into commodities, as Lewis Hyde points out, "the fruits of gift exchange are lost. At that point commerce becomes correctly associated with the fragmentation of community and the suppression of liveliness, fertility, and social feeling. For where we maintain no institutions of positive reciprocity, we find ourselves . . . unable to enter gracefully into nature, unable to draw community out of the mass, and finally, unable to receive, contribute toward, and pass along the collective treasures we refer to as culture and tradition."[21]

In differentiating gifts from commodities, Hyde distinguishes between "worth" and "value," worth referring to a thing that is prized but, as it were, priceless, and value deriving from a comparison between one thing and another. A thing "has no market value in itself except when it is in the market place, and what cannot be exchanged has no exchange value."[22] When Williams complains of his lack of commercial success, he rightly understands that his work, in standing outside the market place, cannot be exchanged and is therefore, within that system, deemed valueless. A market economy cannot translate creative worth into commodity value: "How much does it cost / to love the locust tree / in bloom? // A fortune bigger than / Avery could muster" (P, 117). For Dewey, the valuelessness of intellectual or creative work is at once a measure of its independence and at the same time a mark of its social uselessness. Intellectuals and artists "have attained their liberty," he argues, "in direct ratio to their distance from the scenes of action" (ION, 108). What good is freedom, Williams might ask, if it is freedom to do nothing, to make no difference? This is certainly not what either Williams or Dewey have in mind for the artist, and while Dewey seems confident that a new culture "expressing the possibilities immanent in a machine and material civilization will release whatever is distinctive and potentially creative in individuals" (ION, 109), without an attendant reconstruction of what is meant by work and exchange themselves, Williams is far less certain.

What Dewey manages to do is to remove the idea of the commodity from the profit system: "The enemy is not material commodities, but the lack of will to use them as instruments for achieving preferred possibilities" (ION, 116). He asks us to imagine a society "free from pecuniary domination." In such an imagined society "it becomes self-evident that material commodities are invitations to individual taste and choice, and occasions for individual choice" (ION, 116).

While it may be possible to imagine such a world, there is no obvious answer as to how it might be achieved. Of course material objects, such as the bathtubs and radios Dewey gives as examples, are not enemies of freedom. It is the system of valuation that converts objects into symbols of wealth and power to be narrowly horded or widely distributed that is at issue here. Dewey's conception of the commodity is innocent of the entwined relationship between a system of corporate manufacture and the society driven by the consumption of that system's products. The "lack of will" Dewey claims prevents the useful deployment of commodities is surely a lack of will on the part of those who benefit from a society of "pecuniary domination." For those not so blessed, Williams's idea of the clenched fist seems more appropriate a description of the way commodities can indeed be oppressive in themselves: "in my life the furniture eats me," he writes in *Spring and All* (SA, 113).

Williams's resistance to the monopolization of capital, spiritual or material, is conceived, following his views on service, along the lines of gift exchange, a conception much more skeptical of the liberating potential of commodities than Dewey is prepared to be. Hyde explains the difference between gifts and commodities as "two territories separated by a boundary."[23] While a gift, when it crosses the boundary, either "stops being a gift or else abolishes the boundary," a commodity "can cross the line without any change in its nature; moreover, its exchange will often establish a boundary where none previously existed."[24] In terms of Williams's lexicon, such exchange creates "blockages" and causes "divorce," like the "impossible moat" caused by the decay of the middle class.

The kind of pre-Hamiltonian economy Williams wishes to recover is in part located in the locally grounded proximity to nature enjoyed by America's indigenous population, the kind of culture of contact he describes in the Rasles and Boone chapters of *In the American Grain*. Indians, *Paterson* Book 3 claims, "made money out of sea-shells. Bird feathers. Beaver skins" (P, 125). Value here is constructed directly from natural forms—"made"—yet Williams does not indicate whether the shells and feathers were considered valuable because of what they were as objects or for what they symbolized, although the exchange value of shells and skin seems the most likely function, making them indistinguishable from coins and notes as a medium. There is clearly a suggestion, however, that Williams wants to make the point that Indians saw wealth more as a condition of existence than as an abstract commodity, since he points out that when the Dutch dig up the body of a recently buried Indian priest and make off with the furs encased with the remains, they understand the furs not as part of the man's existence but merely as goods that have a market price. Hyde claims that "commodity exchange will either be missing or frowned upon to the degree that a group thinks of itself as one body, as 'of a piece'."[25] Such a group is, of necessity, small, and Williams's advocacy of the local and his preference for Jefferson over Hamilton suggest a desire for the kind of self-regulation and communal autonomy no longer available in modern corporate America. Yet despite this apparent nostalgia for social totality, Williams is no advocate of small town insularity and is undoubtedly opposed to the notion that America should be "one body, 'of a piece.' "

Indeed, given his celebration of the hybrid and polluted products of urban America, as well as his passion for new forms commensurate with a modern industrial society, it would be a mistake to see Williams as some kind of repressed agrarian. The aim for Williams is toward a retrieval of what he considers locally appropriate, not to restore a golden age, but simply in order not to abandon what might in fact be most suited to the environment: service, duty, free and open exchange, communal solidarity, dispersed rather than consolidated power. The poem seeks to articulate and embody these virtues, not to the exclusion of but in the face of the presence of resistance and deliberate blockage.

As a form of valuation, Williams's relative measure is a means of recognizing differences between things without resorting to an isolation of discrete phenomena: things are only understood through their relational situation to other things, and as situations change, so do relations and meanings. The relation itself is the space of communication and transaction, and this is the imaginative space worked by the poet/citizen to create connections rather than disruption: "the mind is neutral, a bead linking / continents, brow and toe" (P, 211). If the policies of containment enacted by the institutions of capitalism and imperialism—money in the bank, books in the library, correct language usage policed by medieval European monarchies—have destroyed the polis, the freeing up of, in Social Credit terms, the "real" credit (the "radiant gist") is a way of restructuring ties of community and culture into new configurations.

In *Paterson*, the passages concerning money often contain a proliferation of colons. The colon, like scales, serves to measure possible equivalencies, to weigh alternatives. This punctuation of evaluation serves to connect, to generate a conjunctive dialogue between language particles through proximity, which produces meaning (real credit) by weighing up connotations: "MONEY : JOKE (ie., crime / under the circumstances : value / chipped away at accelerated pace.)" (P, 214). Here, money is the equivalent of a criminal joke that makes a mockery of value. Money is also evaluated alongside uranium, which "throws out the fire / —the uranium's the credit—" (P, 214). While uranium is an energizing force, the credit or value generated by creative work that should be let out to circulate, "Money sequestered enriches avarice, makes / poverty : the direct cause of / disaster ." (P, 214–215).

In the following passage, this argument continues, Williams stacking the lines in such a way as to construct a pyramid of compressed terms:

> Money : Joke
> could be wiped out
> at stroke
> of pen
> and was when
> gold and pound were
> devalued

Money :   small time
                reciprocal action relic
    precedent to stream–lined
                turbine ; credit

    Uranium : basic thought—leadward
                Fractured : radium : credit

Curie : woman (of no importance) genius : radium

        THE GIST

    credit : the gist   (P, 217)

Marie Curie liberates the radium, the power, from the pitchblende through her
exploratory probing into the nature of things. The money/joke equation sits at
the top of this pyramid, the compacted observations tumbling and spreading in
a heap until they reach the base line of Curie/woman/genius/radium. Williams
piles up the equivalencies almost like terms in a mathematical equation until he
reaches the most efficient notation: "credit : the gist." It is "THE GIST" upon
which the pyramid balances, the fulcrum of Williams's argument. As the gist,
"Credit makes solid / is related directly to the effort, / work: value created and
received, / 'the radiant gist against all that / scants our lives" (P, 218). We might
remember Dewey's argument that only with a reevaluation of work as a cre-
atively rewarding activity could mass society retrieve some satisfaction from its
labors.

Describing the potlatch gift giving ceremonies of the North Pacific tribes, the
anthropologist H. G. Barnett wrote in 1938 that such ceremonies are "in complete harmony with the emphasis upon liberality and generosity (or their simula-
tion) in evidence throughout the area. Virtue rests in publicly disposing of wealth,
not in its mere acquisition and accumulation. Accumulation in any quantity by
borrowing or otherwise, in fact, is unthinkable unless it be for the purpose of an
immediate redistribution."[26] Lewis Hyde revealingly points out that Barnett's language has "procreation at its root" since "[g]enerosity comes from *genere* (Old
Latin: beget, produce), and the generations are its consequence." At its etymological source "liberality is desire; libido is its modern cousin. Virtue's root is a sex
(*vir*, the man), and virility is its action. Virtue, like the gift, moves *through* a
person, and has a procreative or healing power."[27]

Divorce may refer to various states of severance in *Paterson,* but the trope
most obviously turns upon denial of sexual and matrimonial union. The "gist" is
the procreative force: radium for curing cancer, purchasing power in creating
prosperity, creativity in work, sexual desire in creating life. These are all forms of

giving and receiving, of creative energy directed toward bonding and healing, of making attachments and community building. Without the gist the tribe fractures, degenerates, and eventually dies. Thus, the breakdown of communication between the sexes—emblematic as male and female are in *Paterson* of culture and nature, and of polarities within the self—becomes the ultimate threat to the health of the polis. In *Paterson* Book 1, the flow of the river, as the primal language of nature, becomes intertwined with Dr. Paterson's sexual desire, yet where the current of communication should connect there is nothing but a rather vacant lack of recognition: "We sit and talk, / quietly, with long lapses of silence." In this silence Paterson (the man/town) is "aware of the stream / that has no language, coursing / beneath the quiet heaven of / your eyes / which has no speech" (P, 35). The stream has no language, the eyes have no speech. This is not a silence due to refusal to speak but because of no words. Of what talk there is we have no inkling, as if the talk is there to make the silence evident. The silence carries the burden of significance, a burden of loss and absence:

> We sit and talk and the
> silence speaks of the giants
> who have died in the past and have
> returned to those scenes unsatisfied
> and who is not unsatisfied, the
> silent [. . .]

The giants "live again in your silence and / unacknowledged desire—" (P, 36).

The virtue, or virility, of the poet cannot move "through a person" and dispense its procreative and healing power if desire is "unacknowledged." This is, the poem says later, "A marriage riddle: / So much talk of the language—when there are no / ears" (P, 129). There is nothing to say "save that / beauty is unheeded . tho' for sale and / bought glibly enough" (P, 129). When gift exchange becomes commodity exchange, boundaries are more likely to be erected than abolished. To buy and sell beauty is to invert the flow of virtue, transforming the harmonious union of marriage into violence, and twisting the open hand of generosity back into a perverted clenched fist of the private sphere:

> —and marry only to destroy, in private, in
> their privacy only to destroy, to hide
> > (in marriage)
> that they may destroy and not be perceived
> in it—the destroying. (P, 130)

Only love "stares death in the eye." Virtue "is a complex reward in all / languages, achieved slowly" (P, 220); it is "wholly / in the effort to be virtuous . / This takes connivance, / takes convoluted forms, takes / time!" (P, 221). As the gist, virtue is "work: value created and received" (P, 218): in a fragmented world virtue does not flow like the river but must be constantly reaffirmed and remade with effort. In a universe based not on first principles but on the relative position of relational objects, the creative, procreative gist cannot wait for nature to take its course but must intervene and work to make a world in which life can prosper:

> Without invention nothing is well spaced,
> unless the mind change, unless
> the stars are new measured, according
> to their relative positions, the
> line will not change, the necessity
> will not matriculate: unless there is
> a new mind there cannot be a new
> line, the old will go on
> repeating itself with recurring
> deadliness [. . .] (P, 65)

Williams's avant-garde critique of modern America depends on individual agency in an age in which such agency is thwarted at every turn. His retrieval of a local ground for the epic finally amounts to a trawling of atrophied lives, brutalized environments, and corrupted beginnings. To construct a redeeming language from this cultural wreckage is to utter a howl of despair, and despite the beauty Williams occasionally unearths from his despoiled locale, no amount of liberal glue can hold the fragments together. That Williams knows this is clear, and to turn a howl into another declaration of independence is no mean feat, but it is telling that the belated addition of Book 5, after the almost resigned stoicism that ends Book 4, retreats from the embattled terrain of economic and historical analysis to the domain of the aesthetic. Above all else there is "A WORLD OF ART / THAT THROUGH THE YEARS HAS / SURVIVED!" (P, 244). This is the world of "Pollock's blobs of paint squeezed out / with design! / pure from the tube. Nothing else / is real" (P, 248–249). In many ways this is no retreat at all, for Williams is simply reiterating his long-held commitment to the potentiality latent in artistic practice and the integrity of aesthetic form. In this he continues to share Dewey's democratic faith in the "work of art [as] the truly individual thing," the defiant consummation of liberty against any odds (ION, 121). Yet at this point the aesthetic, for Williams, is no longer situated as a possible countervailing power that might mitigate the full force of economic interests but simply accepted as the only thing "real." The other, previously very real powers, which cause "blockage," prevent communication, and thwart lives, are now consigned to the realm of the unreal and unimportant. The final words of *Paterson* 5 expose the extent to which Williams may have withdrawn from a potentially politicized aesthetics to a simply celebratory mode of formal free play:

We know nothing and can know nothing .

    but

the dance, to dance to a measure

contrapunctally,

        Satyrically, the tragic foot. (P, 278)

The dance may be all "we" could ever have known, but before the dance was a challenge, an act of defiance. Now the gambol seems nothing less than a tragedy.

This may well be a matter of tone. After all, the poem stands as, in Dewey's words, the result of the interaction of materials "through the medium of the artist's distinctive vision and power" (ION, 121). As such, "[i]n its determination, the potential individuality of the artist takes on visible and enduring form" (ION, 121–122). This is a good thing, to be sure, and as a measure of liberty, a powerful one. "The future is always unpredictable," as Dewey writes (ION, 122). Williams would agree with this, beginning *Paterson* with "a plan for action to supplant a plan for action" (P, 10) in good processual pragmatic fashion. Unpredictable the future surely is, and Dewey's conviction in the future is a measure of his buoyant optimism. Williams at times seems less than optimistic, often embattled, doubtful. The unevenness he allows into his work, the occasional despondency, shrillness, fury, are part of his pragmatic, experimental method, keeping the work in tune with events. Perhaps there is even an optimism in that, in giving imperfection its due. Neither Dewey nor Williams are strong on answers, whether they are writing about economic inequality or aesthetic form. They are unswervingly good on questions, challenges, problems. They are unceasingly tenacious in their quest for change, improvement, for increased liberty and equality, for new ideas, new shapes of experience. If art is the measure of how culture might serve society, Williams's contrapunctal dance goes some way to prick the plainsong of corporate America, and this, perhaps, is cause enough for optimism.

Conclusion

What I assume you shall assume.

—Walt Whitman

During 1916, the sixty-year-old John Dewey was treated by the famous guru of physiotherapy, Frederick Matthias Alexander. The philosopher was, apparently, according to Alexander, judging by the way he talked and held his head, "drugged with thought," his mind somehow dissociated from his body.[1] Alexander's method of supposedly altering consciousness by adjusting the posture and movements of the body impressed Dewey sufficiently for him to provide introductions for a number of Alexander's books. Bypassing Freud, Alexander traced psychic disorders, not to the unconscious mind, but to physical imbalance, an imbalance caused by a deep conflict between culture and biology. Readjustment involved, to use the title of Alexander's book of 1923, the constructive conscious control of the individual. To achieve this, lifetime habits of bad posture had to be overruled and replaced, often by the active, physical intervention of the physiotherapist. Such a literally hands-on approach was necessary because, according to Alexander, only when the change is somatically experienced will the lesson be learned: knowing something is not the same as being able to experience it. The organic, holistic emphasis of such a philosophy was not lost on Dewey, who footnotes Alexander in both *Experience and Nature* and *Human Nature and Conduct*. Alexander himself was not averse to extrapolating broad cultural and historical lessons from his breakthrough, lessons Dewey reiterates: "It is as reasonable to expect a fire to go out when it is ordered to stop burning as to suppose that a man can stand straight in consequence of a direct action of thought and desire. The fire can be put out only by changing objective conditions; it is the same with rectification of bad posture" (HNC, 24). It is not enough to constantly tell people what is wrong with their lives, since the old habits will be so ingrained as to feel like nature, only temporarily amenable to new ideas. Through the intervention of a bodily influence, sensational alteration takes the lead, revealing a new reality to the mind, which can then consciously maintain the new state. Only at this point, once "objective conditions" have been changed, can the individual lead a new life on new principles, unrestrained by old habits.

From an article entitled "Dynamic Posture" published in the *Journal of the American Medical Association,* Williams pastes the following into *Paterson* 2: "The body is tilted slightly forward from the basic standing position and the weight thrown on the ball of the foot, while the other thigh is lifted and the leg and opposite arm are swung forward (fig. 6b). Various muscles aided" (P, 59). As a careful, even humorous, delineation of the unconscious act of walking, this functions as a good way for Williams to trope on the notion of measure as the biology of organic form: writing as natural and as coordinated as the commonest of human abilities. The article Williams is borrowing from, however, is not simply about walking, it is about "correct" walking, which should be characterized by "a smooth rhythm," "free muscle and joint action, momentum, balance and rhythm," and "low energy output."[2] Like the Alexander technique, the article is a professional, scientific attempt to provide a biological, therapeutic palliative to bad social conditions. Modern life has caused our bodies, Alexander suggests, to "become relaxed, our muscles atrophied, and our functions put out of gear."[3] Williams's medical journal makes the same point: "Crowded city pavements and dirty fume-laden air usually promote bad walking posture, whereas the varied topography and surfaces and the clean air make good walking posture easier"[4]: organicism as pastoralism, politics realigned as biology, failure to adjust (and, therefore, to survive) as personal failure, rural privileged over urban (and urban life, therefore, seen as a Fall), modification over revolution. Being told to stand up straight never said so much about notions of social organization.

LOOSE-LIMBED DEMOCRACY

Williams shares with Dewey the belief in democracy as a way of life. The overarching organicism of this conception suggests that democracy is not, however, just a way of life to be chosen from various possible ways of living. As natural—organic—democracy is the way life *is.* The profound effect of Darwin on Dewey, and of the study of medicine on Williams, enable them to sanction their view of democracy by appealing to the empirical evidence of biology: this is how we are made, this is what we are. If democracy is natural, then, and America is founded on the principles of democracy, it must follow that America is the fruit of a natural process. As both Williams and Dewey understand, however, the logic of this deduction is not borne out by an examination of political, social, and everyday life in America. If, on their terms, democracy has failed, or is failing, then nature is not taking its proper course. Something must be wrong with the organism. Not surprisingly, Williams's and Dewey's cultural and social criticism is not based so much on the rigors of political science as on the practice of medical diagnosis. Their holistic perspective is concerned with adjustment, realignment, therapeutic intervention, treatment, cure. The body is sick, it must be helped. This is certainly a different way of approaching and responding to social problems than, say, the analysis of class, power, vested interests, and so on, which implies a recognition of inherent and intractable structural conflicts. As a natural thing, America has all the right organs, they are simply out of sorts.

In Williams's and Dewey's usage, the basic units of their liberal vocabulary are often uttered with the assured lack of ambiguity enjoyed by the most unadorned of nouns. Chicken, wheelbarrow, community, experiment, art, education, democracy. Their beliefs seem as free of clutter as Williams's poetry: democracy is a creative process akin to the creativity of artistic practice; communication is the basis for community building; education is the primary means of social improvement; scientific method is the paradigm for subject-object interaction. This vocabulary, bracing in its simplicity and optimism, (and also, perhaps, in its familiarity), is, as far as Williams and Dewey see it, no longer clean, no longer healthy. Their therapeutic response to cultural and social breakdown is largely based on an excavation of what might remain of an unsullied American ground. Such a response is deeply romantic in tenor. There is the belief in the authenticity and innocence of less "civilized," more "primitive" peoples and of children, whose close proximity to a state of nature means that they live an inherently more democratic, because more natural, existence. Leading on from this is the hope that "we" can learn from these groups—American Indians, African tribes, school children, immigrants, perhaps—and retrieve the virtue that we have lost.

From here, it is but a short step to arrive at the trope of communication as free exchange of gifts. Williams gets this from the Abnaki Indians, from Elsie's splash of Indian blood, from his own Spanish lineage, from *Paterson's* brutalized "beautiful thing": natural generosity hurt but not completely desecrated by greed. In *Art as Experience,* Dewey similarly refers to the unity of art and life in primitive societies, the relatedness of thought and action, beautiful and useful, and so on. All this, we are told, we have lost and must regain if we are to survive. The retrieval begins at school, for children we can trust to appreciate the good and the natural when they see it. Science gives us the method. The materials are at hand, the evidence will bear out the practice.

Faced with such a powerful optimism, how does such an approach to social and cultural insufficiency bear up to a more skeptical eye? The major obstacle to the realization of the pragmatic liberal ambition is the intractability of present conditions. While the necessity, for example, for a strong educational system that can prepare children to join society as responsible and valuable citizens is not to be disputed, it is expecting too much to place the burden of social transformation in the classroom. Power resides elsewhere, unperturbed by storms in the inkwells. Likewise, the difficulty with using science as the model of inquiry rooted in modern conditions is that, as Casey Nelson Blake observes, the progressive notion of science "often equated technical and critical reason and confused the work of the efficiency expert with the experimental spirit of the scientific community." Consequently, the contradiction arises in which "[p]rogressives could in one breath endorse the liberating potential of rational discourse within the scientific profession as an antidote to the factory system and in the next hail the technolog-ical and organizational achievements of industrialization."[5] Adjustment can often sound like accommodation.

More deeply troublesome than the romantic emphasis on education and a kind of science of organic reason, however, is the broader meaning and implica-tions of democracy itself. For both Dewey and Williams, democracy begins with the aesthetic. The interaction or communication between the self and the world is a way of becoming included, of connecting. The experience of connection is aesthetic inasmuch as it constitutes a realization of formal, relational union. Like the creation and appreciation of art, this unifying experience is not totalizing but processual: it is the experience of this process in itself, not of any final object, that is of primary significance. A democratic society should, then, in its recognition of individual liberty and communal responsibility, be created and appreciated—ex-perienced—as a form of art.

This is a proposition, not a description. The kind of democratic socialism Dewey and Williams articulate is nowhere close to what actually happens in America. Given that they know this, which they undoubtedly do, and that their work is therefore adversarial, provocational, combative, even as a proposition the correspondence between the aesthetic and the democratic struggles to wholly convince. Formal cohesion is by no means conclusively an indicator of mutual support and agreement—repression and exploitation can be as elegantly struc-tured and self-justifying as dutiful, interactional respect. Art is not automatically coterminous with democracy. Any notional freedom for art must be fought for, established, and maintained in the same way as social and political liberties. Not that either Dewey or Williams claims art, or imagination, or creativity, as founda-tional, although Williams comes close. It is hard, however, to see from where a true aesthetic democracy will spring, since their belief in communal self-creation situates the power or will for change within a society that, on the evidence, seems to have its very existence as a true democracy contradicted at all points.

In an important sense, it must be said, this appraisal is too monolithic and does not take into consideration the possibility, perhaps the inevitability, of resid-ual and emergent cultural spaces and communities. Indeed, surely Williams and Dewey themselves represent the strength of such spaces. Capitalism is nowhere as totalized a structure as Adorno would have us believe. Nevertheless, in looking to the so-called community to change itself from within, Williams and Dewey still refuse to recognize the full weight of reified consciousness. Both men are prepared to take an adversarial stance, but they do so reluctantly, since the whole point of their liberalism is that it is public, inside, not agitating from without. Pound longed for, and eventually got, his perfect readership, but Williams was after something far less rarefied: a *general* public of sophisticated, tuned-in readers: a conversation, not a pronouncement.

It may well be true, as Dewey claims, that "[n]o man and no mind was ever emancipated by being left alone" (PP, 340), or, as Williams puts it, "[l]iberty . . . has the significance of inclusion rather than a breaking away" (SE, 208), but the tautology remains: without liberty, how can liberty be imagined, and thus achieved? What is the common good without consensus? Without consensus, who is to say who is included or excluded?

Since, for Dewey, the individual is defined through societal and communal—contextual—relations, then the democratic individual must be dependent, to some degree, upon the existence of a democratic community. If, however, this community does not exist, and must be worked toward, then how is it possible for the individual to have, a priori, democratic characteristics? Contextualism surely suggests that context and individual elements are interdependent and mutually defining. Even if we accept that societies contain degrees of democracy that fund an individual's democratic traits, how can we be sure that this individual selects democracy as the right, or good, or even useful, qualities he or she wishes to cultivate? To live democratically, following the logic of contextualism, is to live, by and large, in agreement with the values of the community. Any problems that may arise are solved through discussion and collective experimentation. The existence of a common good must be assumed for this to be tenable, yet where, in early twentieth-century America, is this common good to be located? Where is the communal homogeneity that would be necessary for consensually derived decisions to be arrived at? Dewey cannot answer this at a national level and must therefore stress the importance of the local, of small scale communal autonomy. Even given the efficacy of this model at local level, however, where is the guarantee that all local units will act democratically? There is none, unless we appeal to some innate human quality that will ensure the democratic impulse. For surely social organization can be grounded on totalitarian or feudalistic principles just as effectively at the smallest social level as at the national. In its insistence that pragmatism is nonideological, that it is a method, a means of inquiry, a way of doing things, there is, of course no guarantee that pragmatism is inherently liberal and progressive. (Mussolini was an admirer of pragmatism.) Yoking democracy and pragmatism is a historical contingency; the terms are not interchangable.

What is perhaps most striking about the American convergence of romantic and republican anticapitalism is, as Casey Nelson Blake quite rightly points out, that it neglects a rigorous examination of the public sphere as an arena of conflict and subordinates questions of class or rights to an ideal of community: "Both the romantic and republican indictments of modern industrial society stressed the need for personal fulfilment in small-scale communities knit together by shared cultural traditions, mutual aid, and a sense of the common good." This brand of radicalism focused primarily on the moral, aesthetic, and personal, the failure of modern life to give meaning to individuals being "its most damning feature from the perspective of those raised on a republican conception of citizenship and a romantic belief in the authority of the creative imagination."[6] The most characteristic aspect of this strain of cultural criticism, evident in both Williams and Dewey and attacked aggressively by Marxists such as Mills and Eastman, is its combination of fervent belief and optimism with a hopeless vagueness over specifics, of faith in technology and material progress with an often cloying nostalgia for a notional *Gemeinschaft* capable of dissolving social and economic conflict and exploitation through the invocation of a prelapsarian polis, the very acme of Aristotelian virtue, which was or will be but never *is*.

PURE PRODUCTS: US, HERE, NOW

Williams's constant stress upon the importance of a sense of place becomes more curious and complex once it is considered that the kind of local relationships he argues for are probably more imagined than real. Rutherford, New Jersey, was the first commuter town to serve New York City and was inevitably dependent upon the city for its population and identity. Both Van Wyck Brooks and Randolph Bourne hailed from New Jersey also and, as Brooks notes, "it was in the nature of our suburban world that everybody had come from somewhere else."[7] Bourne, likewise, saw the inhabitants of New Jersey as "nomadic," so tied to the demands of the metropolis that there was no time for "the cultivation of that ripening love of surroundings that gives quality to a place, and quality too, to the individual life."[8]

While Williams's practice was in New Jersey, his intellectual life was in the city. His own nomadic existence reveals his refusal, or inability, to root himself completely to one or the other of his careers and their attendant lifestyles. As the modernist-as-commuter, Williams's ambivalent and often contradictory attitudes toward the small town and the city become clearer. While extolling the virtues of the Jeffersonian ideal of small self-governing communities based on shared values and customs, he could simultaneously rail against the small-mindedness and claustrophobia that often accompanied small town life. And while the city embodied the pluralistic, visceral body of modern America, the speed, vibrancy, and danger so enticing to the poet-adventurer, it was also the site of terrible suffering brought about by the power of the same corporate capitalism that made the modern urban spectacle possible. Williams never completely came down on one side or the other, and his ambivalence is emblematic of the conflicting loyalties of the progressive liberal: distainful of the hypocritical and outmoded Victorianism of the small town, fearful and in awe of what might come along to replace it.

Williams is not of the city, he approaches it, and not without suspicion. For all his talk of a pluralism of custom and language, there is a suburban anxiety in Williams's urban perspective, which jars with his more romantic evocations of the exotic primitive. "I was getting up closer to the city, approaching the mouth of the river, identified with the mouth of the Hudson," he explains, describing the movement of *Paterson*, Book 4.

> If you are going to write realistically of the conception of filth in the world, it can't be pretty. What goes on with people isn't pretty. With the approach to the city, international character began to enter the innocent river and pervert it; sexual perversions, such things that every metropolis when you get to know it houses. Certain human elements can't take the gaff, have to become perverts to

satisfy certain longings. When human beings herd together, have to face each other, they are very likely to go crooked. What in the world is the artist to do? He is not a moralist. He sees things, reacts to them, must take them into consideration. (IWWP, 79)

While he accepts that he must face the reality of the city and its poverty, the juxtaposition of the "innocent" river, surging from the uncorrupted American hinterland toward the perversions of the city, sounds more like Henry James on New York than Williams, especially in its elision of the "international character" with "sexual perversion."

The kind of communities Dewey and Williams describe tend toward the idiosyncratic and specific. Yet the most cohesive social groupings, the communities that exhibit the strongest Jeffersonian traits of self-regulation and internal unity are, ironically (but predictably), the most marginalized: those of immigrants, ethnic minorities, isolated rural settlements. Such communities enjoy their autonomy by virtue of their disconnectedness; they are groups untouched by national prerogatives due to either geographical, racial, or linguistic exclusion. The peculiarities of idiom and custom found in such communities may well be locally and experientially generated, but it is their removal from national affairs and influences that marks their distinctiveness. Such communities cannot adequately be held up as either representative of, nor even necessarily desirable for, the nation. This, perhaps, is part of their attraction for Dewey and Williams, who see local independence as the mainstay against a homogenizing and suffocating nationalism. Their loose federalism means that small settlements can enjoy the liberty to preserve their idiosyncrasies. If we go along with this, talk of America and American characteristics, language, customs, and so on, becomes irrelevant. Taken still farther, while the citizens of these autonomous communities may be able to talk to one another, can they and do they want to talk to anyone else? In such a view, community and nationhood cancel each other out. Surely the freedom to be left alone is not adequate. Left alone to do what? Left to institutionalize a rigid and vicious caste system in the Southern states? Left to establish a criminal city-state in Chicago based on charismatic leadership?

The word *community* in liberal discourse very easily becomes a synonym for virtue. Communities are made up of the good people. But who decides? What about everyone else? Who is in, who is out? Who are "we"? "We," notes C. Wright Mills, is "the most tricky word in the vocabulary of politics."[9] Williams liked to claim that "the local is the only universal," that anywhere is everywhere, and as an ontological affirmation of existence, this is probably as good as any. As a recognition of the groundedness of the inherently contextualized nature of being, it also works. To specify the locality, to make note of America as a place with a history as well as a geography, however, is to move from ontology to society, to politics, and, perhaps most significantly, to nationality. For every anywhere is always somewhere, freighted with a past and an identity independent, to some extent, from the individual dweller. While Williams is surely correct in acknowledging the specifics, the particularities, of his own place, of recognizing the interpenetration of location and identity, his acceptance of America as an entity, as an idea and an ideology, often leads him away from the concrete and into the abstract, the general, the shaky rhetoric of nationalism. The democratic foundations of the American nation provide Williams with a vocabulary for artistic and individual freedom. Thus, America is the place of potentiality, of process, of experimentation: the great opportunity. Yet creative freedom is also seen as necessary for all artists, wherever they find themselves. While Williams is far from xenophobic and often speaks of creativity as a kind of transnational community—anywhere *is* everywhere—it is nonetheless true that Williams claims a special place for America: America as exemplum, as beacon of freedom, which can tend to universalize the American experience. All true artists become honorary Americans by virtue of their artistic freedom. As such, *Williams's* locality is the only universal, *his* anywhere is everywhere.

The *New Republic,* of which Dewey was a founding editor and major contributor, was set up by Herbert Croly in 1914 to be an organ for the integration of political, economic, and cultural nationalisms.[10] Croly believed that art could "convert the community into a well-informed whole".[11] While Williams was himself more in sympathy with the polyglot *transition* than with the naturalism of either *New Republic* or *The Seven Arts,* his Americanist position maintains the contradictions of Croly's, Dewey's, and Brooks's organic nationalism. For the modern liberal democratic ethos tends to universalize as it individuates, stressing the uniqueness and freedom of each citizen even as it presents this uniqueness as universal: the self-expression of a unity. "It is one of the contradictions of cultural nationalism," writes David Bennett, "that it should invoke universal values as local ones." To retain "the concept of an autonomous human subject, whose self-realization is the goal of this particular nation," nationalist ideology "cannot help but re-present national interests as universal."[12] Williams's refusal to be defined by any terms other than his own—the terms of the American individualist—means that historical and cultural context (inherited national identity) must somehow be voided and re-placed, rearticulated, reshaped by the self. "[Y]ou must begin with nothing" (VP, 98), he says. From nothing, Williams builds a context as he believes it should be, retrieving from the past (as in *In The American Grain,* and in *Paterson*) an America in his own image. America is no longer an oppressive reminder of failed democracy, but through art, as art, even, it becomes "a country by itself" (VP, 251). The creative will to power recognizes the necessity of context, absorbs it, evaporates it, reconstitutes it as a manifestation of the self. As with Emerson, Thoreau, Whitman, so with Williams. The "we" contracts to the "I", which becomes the "I" as "we". E Pluribus Unum: "Whenever I say, 'I' I mean also 'you'. And also, together, as one, we shall begin" (SA, 89). Not forgetting that "we" is the most tricky word in the vocabulary of politics.

Michael Billig has suggested that the nationalism of Western democratic nation-states is "not straightforward" because "it does not present itself as nationalist . . . The denial of 'our' nationalism is nationalist, for it is part of the common-sense imagining of 'us', the democratic, tolerant, reasonable nation."[13] Pragmatism's antifoundationalism, its insistence that meaning and value are derived through communication and consensus, means that a sense of community must come before knowledge or beliefs; who "we" are determines what we are and how we understand the world. As Billig points out, however, the use of "we" is extremely useful in political rhetoric, through which "sectional interests can be presented as if they were universal ones."[14] Tricky indeed. The use of "we", "as it integrates 'us', also directs 'us'. This might be called the syntax of hegemony."[15] The liberal emphasis on inclusion, when coupled with the use of a somehow pre-existing "we", suggests that those not included—"them"—need to be brought into the fold, need to become like "us" so they can enjoy "our" freedom.

Such a perspective sheds some light on, although it does not fully explain, the seemingly undaunted sense of optimism both Dewey and Williams display in their belief in the eventual resolution of social inequality. As Ernest Gellner has said, "A certain cheerfulness seems to be of the very essence of Pragmatism, and is in effect one of its defining traits."[16] For Gellner, this cheerfulness reveals, however, a "crucial error" at the heart of the pragmatist world view. The "relevant antithesis of cheerfulness," says Gellner, is "a sense of crisis," and crisis, "in turn, must be distinguished from a problem." A problem may be a serious difficulty but it "does not call for a revaluation of the very criteria of what is to count as a solution, for any overall reassessment of all the criteria of all the criteria of solution themselves" (G, 242). "Talk of 'problems' prejudges too much, and does so on the optimistic, complacent side" (G, 243). The point about cheerfulness "as a strategy or style" is, then, that it refuses to register crisis, assuming that any difficulty, as a problem, is within the realm of solvability: there is a "willingness to try and use any tool that is to hand, inspired by a confident expectation that though any one tool or effort may fail, by and large one's kit contains adequate tools, that all-in-all our criteria are sound" (G, 243). It is the suspension of this set of assumptions that would reveal a crisis but, according to Gellner, crisis is outside the pragmatist vocabulary. There is indeed, in Dewey, a familiar avoidance of insoluble dilemmas by an appeal to the correct usage of resources. For instance, within the same essay Dewey can move from outright condemnation to optimistic mediation. He claims that "our consciously inherited social philosophy . . . appears to be a legalistic individualism used to sanction economic inequality and industrial disorganization," which sounds very much like a crisis. But no, just when his critique could move in for the kill, we find a few lines later that "[w]e have the material for a genuinely unified ideal, much as that material requires focusing and articulation."[17]

Gellner suggests that this cheerfulness is based on what he calls the "Continuity Thesis" between biological and human history (G, 248–249). The twin inspirations behind pragmatism, Darwinian evolution and nineteenth-century socioeconomic and intellectual history, seem to be "success stories" in that they appear to have been "unplanned, and attained by uncoordinated or even in the main unconscious individual effort, by repeated trial-and-error, by endeavor which does not spurn the successive utilization of quite diverse methods or paths, and which receives both its impetus and its checks in the hurly-burly of concrete struggles" (G, 246). Now, the problem with selecting these models as a basis for universal human existence is that they are "most untypical of the rest of human history proper," since the characteristic condition of history is not instability and growth but "stalemate-equilibrium or acute crisis. Sustained growth is alas untypical" (G, 249). Only on its own terms can biological history and its patterns be seen as typical; this is no validation for using it as an "analogy or parable" for human history. Likewise, to base a philosophy on the economic history of nineteenth-century North America is nothing more than "absurd" (G, 249). Underlying these analogies is the assumption that the American experience is not "*one* social climate amongst others, but . . . the natural and well-nigh inevitable condition of mankind" (G, 250). This perspective betrays a tendency to epistemological and cultural nationalism. As Gellner points out, "the mind of a pragmatist turns easily to Atlantic economic history of the nineteenth century, or the history of science *after* the seventeenth century, or to the evolution of the whole species: but one does not often see it lingering on the ancient Near East, on the Middle Ages, or on Chinese, Hindu or Muslim civilization" (G, 251).

Behind the pragmatist defense of pluralism, then, lies an acceptance of a notional natural process that is, in fact, culturally and historically specific, yet taken as a given. Such an acceptance can lead to the advocacy of process at the level of individuals, but always process within the perimeters of a governing paradigm of what is known as the "natural" condition of mankind.[18] Micro-process functions within macro-stasis. What presents itself as fluidity and change is restricted in range to what is possible within existing conditions. Horace Kallen's pragmatically informed notion of cultural pluralism, supported by Dewey, is typical in this regard, with its emphasis on difference circumscribed by a unifying harmony of interests. Setting forth his vision of an American cultural pluralism, Kallen suggests that while the common language would be English, "each nationality would have for its emotional and involuntary life its own peculiar dialect or speech, its own individual and inevitable aesthetic and intellectual forms."[19] The fact that "peculiar" dialect or speech are not considered languages in their own right but secondary, localized diversions from English, is symptomatic of Kallen's assumptions about the naturalness of American cultural and political forms. "The political and economic life of the commonwealth," he claims, "is a single unit and serves as the foundation and background for the realization of the distinctive individuality of each *natio* that composes it," but this assumes that the foundation and background is secure and egalitarian to begin with. Furthermore, Kallen's notion of ethnic groups is stable and fixed, his rejection of assimilation leading to a static conception of society: "In historic times so far as is known no new ethnic types have originated, and from what is known of breeding there comes no assurance that the old types will disappear in favor of the new."[20] This view takes no account of historical change and of ethnogenesis, deriving its analysis from present conditions it accepts as the model for universal application. It is a form of cheerfulness that, in its acceptance of what is, almost converges with the separatist racist polemics with which it argues. While preserving the rights of each group within the commonwealth to maintain its individual identity, the commonwealth itself is left untouched. Groups within the commonwealth, after all, can only maintain their difference so long as they agree with the overriding principles that hold the commonwealth together. There is no place in this system for conflict or crisis.

Founded on a background theory of the natural order of things, pragmatic proposals such as Kallen's, as Gellner claims, take the American tradition as nature and fit everything into this mold. In denying conflict in favor of harmony, Kallen is reading reality through American ideology and smoothing over ethnic and class antagonisms by a transcendent appeal to a notional organic holism. Organicism can serve to justify sameness as well as diversity. It is the former, Gellner argues, that truly characterizes pragmatism:

> The sense of continuity, the eager erosion of those "dualisms" and radical dis-continuities with which other philosophers operated, results in a curious stan-dardization of everything, a new dusk in which all the cows are the same shade of grey, in which all cognitive advances partake in the same status of corrigible adjustments in some big cognitive corporation. Small differences are not denied, of course, but being so small and numerous, like the petty shareholders in a property-holding democracy, they cannot really defy the great organizations, those great "corporate bodies", which only face experience collectively. (G, 257)

He concludes that "pragmatism is indefensible, because radical cataclyms do occur. When they do, cheerfulness, in the sense defined—a happy reliance on the existing stock of tools and ideas, without any effort at a prior philosophy—simply is not a workable strategy." Pragmatism is distinctively American in that "it emerged from a society which takes cognitive growth altogether for granted; and it does this because it only came into being at a time when such growth had indeed become the norm" (G, 259).[21]

THIS RHETORIC IS REAL

What should not be missed in criticizing the inadequacy of liberalism as con-ceived by Dewey, Williams, and by many of their contemporaries, is their over-whelming belief in the provocational public role of the intellectual and the artist, public in the very ordinary sense of being part of everyday life, inside it, working with and being worked upon by its elements. This willingness to face actual social conditions, to struggle with the inadequacies of American democracy, reveals an indefatiguable belief in the power of human agency to effect change. Such a faith is deeply ingrained in the American romantic, pragmatic, and republican tradi-tions, and both Dewey and Williams display both the fervor of the convictions and the limitations that trouble, and continue to trouble, these traditions. They do not solve the moral and political dilemmas they face, but in tenaciously prodding issues, in insisting upon the need for further discussion, for more work to be done, Dewey and Williams, in their respective spheres of influence, demand attention.

Williams, in particular, when he shifts from the broad strokes of his strident Americanism to the complexities and paradoxes of maintaining artistic integrity and a commitment to social responsibility, is incisive in his grasp of the dilemmas facing the citizen of a modern liberal democracy. The power of the poet, he believes, lies in the ability to see. Sight can reveal joy, but it also "gives us a sorrow which is a pity for if I see far and feel deeply how can I fail to see the misery of men? But how unnecessary it is, for if I saw it was necessary I would not pity but I would go my own way. But because these people can be well I pity them and do not pity a stone. Now comes service" (EK, 184). Faced with the injustice of human misery, some form of action is required. So far, this is the typical liberal humanitarian response. Williams, however, recognizing the prerogatives of individualism and self-preservation, not to mention political impotency, struggles to locate the nature of responsibility.

> But how shall I serve? I cannot love these people as they are for I cannot love dirt and laziness and ignorance—merely by loving life which is what they might be. For after I have rid myself of the encumbrances which hold me from going about freely and which the hungry are eager for, that is, money, etc., what is there left for me to do? Is my service at an end? (EK, 185)

The burden of the poet as seer defines the nature of his or her service: the poet, in being faithful to the vision, to the uniqueness of the individual self, is confirming, stating, demonstrating freedom; in short, "to put into form what we see . . . is our only service." This putting into form is a manifestation, an act, an articulation of vision and understanding. As such, it is a gift to the world, and, in generosity, a bond, a union—contact—is established. "[T]he knowledge I have is in itself nothing; I must give it, I must love" (EK, 185).

There is a sense of longing in this faith in human connectedness, a poignancy, a pathos that reveals the extent of Williams's recognition that art must finally, perhaps inevitably, find solace only in itself. The extent to which we might feel this recognition is an anticlimactic moment, after so many assertions made about the social power of art, depends upon the degree to which we are convinced that it is, in fact, a retreat. Faced with the rapid incorporation of American life, Dewey and Williams are emblematic of a generation of liberals who believed there was still time to redirect the drive to national consolidation through the activation of an alternative indigenous tradition. Inside the language of free enterprise, self-preservation, and American exceptionalism, they spoke an idiom that inflected the keywords of capitalist nationalism to say things such as creative freedom, communal responsibility, and united plurality. The optimism of this idiom resides in the fact that those meanings are latent in the language, part of the nation's identity, however deeply they may be buried. The constant reiteration of these meanings reveals a determination to keep alive a strain of public discourse often stifled by the bellows from the market place. To believe in endless process, as Dewey and Williams do, is to reject surrender, or silence. What this belief in process also means, however, is that just as incorporation will never finalize its goal, neither will any adversarial act ever conclusively prevent its advance. What knowledge Williams might have must be transmitted, over and over again. To "put into form what we see" is not a solution to political or social problems, but it is a challenge to forces of domination, a proof of some kind of autonomy, and an offering to a culture unaccustomed to receiving gifts. The effects of this service remain undefined, and despite his faith in the transformative power of art, Williams must, however reluctantly, for once agree with Eliot that "[a]t the moment when one writes, one is what one is, and the damage of a lifetime, and of having been born into an unsettled society, cannot be repaired at the moment of composition."[22]

What ultimately saves Williams and his brand of Deweyan liberalism from the fatalism and despair that such an acceptance might engender, is his awareness, cheerful or otherwise, that that which is not fully formed does not need repair so much as it requires articulation. For Williams, each moment of composition calls into being a new world, a previously unimagined space without preconditions. This could be a prospective true space for democracy. Perhaps the testimony of its presence is not enough, but it is evidence of possibility, and therefore of a future: "It is spring. That is to say, it is approaching THE BEGINNING" (SA, 94).

NOTES

INTRODUCTION

1. Take, for example, Horace Kallen's assessment of Dewey's influence in 1939: "As I see it, it will be Dewey, not Ford, not Edison, not Roosevelt, who, when the last word has been said and the last vote has been counted, will figure as the pregnant symbol of what is best in the America of today and most hopeful for the Americanism of tomorrow." Kallen quoted in Cornel West, *The American Evasion of Philosophy: A Genealogy of Pragmatism* (London: Macmillan, 1989), p 71. In the same year, Alfred North Whitehead concluded that "We are living in the midst of the period subject to Dewey's influence." Paul Arthur Schilpp, ed. *The Philosophy of John Dewey* (La Salle, Illinois: Open Court, 1939), p 477.

2. Cary Wolfe, in his study of Emerson and Pound, explains his own linking of two disparate writers in terms that might serve to describe the point of my own particular coupling. The connection between his two subjects, writes Wolfe, is of "ideological kinship in a broad cultural logic whose operations extend far beyond the ability of the individual to master them by personal fiat or disarm them by soul-searching and self-reflection." Cary Wolfe, *The Limits of American Literary Ideology in Pound and Emerson* (Cambridge: Cambridge University Press, 1994), p 4.

3. See Cornel West on Dewey's decision, on his move to the University of Chicago in 1894, to practice "professional caution and political reticence" after a brief involvement with left-wing radicals. Dewey "remained committed yet directed his energies into middle-class channels, especially education." *The American Evasion of Philosophy*, pp 83–84.

4. Jeffrey Walker, *Bardic Ethos and the American Epic Poem: Whitman, Pound, Crane, Williams, Olson* (Baton Rouge: Louisiana State University Press, 1989), p 15.

CHAPTER ONE

1. Karl Marx, *Selected Writings*, ed. David McLellan (Oxford: Oxford University Press, 1977), p 28. See Dewey, *The Public and its Problems*, p 299: "The idea of a natural individual in his isolation possessed of full-fledged wants, of energies to be expended according to is own volition, and of a ready-made faculty of foresight and prudent calculation is as much a fiction in psychology as the doctrine of the individual in possession of antecedent political rights is one in politics."

2. Ralph Waldo Emerson, *Essays and Lectures* (New York: Library of America, 1983), pp 567–568.

3. George Kateb, *Emerson and Self-Reliance* (Thousand Oaks, CA: Sage, 1995), p 189.

4. John Dewey, "Creative Democracy—The Task Before Us," LW 14, 224–230, p 227. For Marx's view on the individual and democracy see, for example, Josef Chytry, *The Aesthetic State: A Quest in Modern German Thought* (Berkeley: University of California Press, 1989), p 241: "Democracy is the 'truth' or summation of all other institutional forms: it is the actualization of finite individualism on the political level. The republican form of government may be an essential step toward the 'Aufhebung des Staates,' the end to a state apparatus separate from direct exercise of executive and legislative power. But democracy proper is the only appropriate institutional expression of the finite individual's awareness of himself as the true basis of the political structure that demands his loyalty when he consciously engages with others in the creative activities of the polity as his own work (Werk) and free product (freies Produkt)." On Emerson and democracy, see Kateb, *Emerson and Self-Reliance*, especially chapter 6.

5. John Dewey, "Creative Democracy—The Task Before Us," LW 14, 224–230, p 228. Cf. Whitman, *Democratic Vistas*, in *Complete Poetry and Selected Prose and Letters*, p 657: "As the greatest lessons of Nature through the universe are perhaps the lessons of variety and freedom, the same present the greatest lessons also in New World politics and progress."

6. On the question of degrees of democracy, see Frank Cunningham, *Democratic Theory and Socialism,* (Cambridge: Cambridge University Press, 1987), pp 25–33: "[D]emocracy is always a matter of degree. Instead of asking whether something is or is not democratic, one should ask *how democratic* it is" (p 25). "Regarded as an idea, democracy is not an alternative to other principles of associated life. It is the idea of community life itself" (Dewey, PP, 328).

7. Dewey, "Creative Democracy—The Task Before Us," LW 14, p 229.

8. Richard Rorty, *Objectivity, Relativism, and Truth* (Cambridge: Cambridge University Press, 1992), p 178.

9. John Dewey, "Philosophy and Democracy," MW 11, 41–53, p 48. Further references to this work are included in the text as PD.

10. Williams opens *Paterson* Book One by offering the conundrum that "by multiplication a reduction to one" (P, 10). This is elaborated to suggest a natural multiplication of specific objects, each individually itself:

> from mathematics to particulars—
> > divided as the dew,
> floating mists, to be rained down and
> regathered into a river that flows
> and encircles:
> > shells and animalcules
> generally and so to man [. . .] (P, 13)

11. Sacvan Bercovitch, *The Rites of Assent: Transformations in the Symbolic Construction of America* (London: Routledge, 1993), pp. 12–13. See also Ronald D. Rotunda, *The Politics of Language: Liberalism as Word and Symbol* (Iowa City: University of Iowa Press,

1986), p 10: "In the United States . . . democracy offers its holders no great advantage since everyone holds it. . . . Although liberalism has no precise meaning in this country, whenever people have tried to give it a meaning they have often included themselves in the definition, or in the 'true definition'. . . . "

12. Louis Hartz, *The Liberal Tradition in America* (New York: Harcourt, 1955), pp 5–6.

13. See, for example, Peter Wagner, *A Sociology of Modernity: Liberty and Discipline* (London: Routledge, 1994), p 53. "[T]he weakness of the welfare state in the US stems from the impossibility of defining obligations with regard to national citizenship. At least in social terms, there is no strong sense of inclusive boundaries, which could enable the poor as 'our poor', to whom one has moral obligations." More generally, "the emphasis on plurality itself does not solve any problem."

14. Robert W. Clopton and Tsuin-chen On, eds., *John Dewey: Lectures in China, 1919–1920* (Honolulu: University Press of Hawaii, 1973), p 73.

15. Ibid., p 71.

16. Ibid.

17. Ibid., p 80. My italics.

18. Richard J. Bernstein, *Praxis and Action* (Philadelphia: University of Pennsylvania Press, 1971), p 228.

19. Ibid., p 229.

20. C. Wright Mills, *The Power Elite* (New York: Oxford University Press, 1956), p 300.

21. Ibid., pp 300–301.

22. Ibid., p 301.

23. Ibid., pp 305–306.

24. John Dewey, "Democracy is Radical," LW 11, pp 298–299.

25. J. Hillis Miller, *Poets of Reality: Six Twentieth Century Writers* (Oxford: Oxford University Press, 1966), 285–359, p 288.

26. John Dewey, "Experience, Knowledge, and Value: A Rejoinder," LW 14, p 29.

27. Donald E. Pease, *Visionary Compacts: American Renaissance Writings in Cultural Context* (Madison: University of Wisconsin Press, 1987), p 126.

28. Alfred North Whitehead, *Science and the Modern World* (1925. New York: Mentor, 1948), p 87.

29. William Carlos Williams, "The Fatal Blunder," *Quarterly Review of Literature* 2 (1944): 125–26, p 126.

30. Carl Rapp, *William Carlos Williams and Romantic Idealism* (Hanover, NH: University Press of New England, 1984); Donald W. Markos, *Ideas and Things: The Poems of William Carlos Williams* (Cranbury, NJ: Associated University Press, 1994).

31. Rapp, *William Carlos Williams and Romantic Idealism,* p 13.

32. Ibid., p 22.

33. Ibid., p 25.

34. Ibid., p 84.

35. Markos, *Ideas and Things,* p 25.

36. Bernstein, *Praxis and Action,* pp 29–30.

37. As Bakhtin writes, "In dialogue the destruction of the opponent also destroys that very dialogic sphere in which the word lives." Gary Saul Morson, ed., *Bakhtin: Essays and Dialogues on his Work* (Chicago: University of Chicago Press, 1986), p 182.

38. Michael Oakeshott, "The Voice of Poetry in the Conversation of Mankind," in *Rationalism in Politics and Other Essays* (London: Methuen, 1962), 197–247, p 198. While a conversation "may have passages of argument and a speaker is not forbidden to be demonstrative," there "is no 'truth' to be discovered, no proposition to be proved, no conclusion sought." The participants in a conversation "are not concerned to inform, to persuade, or to refute one another, and therefore the cogency of their utterances does not depend upon their all speaking in the same idiom; they may differ without disagreeing."

39. John Dewey, *Characters and Events: Popular Essays in Social and Political Philosophy,* Volume I, ed. Joseph Ratner (New York: Holt, 1929), p 126. Abbreviated in the text as CE I followed by page number.

40. Gadamer, in *Truth and Method,* suggests that "Dialogue is nothing but the mutual stimulation of thought[,] . . . a kind of artistic construction in the reciprocity of communication." Any prearranged agreement of terms or idiom is irrelevant because the construction is achieved in the meeting itself, in the interaction of utterances as manifested and engaged thought: "utterance is not merely an inner product of thought, but is also communication and has, as such, an external form . . . " Hans-Georg Gadamer, *Truth and Method,* trans. Joel Weinsheimer and David G. Marshall (London: Sheed and Ward, 1989), pp 165–66.

41. Oakeshott, *Rationalism in Politics ,* pp 201–202.

42. The concept of play is used by Gadamer in order to understand the kind of purposive purposelessness of art. In art, as in play, "all those purposive relations which determine active and caring existence have not simply disappeared, but in a curious way acquire a different quality" (*Truth and Method,* p 91). As with Oakeshott's conversationalists, in order to make play wholly play, the game must be taken seriously; not the game as an object but the mode of being of play itself. Just as, for Gadamer, "the work of art has its true being in the fact that it becomes an experience changing the person experiencing it," play also "merely reaches presentation through the players"; the players are not the subjects of the play anymore than the conversationalists are the subject of the conversation. It is the *experience* of play, conversation, and art that constitutes the generative and transformational energy that offers a kind of cultural praxis not geared to end results. Conversation, writes Oakeshott, "is not an enterprise designed to yield an extrinsic profit" (*Rationalism in Politics,* p 198). "The movement which is play," confirms Gadamer, "has no goal which brings it to an end; rather it renews itself in constant repetition." (*Truth and Method,* p 93).

43. Similar criticisms have been leveled at Richard Rorty's neopragmatist notion of conversation. See Susan C. Jarrett, "In excess: radical extensions of neopragmatism," in Steven Mailloux, ed., *Rhetoric, Sophistry, Pragmatism* (Cambridge: Cambridge University Press, 1995), 206–227; Frank Lentricchia, "Rorty's Cultural Conversation," *Raritan* 3 (Summer 1983): 136–141; Jo Burrows, "Conversational Politics: Rorty's Pragmatist Apology for Liberalism," in *Reading Rorty: Critical Responses to* Philosophy and the Mirror of Nature *(and Beyond)* (Oxford: Blackwell, 1990), 322–338. Lentricchia notes that "[N]o single anchoring goal or telos for the conversation is possible because our various vocabularies will never project or describe the same thing. The voices, staying closer to the

metaphor, will tend to merge in a cacophony, a Babel-like chorus of unconstrained and incommensurate interpretation . . . Rorty's conversation sounds like no conversation at all" (p 137). Likewise, Burrows asks: "What are the political preconditions for conversational practices? Are these practices 'benign' (i.e. non-confrontational), and if so, how can this be squared with political reality? Are the limitations on the selection of the subject-matter of conversation analogous to the constraints on the choice of theme for a poem or novel? Is participation likely to be restricted to those fortunate enough to be able to view their lives 'ironically', in a spirit of Derridean playfulness? In short, what determines the style and content of conversation, and who gets to take part?" (p 322).

44. C. Wright Mills, *Sociology and Pragmatism: The Higher Learning in America* (1942: New York: Oxford University Press, 1964), p 392.

45. Ibid., pp 392–393.

46. Ibid., p 394.

47. Ibid., p 405.

48. FC, 176. The letter from Williams to Pound is quoted by Thomas Parkinson, "Pound and Williams," in George Bornstein, ed., *Ezra Pound Among the Poets* (Chicago: University of Chicago Press, 1985), 149–167, p 162.

49. Ralph Waldo Emerson, "Quotation and Originality," in *The Portable Emerson* (New York: Viking, 1946), p 292. We might also remember, with reference to this poem, Walter Benjamin's observation that the "cultural treasures" the historian surveys "have an origin which he cannot contemplate without horror." See Walter Benjamin, "Theses on the Philosophy of History," in *Illuminations: Essays and Reflections* , trans. Harry Zohn (London: Cape, 1970), p 258.

50. Theodor W. Adorno, *Aesthetic Theory*, trans. C. Lenhardt (London: Routledge, 1984), p 71. "If oneness in art works inevitably implies the use of force against the many," says Adorno, "then it follows that the many must also fear oneness."

51. On the significance of the National Origins Act and the Indian Citizenship Act for an understanding of American nativism, see Walter Benn Michaels, *Our America: Nativism, Modernism, and Pluralism* (Durham, NC: Duke University Press, 1995), pp 30–32. Michaels also has pertinent things to say about Williams. See pp 74–77, 82–85.

52. Alexis de Tocqueville, *Democracy in America*, trans. Henry Reeve (Oxford: Oxford University Press, 1946), pp 336–337.

53. Sacvan Bercovitch, *The Rites of Assent*, p 14.

4. See Carroll F. Terrell, "Louis Zukofsky: An Eccentric Profile," in Carroll F. Terrell, ed., *Louis Zukofsky: Man and Poet* (Orono, Maine: National Poetry Foundation, 1979), pp 36, 51–52.

55. Mary Oppen, *Meaning a Life: An Autobiography* (Santa Barbara: Black Sparrow, 1978), p 94.

56. Count Hermann Keyserling, *America Set Free* (London: Cape, 1930), pp 112–113.

57. John Dewey, "Nationalizing Education," MW 10, p 204.

58. John Dewey to Horace M. Kallen, 31 March 1915, quoted in Robert B. Westbrook, *John Dewey and American Democracy* (Ithaca and London: Cornell University Press, 1991), pp 213–214.

59. Ibid.

60. John Dewey, "Nationalizing Education," MW 10, p 210.

61. John Dewey, "Universal Service as Education," MW 10, 183–90, p 186.

62. William Carlos Williams, "Letter to an Australian Editor," 1946, rpt. *William Carlos Williams Review* 17: 2 (Fall 1991): 8–12, p 11.

63. Ibid.

CHAPTER TWO

1. William Morris quoted in Raymond Williams, *Culture and Society, 1780–1950* (London: Chatto, 1958), p 158.

2. The prominence and significance of marriage in Williams's writing has been well documented. See, for example, Ann W. Fisher-Wirth, *William Carlos Williams and Autobiography: The Woods of his Own Nature* (University Park: Pennsylvania State University Press, 1989), Chapters 3 and 4; Barry Ahearn, *William Carlos Williams and Alterity: The Early Poetry* (Cambridge: Cambridge University Press, 1994), Chapter 2; Ron Callan, *William Carlos Williams and Transcendentalism: Fitting the Crab in a Box* (London: Macmillan, 1992).

3. As Stanley Cavell writes, "Human forms of feeling, objects of human attraction, our reactions constituted in art, are as universal and necessary, as objective, as revelatory of the world, as the forms of the laws of physics." Stanley Cavell, *The Senses of Walden,* (New York: Viking, 1974), p 104.

4. Samuel Taylor Coleridge, *Biographia Literaria,* Chapter XIII (London: Dent, 1917), pp 159–60.

5. Stanley Cavell, *Pursuits of Happiness: The Hollywood Comedy of Remarriage* (Cambridge: Harvard University Press,1981), pp 126–27.

6. Ibid., p 103.

7. See Fisher-Wirth, *William Carlos Williams and Autobiography*, p 52: "Whereas adultery is a statement of man's freedom, an assertion of desire independent of social order, and therefore an assertion of art, marriage is a statement of man's presence in the world, a promise of his commitment to the world, without which commitment there would be no art and no one to be free."

8. John Dewey, "Art into Education—Education into Art," LW 2, 111–115, p 111.

9. Ibid., 112. Dewey is quoting from *Science and the Modern World* (1925. New York: Mentor, 1964), p 176.

10. Dewey and Williams were not alone in derogating the popular taste. For example, Randolph Bourne, a critic deeply influenced by Dewey, makes the observation that because modern industrial labor sapped the vitality of the worker, "the clerk dulled and depressed by the long day, and the factory worker—his brain a-whirl with the roar of the machines—must seek elation and the climax which the work should have given them, in the crude and exciting pleasures of the street and the dance and the show." Randolph Bourne, "In the Mind of the Worker," *Atlantic Monthly* 113 (June 1914): 375–382, p 378.

11. Cary Nelson has observed that the "subject matter of ordinary life enters modern poetry quite prominently, but it is offset by a higher degree of distanciation. Williams's 'The Red Wheelbarrow' is perhaps the locus classicus of the risk in modern poetry that the distinction between form and the everyday will collapse." Cary Nelson, *Repression and Re-*

covery: Modern American Poetry and the Politics of Cultural Memory, 1910–1945 (Madison: University of Wisconsin Press, 1989), p 67.

12. John Dewey, "The Need for a Recovery of Philosophy," MW 10, 3–48.

13. Ibid., p 6.

14. Ibid.

15. Art, writes Adorno, "is social primarily because it stands opposed to society. Now this opposition art can mount only when it has become autonomous. By congealing into an entity unto itself—rather than obeying existing social norms and thus proving itself to be 'socially useful'—art criticizes society just by being there. . . . Radical modernism preserves the immanence of art by letting society into its precincts but only in dimmed form, as though it were a dream. . . . If any social function can be ascribed to art at all, it is the function to have no function." *Aesthetic Theory*, pp. 321–322.

16. Cecelia Tichi, *Shifting Gears: Technology, Literature, Culture in Modernist America* (Chapel Hill: University of North Carolina Press, 1987), pp 242–243.

17. Peter Schmidt, in *William Carlos Williams, The Arts, and Literary Tradition* (Baton Rouge: Louisiana State University Press, 1988), takes this line, placing Williams's improvisations in the context of French and New York Dada experiments in automatic writing. Schmidt sees Williams's work as closer to therapy than art. See Chapter 3, pp. 90–135.

18. Thomas M. Alexander, *John Dewey's Theory of Art, Experience and Nature: The Horizons of Feeling* (Albany: State University of New York Press, 1987), p 262.

CHAPTER THREE

1. Brian A. Bremen, *William Carlos Williams and the Diagnostics of Culture* (Oxford: Oxford University Press, 1993), p 3.

2. Williams quoted in Bremen, p 4.

3. Gail McDonald, *Learning to be Modern: Pound, Eliot, and the American University* (Oxford: Oxford University Press, 1993), p 62.

4. Ibid.

5. Burton Bledstein, *The Culture of Professionalism: The Middle Class and the Development of Higher Learning in America* (New York: Norton, 1976), pp 288–289.

6. Gerald Graff, *Professing Literature: An Institutional History* (Chicago: University of Chicago Press, 1987), p 62.

7. John Dewey, "Logical Conditions for a Scientific Treatment Of Morality," MW 3, pp 3–4.

8. John Dewey, *How We Think*, MW 6, pp 236–237, 201, 232.

9. Ibid., pp 201.

10. Ibid., p 232.

11. Ibid.

12. John Dewey, "Science as Subject-Matter and as Method," MW 6, p 78.

13. John Dewey, "The Problem of Truth," MW 6, p 31.

14. John Dewey, "Intelligence and Morals," MW 4, p 39.

15. Quoted in Alfred Kazin, *On Native Grounds: An Interpretation of Modern American Prose Literature* (New York: Harcourt, 1942), p 171.

16. Richard Rorty, *Consequences of Pragmatism (Essays: 1972 – 1980)* (Brighton: Harvester, 1982), p 63.

17. Kazin, *On Native Grounds*, pp 142, 144.

18. John Dewey, *Reconstruction in Philosophy*, MW 12, p 186.

19. Ezra Pound, *The Selected Letters of Ezra Pound, 1907–1941,* ed. D.D. Paige (London: Faber, 1950), p 180.

20. Ezra Pound, *Selected Prose 1901–1965* , ed. William Cookson (London: Faber, 1973), p 449.

21. T. S. Eliot, *The Idea of a Christian Society* (1939), in *Christianity and Culture* (New York: Harcourt, 1968), p 32.

22. Michael W. Apple, *Ideology and Curriculum* (London: Routledge, 1979), p 47.

23. Ibid., p 48.

24. Marvin Lazerson, *Origins of the Urban School* (Cambridge: Harvard University Press, 1971), pp x–xi.

25. Apple, *Ideology and Curriculum* , p 70.

26. Franklin Bobbitt, *The Curriculum* (New York: Arno, 1971), p 131. Emphasis in original.

27. Edward A. Ross, *Principles of Sociology* (New York: Century, 1920), p 409.

28. John Dewey, "Education from a Social Perspective," MW 7, pp 115–116.

29. Ibid., p 127.

30. Ibid., p 120.

31. F. W. Taylor quoted in Apple, *Ideology and Curriculum* , p 182.

32. John Dewey, "Some Dangers in the Present Movement for Industrial Education," MW 7, p 99.

33. Ibid., p 102.

34. John Dewey, "Learning to Earn," MW 10, p 146.

35. John Dewey, "Education vs. Trade-Training: Reply to David Snedden," MW 8, p 412.

36. Irving Babbitt, *Democracy and Leadership* (Boston: Houghton, 1924), p 313.

37. Ibid., pp 257, 312.

38. Ibid., p 312.

39. Robert Scholes, *Textual Power: Literary Theory and the Teaching of English* (New Haven: Yale University Press, 1985), pp 131–132.

40. Ezra Pound, *ABC of Reading* (London: Faber, 1951), pp 17–18.

41. Scholes, *Textual Power,* p 131.

42. Flexner quoted in Cecelia Tichi, *Shifting Gears,* pp 253–255.

43. Osler quoted in ibid., p 255.

44. Paulo Freire, *Pedagogy of the Oppressed* (New York: Herder and Herder, 1972) p 75.

45. Ibid., p 76.

46. Ibid.

47. Ibid., p 77.

CHAPTER FOUR

1. Ralph Waldo Emerson, *Essays and Lectures* (New York: Library of America, 1983), p 16.

2. Mike Weaver, *William Carlos Williams: The American Background* (Cambridge: Cambridge University Press, 1971), p 32.

3. John Dewey, "Americanism and Localism," *Dial* 68 (June 1920): 684–688, p 687. Further references are included in the text, abbreviated as AL. Reprinted in MW 12, pp 12–16.

4. *Contact: Numbers 1–5, 1920–1924* (New York: Kraus Reprint, 1967), *Contact* 2., not paginated.

5. James Oppenheim, "Poetry—Our First National Art," *Dial* 68 (Feb. 1920): 238–242, p 238.

6. See Weaver, *The American Background*, pp 32–36.

7. See Raven I. McDonald Jr., introduction to H. L. Mencken, *The American Language*, 4th ed. (London: Routledge, 1963), pvii.

8. H. L. Mencken, *The American Language*, p 99.

9. William Carlos Williams, "Yours, O Youth," *Contact* 3, p 14. Reprinted in SE 32–37.

10. Malcolm Cowley, *Exile's Return: A Literary Odyssey of the 1920's* (London: Bodley Head, 1934), p 28.

11. Pierre Bourdieu claims that "in order for one mode of expression among others to impose itself as the only legitimate one, the linguistic market has to be unified and the different dialects (of class, religion or ethnic group) have to be measured against the legitimate language or usage." Bourdieu goes on to remark that "only when the making of the 'nation', an entirely abstract group based on law, creates new usages and functions does it become indispensable to forge a *standard* language, impersonal and anonymous like the official uses it has to serve, and by the same token to undertake the work of normalising the products of the linguistic habitus. The dictionary is the exemplary result of this labor of codification and normalization." Pierre Bourdieu, *Language and Symbolic Power,* ed. John B. Thompson, trans. Gino Raymond and Matthew Adamson (Cambridge: Polity, 1991), pp 45, 48.

12. Stuart and Elizabeth Ewen, "Americanization and Consumption," *Telos* 37 (1978): 42–51, p 47.

13. Furniss quoted in Ibid., p 46.

14. Henry James, *The Question of Our Speech. The Lesson of Balzac. Two Lectures* (Boston: Houghton, 1905), pp 40–41. Further references are in the text abbreviated as J and page number.

15. Bourdieu, *Language and Symbolic Power,* p 55.

16. Raymond Williams quoted in Eugene Rochberg-Halton, *Meaning and Modernity: Social Theory in the Pragmatic Attitude* (Chicago: University of Chicago Press, 1986), p 111.

17. Gunther Barth, *City People: The Rise of Modern City Culture in Nineteenth Century America* (Oxford: Oxford University Press, 1980), p 61.

18. For an insightful examination of the pervasiveness of the car in American poetry

and culture, see Eric Mottram, "'That Dark Instrument'—The American Automobile," *Talus* 3 (Spring 1988): 12–32.

19. J. J. Flink's *Car Culture* (Cambridge: MIT Press, 1975), and John B. Rae's *The Road and the Car in American Life* (Cambridge: MIT Press, 1971) provide good surveys of the impact of the automobile on American life.

20. For the influence of driving on Williams's aesthetics, see, for example, Roy Miki, "Writing and Driving," in *William Carlos Williams: Man and Poet* , ed. Carroll Terrell (Orono, Maine: National Poetry Foundation, 1983), pp 111–128; Cecelia Tichi, *Shifting Gears*, pp 245–256.

21. William Carlos Williams, "The Fatal Blunder," *Quarterly Review of Literature* 2 (1944): 125–126, p 126.

22. Henry David Thoreau, *The Portable Thoreau*, ed. Carol Bode (Harmondsworth, England: Penguin, 1947), p 593.

23. Jacques Derrida, in "Structure, Sign and Play in the Discourses of the Human Sciences," suggests that "the centre also closes off the play which it opens up and makes possibleThe concept of centred structure is in fact the concept of play based on fundamental ground, a play constituted on the basis of a fundamental immobility and a reassuring certitude which itself is beyond the reach of play." Jacques Derrida, *Writing and Difference*, trans. Alan Bass (1978. London: Routledge, 1990), p 279.

24. Henry Ford quoted in Flink, *Car Culture*, p 86.

25. Roland Barthes, *Mythologies* (London: Paladin, 1973), p 95.

26. This kind of rationalization of the landscape was predicted by Thoreau in 1862 when he wrote that "at present . . .   the best part of the land is not private property; the landscape is not owned, and the walker enjoys comparative freedom. But possibly the day will come when it will be partitioned off into so-called pleasure grounds, in which a few will take a narrow and exclusive pleasure only—when fences shall be multiplied, and man-traps and other engines invented to confine men to the *public* road." Henry David Thoreau, "Walking," in *The Portable Thoreau*, p 602.

27. Flink, *Car Culture*, p 166.

28. Marshall Berman, *All That is Solid Melts Into Air: The Experience Of Modernity* (New York and London: Verso, 1983), pp 298–99.

29. Alexis de Tocqueville, *Democracy in America*, p 336.

30. Ibid., p 337.

31. Cf. Adorno, *Aesthetic Theory*, p 362. "The unity of the social criterion of art with the aesthetic one hinges on whether art is able to supersede empirical reality while at the same time concretizing its relation to that superseded reality."

32. David Frail, *The Early Politics and Poetics of William Carlos Williams* (Ann Arbor: UMI Research Press, 1987), p 175.

33. For other examples of anti-Puritan cultural criticism of the time, see, for example, Brooks's *The Wine of the Puritans* (1908) and *America's Coming of Age* (1915), Frank's *Our America* (1919), and Mumford's *The Golden Day* (1926).

34. John Dewey, "The Need for A Recovery of Philosophy," MW10, p 4.

35. Ibid., p 10.

36. Ibid., p 47.

37. Ibid., pp 47–48.

38. Ibid., p 48.

39. Henry David Thoreau, *Walden* (1864. New York: Bantam, 1963), p 181. This fusion of horizons between past and present is what Williams is looking for, the kind of incarnational hermeneutics described by Gadamer where written history "is not a document, as a piece of the past, that is the bearer of tradition but the continuity of memory. Through it tradition becomes part of our own world, and thus what it communicates can be stated immediately. Where we have a written tradition, we are not just told a particular thing; a part of humanity itself becomes present to us in its general relation to the world." Hans-Georg Gadamer, *Truth and Method*, p 390.

40. Vera M. Kutzinski, *Against the American Grain: Myth and History in William Carlos Williams, Jay Wright, and Nicolas Guillen* (Baltimore: Johns Hopkins University Press, 1987), chapter 1.

41. Edmundo O'Gorman, *The Invention of America: An Enquiry into the Historical Nature of the New World and the Meaning of its History* (1958. Westport, CT: Greenwood, 1972), p 137.

42. Kenneth Burke, "Subjective History," *New York Herald Tribune Books,* 14 March 1926, p 7.

43. D. H. Lawrence, "American Heroes," *The Nation* , 14 April 1926, pp 413–414.

44. Emerson writes that "there is properly no history, only biography. Every mind must acknowledge the whole lesson for itself—must go over the whole ground. What it does not see, what it does not live, it will not know." Thoreau pushes history even further into the subjective by claiming that "the *past* cannot be *presented*; we cannot know what we are not. But one veil hangs over past, present, and future, and it is the province of the historian to find out, not what was, but what is. Biography, too, is liable to the same objection; it should be autobiography. . . . If I am not I, who will be?" Ralph Waldo Emerson, *Essays and Lectures* (New York: Library of America, 1983), p 240; Henry David Thoreau, *A Week on the Concord and Merrimack Rivers* (1849. Princeton, NJ: Princeton University Press, 1989), pp 154–155.

45. Ralph Waldo Emerson, *The Portable Emerson*, p 292.

46. Bryce Conrad, *Refiguring America: A Study of William Carlos Williams's* In the American Grain (Urbana and Chicago: University of Illinois Press, 1990), chapter 2.

47. Van Wyck Brooks, "The Culture of Industrialism," *Seven Arts* (April 1917): 655–666, rpt. in Alan Trachtenberg, ed.,*Critics of Culture: Literature and Society in the Early Twentieth Century* (New York: John Wiley, 1976): 89–98, p 90.

48. Waldo Frank, "The Land of the Pioneer" (1919), rpt. in Trachtenberg, *Critics of Culture*, 119–144, p 120.

49. Marcel Mauss, *The Gift:The Form and Reason for Exchange in Archaic Societies* (1950. London: Routledge, 1990), p 14.

50. Ibid., p 12.

CHAPTER FIVE

1. John Dewey, *Impressions of Soviet Russia,* LW 5, pp 114–116, 24, 52–8, 61, 109.

2. William Carlos Williams, "An American Poet," in James E. B. Breslin, ed., *Something to Say: William Carlos Williams on Younger Poets* (New York: New Directions, 1985),

p 77. "Without saying that Lewis is important as a poet . . . I will say that he is tremendously important as an instigator to thought about what poetry can and cannot do to us today." The power of Lewis's work lies, then, not so much in its aesthetic excellence but in its commitment to poetry as a form of social praxis.

3. Ibid., p 80.

4. John Dewey, "The Need for a New Party," LW 6, p 169.

5. Dewey quoted in Casey·Nelson Blake, *Beloved Community: The Cultural Criticism of Randolph Bourne, Van Wyck Brooks, Waldo Frank, and Lewis Mumford* (Chapel Hill and London: University of North Carolina Press, 1990), p 87.

6. Edward J. Bordeau, "John Dewey's Ideas About the Great Depression," *Journal of the History of Ideas* 32.1 (January-March 1971): 67–84, p 69.

7. Dewey quoted in ibid., p 71.

8. Ibid., p 74.

9. Dewey quoted in ibid., 78.

10. John Dewey, "I Believe," LW 14, p 91.

11. John Dewey, "Democracy and Educational Administration," LW 11, pp 217–18.

12. Ibid., pp 218–219.

13. John Dewey, "Why I Am Not a Communist," LW9, p 93.

14. Ibid., p 94.

15. John Dewey, "Liberty and Social Control," LW 11, p 360.

16. Ibid., p 361.

17. Ibid., pp 361–362.

18. John Dewey, "Liberty and Equality," LW 11, p 370.

19. John Dewey, "I Believe," LW 14, pp 94–95.

20. John Dewey, "The Need for a New Party," LW 6, p 163.

21. John Dewey, "I Believe," LW 14, pp 95–96.

22. John Dewey, "No Halfway House for America," LW 9, p 289.

23. Ibid., pp 289–290.

24. John Dewey, "Imperative Need: A New Radical Party," LW 9, pp 76–77.

25. John Dewey, "Is There Hope for Politics?" LW 6, p 188.

26. John Dewey, "Why I Am Not a Communist," LW9, p 95.

27. Williams quoted in Paul Mariani, *William Carlos Williams: A New World Naked* (New York: McGraw Hill, 1981), p 330.

28. Ibid.

29. Letter to Fred and Betty Miller, July 1934, quoted in Mariani, *A New World Naked* , p 360.

30. Ibid.

31. *Partisan Review* 3. 2 (April 1936): 3–16.

32. Ibid., pp 13–14.

33. Ibid., p 13.

34. John Dewey, "Why I Am Not a Communist," LW9, p 94.

35. William Carlos Williams, "The New Poetical Economy," *Poetry* 44 (July 1934):

220–225, rpt. in Burton Hatlen, ed., *George Oppen: Man and Poet* (Orono, Maine: National Poetry Foundation, 1981): 267–270, p 267.

36. Ibid., p 270.

37. Ezra Pound, *The Literary Essays of Ezra Pound,* p 9.

38. For Zukofsky's influence on Williams, see Paul Mariani, *William Carlos Williams: A New World Naked,* pp 273–382 passim; Peter Quartermain, *Disjunctive Poetics: From Gertrude Stein and Louis Zukofsky to Susan Howe* (Cambridge: Cambridge University Press, 1993), Chapter 5; Sandra Kumamuto Stanley, *Louis Zukofsky and the Transformation of a Modern American Poetics* (Berkeley: University of California Press, 1994); Neil Baldwin, "Zukofsky, Williams, and *The Wedge:* Toward a Dynamic Convergence," in Carroll F. Terrell, ed., *Louis Zukofsky: Man and Poet* (Orono, Maine: National Poetry Foundation, 1979), pp 129–142.

39. *Poetry* 37 (Feb. 1931): 268–284, p 268.

40. Ibid., p 273.

41. Oppen quoted by Rachel Blau DuPlessis, "Objectivist Poetics and Political Vision: A Study of Oppen and Pound," in *George Oppen: Man and Poet,* pp 123–148, p 127.

42. Ibid., p 126.

43. Louis Zukofsky, "An Objective" quoted in *George Oppen: Man and Poet,* p 127.

44. William Carlos Williams, "Comment," *Contact* 1.1 (Feb. 1932), p 8.

45. Ibid.

46. Williams quoted in CP 1, p 542.

47. In *The Freeman* in 1920 Williams described Coffey's action as "a light in the dark, a diagnosis"; in Maxwell Bodenheim's novel *Crazy Man* (1924) Coffey is portrayed as a Christ–figure, and in Conrad Aiken's *Conversation* (1940) he is an idealist (CP 1, 537).

48. Joseph Freeman on Mike Gold, quoted in James Burkhart Gilbert, *Writers and Partisans: A History of Literary Radicalism in America* (New York: John Wiley, 1968), p 76.

49. George Oppen quoted in L.S. Dembo, "The 'Objectivist' Poet: Four Interviews," *Contemporary Literature* 10 (Spring 1969): 155–219, p 161.

50. Robert von Hallberg, "The Politics of Description: W.C. Williams in the 'Thirties," *ELH* 45 (1978): 131–151, p 132.

51. Zukofsky quoted by Hallberg, p 146.

52. Williams quoted in Mariani, *A New World Naked,* p 370.

53. John Dewey, "Why I Am Not a Communist," LW9, p 92.

CHAPTER SIX

1. G. W. F. Hegel, *Aesthetics: Lectures on Fine Art, Volume II,* trans. T. M. Knox, (Oxford: Oxford University Press, 1975), p 1044. Further references are cited in the text, abbreviated by H.

2. Alec Marsh, *Money and Modernity: Pound, Williams, and the Spirit of Jefferson.* (Tuscaloosa: University of Alabama Press, 1998), p 228. Marsh convincingly argues that *Paterson* is deeply indebted to Deweyan pragmatism, both formally and in its critique of corporate America. See chapters 6 and 7.

3. Northrop Frye, *Anatomy of Criticism: Four Essays* (Princeton: Princeton University

Press, 1957), p 54. Elsewhere, Frye expands: "The function of the epic in its origin, seems to be primarily to teach the nation, or whatever we call the social unit which the poet is addressing, its own traditions. These traditions are chiefly concerned with the national religion and the national history, and both are presented in terms of the activities of 'Giant Forms,' or beings at once human and divine, who are called 'Gods' in the religious context and 'heroes" in the historical one." Northrop Frye, *Fearful Symmetry: A Study of William Blake* (Boston: Beacon, 1947), p 316.

4. See Margaret Glynne Lloyd, *William Carlos Williams's Paterson: A Critical Reappraisal* (Cranbury, NJ: Associated University Press, 1980), pp 241–242 for a survey of critical responses to *Paterson.*

5. John Malcolm Brinnin and James Breslin both refer to the fragmented condition of the modern world, a condition that rules out the epic form. Brinnin: *Paterson's* structure, "suggested partly by an available cultural situation, is nevertheless mostly the device of an author who, in despair, creates what he has failed to inherit—a body of myth, a roster of dramatis personae, a religious sanction. The official facades of democracy and Christianity cannot disguise the fact that the contemporary world is characterised more by disparity than by unity. Consequently, the poet is denied the advantage of a homogeneous community where the deeds of religious and political heroes reflect common ideals." John Malcolm Brinnin, "William Carlos Williams," in Leonard Unger, ed., *Seven Modern American Poets,* (Minneapolis: University of Minnesota Press, 1967), p 110. Breslin: "Williams's attempt to put the totality of his world in a single work pushed him toward the epic, the most sublime of all literary forms; yet, as he well knew, the serene tone, graceful continuity, and monumental beauty of the epic were impossible in his fragmented world." James Breslin, *William Carlos Williams: An American Artist* (New York: Oxford University Press, 1970), p 170.

6. Theodor W. Adorno, *Prisms* (London: Routledge, 1967), p 32.

7. John Dewey, *Logic: The Theory of Inquiry,* LW 12, p 72.

8. Ibid.

9. John Dewey, "A Naturalistic Theory of Sense-Perception," LW 2, p 52.

10. For the influence of Einstein's theory on the arts, see Alan J. Friedman and Carol C. Donley, *Einstein as Myth and Muse* (Cambridge: Cambridge University Press, 1985).

11. Heisenberg quoted in Friedman and Donley, p 127. See Marsh on *Paterson* in *Money and Modernity,* p 225: "Each thought's local context on the page, added to the poet's local context when putting the thought on the paper, conspires to create conjunctive relations, which the reader must take into account."

12. Hegel claims that there are "*two* sorts of a nation's reality. First, an entirely *positive* or *factual* world of the most specialized usages of precisely this individual people, at this specific period, in this geographical and climatic situation, with these rivers, mountains, and woods, in short with this natural environment. Secondly, the *substance* of the nation's *spiritual* consciousness in respect of religion, family, community, and so forth" (*Aesthetics,* p 1056). However, if the epic is "to win the abiding interest of other peoples and times too, then the world it describes must not be only that of a *particular* nation; it must be such that what is *universally* human is firmly impressed at the same time on the particular nation described and on its heroes and their deeds" (*Aesthetics,* pp 1057–1058).

13. Eric A. Havelock, *Preface to Plato* (Oxford: Blackwell, 1963), p 91.

14. Ibid., pp 146, 91.

15. Ibid., p 153. See *Paterson*, 60: "What do I do? I listen, to the water falling [. . .] This is my entire occupation."

16. Published as "(Revolutions Revalued): The Attack on Credit Monopoly from a Cultural Viewpoint" in *A Recognizable Image*, p 97–118.

17. Quoted in Mike Weaver, *William Carlos Williams: The American Background*, p 106.

18. CH. Douglas, The *Monopoly of Credit* (London: Chapman and Hall, 1931), p 14.

19. On Social Credit see Peter Makin, *Pound's Cantos*, (London: George Allen, 1985), pp 101–114; Peter Nicholls, *Ezra Pound: Economics, Politics and Writing*, (London: Macmillan, 1984), pp 20–30, 51–59. On Social Credit and Williams see Mike Weaver, *The American Background*, pp 103–114; Brian A. Bremen, *William Carlos Williams and the Diagnostics of Culture*, pp 187–197.

20. Alec Marsh, *Money and Modernity*, p 5.

21. Lewis Hyde, *The Gift: Imagination and the Erotic Life of Property* (New York: Random, 1983), pp 38–39.

22. Ibid., p 60.

23. Ibid., p 61.

24. Ibid.

25. Ibid.

26. H.G. Barnett quoted in ibid., p 35.

27. Ibid.

CONCLUSION

1. F. M. Alexander quoted in Bruce Wiltshire, "Body-mind and Subconsciousness: Tragedy in Dewey's Life and Work", in John J. Stuhr, ed., *Philosophy and the Reconstruction of Culture: Pragmatic Essays After John Dewey* (Albany: State University of New York Press, 1993); 257–272, p 260.

2. Beckett Howorth, "Dynamic Posture," *Journal of the American Medical Association* CXXXI. 17 (24 August 1946): 398–404, quoted in Mike Weaver, *The American Background*, p 206.

3. F. M. Alexander, *Man's Supreme Inheritance: Conscious Guidance and Control in Relation to Human Evolution in Civilization* (1910. London: Chaterson, 1943), p 6.

4. Howorth quoted in Weaver, p 206.

5. Casey Nelson Blake, *Beloved Community*, p 78.

6. Blake, *Beloved Community*, pp 3–4. Blake is referring to the Young Americans, but his assessment is equally applicable to Dewey and Williams.

7. Van Wyck Brooks quoted in Blake, *Beloved Community*, pp 5–6.

8. Randolph Bourne quoted in Blake, p 15. From "The Social Order in an American Town," *Atlantic Monthly* 111 (Feb. 1913), p 233.

9. C. Wright Mills, *The Marxists* (New York: Dell, 1962), p 19.

10. David Bennett, "Defining the 'American' Difference: Cultural Nationalism and the Modernist Poetics of William Carlos Williams," *Southern Review* 20 (Nov. 1987): 271–280, p 271.

11. Ibid.

12. Ibid., p 279.

13. Michael Billig, "Nationalism and Richard Rorty: The Text as a Flag for *Pax Americana*," *New Left Review* 202 (Nov.-Dec. 1993): 69–83, pp 71–2.

14. Ibid., p 76.

15. Ibid., p 77.

16. Ernest Gellner, *Spectacles and Predicaments* (Cambridge: Cambridge University Press, 1979), p 241. Further references cited in the text by G and page number.

17. John Dewey, "Universal Service for Education," MW 10, 1916, 183–190, pp 188–189.

18. See Alistair MacIntyre, *Whose Justice: Which Rationality* (London: Duckworth, 1988), p 392: "Liberalism . . . is often successful in pre-empting the debate by reformulating quarrels and conflicts with liberalism, putting in this or that particular set of attitudes or policies, but not the fundamental tenets of liberalism with respect to individuals and the expression of their preferences . . . [T]he contemporary debates within modern political systems are almost exclusively between conservative liberals, liberal liberals and radical liberals. There is little place in such political systems for the criticism of the system itself, that is, for putting liberalism in question."

19. Horace M. Kallen, *Culture and Democracy in the United States: Studies in the Group Psychology of the American Peoples* (New York: Boni and Liveright, 1924), p 124. For a convincing critique of Kallen's position see Werner Sollors, "A Critique of Pure Pluralism," in Sacvan Bercovitch, ed., *Reconstructing American Literary History* (Cambridge: Harvard University Press, 1986), pp 250–279.

20. Ibid., p 119.

21. This is also Rush Welter's conclusion. Discussing Herbert Croly, Walter Lippmann, and Dewey, Welter suggests that their "political failure was implicit in their philosophy. They took reform for granted because it was going on when they wrote . . . For all their incisive criticisms of progressive individualism, Croly and Lippmann virtually ignored vested interests and vested intelligence and they were innocent of any social theory of politics that might at least have provided them with a sense of the necessary dynamics of political change. Meanwhile Dewey simply defined every social problem as a problem of education, and ignored the practical possibility that education however reformed might be powerless to overcome refractory social habits." Rush Welter, *Popular Education and Democratic Thought in America* (New York: Columbia University Press, 1962), p 282.

22. T. S. Eliot, *After Strange Gods: A Primer of Modern Heresy* (London: Faber, 1934), p 25.

BIBLIOGRAPHY

Adorno, Theodor W. *Aesthetic Theory.* Translated by C. Lenhardt. London: Routledge, 1984.

———. *Prisms.* Translated by Samuel and Shierry Weber. London: Neville Spearman, 1967.

Ahearn, Barry. *William Carlos Williams and Alterity: The Early Poetry.* Cambridge: Cambridge University Press, 1994.

Alexander, Frederick Matthias. *Man's Supreme Inheritance: Conscious Guidance and Control in Relation to Human Evolution in Civilization.* 1910. London: Chaterson, 1943.

Alexander, Thomas M. *John Dewey's Theory of Art, Experience, and Nature: The Horizons of Feeling.* Albany: State University of New York Press, 1987.

Apple, Michael W. *Ideology and Curriculum.* London: Routledge, 1979.

Aristotle. *Poetics.* In *Philosophies of Art and Beauty: Selected Readings in Aesthetics from Plato to Heidegger.* Edited by Albert Hofstadter and Richard Kutius. Chicago: University of Chicago Press, 1964.

Babbitt, Irving. *Democracy and Leadership.* Boston and New York: Houghton, 1924.

Barth, Gunther. *City People: The Rise of Modern City Culture in Nineteenth Century America.* Oxford: Oxford University Press, 1980.

Barthes, Roland. *Mythologies.* London: Paladin, 1973.

Benjamin, Walter. *Illuminations: Essays and Reflections.* Translated by Harry Zohn. London: Cape, 1970.

Bennett, David. "Defining the 'American' Difference: Cultural Nationalism and the Modernist Poetics of William Carlos Williams." *Southern Review* 20 (Nov. 1987): 271-280.

Bercovitch, Sacvan, ed. *Reconstructing American Literary History.* Cambridge: Harvard University Press, 1986.

Bercovitch, Sacvan. *The Rites of Assent: Transformations in the Symbolic Construction of America.* London: Routledge, 1993.

Berman, Marshall. *All That Is Solid Melts into Air: The Experience of Modernity.* New York and London: Verso, 1983.

Bernstein, Michael Andre. *The Tale of the Tribe: Ezra Pound and the Modern Verse Epic.* Princeton: Princeton University Press, 1980.

Bernstein, Richard J. *Praxis and Action.* Philadelphia: University of Pennsylvania Press, 1971.

———. *Philosophical Profiles.* Philadelphia: University of Pennsylvania Press, 1986.

Billig, Michael. "Nationalism and Richard Rorty: The Text as a Flag for *Pax Americana*." *New Left Review* 202 (Nov.-Dec. 1993): 69–83.

Blake, Casey Nelson. *Beloved Community: The Cultural Criticism of Randolph Bourne, Van Wyck Brooks, Waldo Frank, and Lewis Mumford*. Chapel Hill and London: University of North Carolina Press, 1990.

Bledstein, Burton. *The Culture of Professionalism: The Middle Class and the Development of Higher Learning in America*. New York: Norton, 1976.

Bobbitt, Franklin. *The Curriculum*. New York: Arno, 1971.

Bordeau, Edward J. "John Dewey's Ideas About the Great Depression." *Journal of the History of Ideas* 32.1 (January-March 1971): 67–84.

Bornstein, George, ed. *Ezra Pound Among the Poets*. Chicago: University of Chicago Press, 1985.

Bourdieu, Pierre. *Language and Symbolic Power*. Edited by John B. Thompson. Translated by Gino Raymond and Matthew Adamson. Cambridge: Polity, 1991.

Bourne, Randolph. "In the Mind of the Worker." *Atlantic Monthly* 113 (June 1914): 375–382.

Bremen, Brian A. *William Carlos Williams and the Diagnostics of Culture*. Oxford: Oxford University Press, 1993.

Breslin, James E. B. *William Carlos Williams: An American Artist*. New York: Oxford University Press, 1970.

———. "William Carlos Williams and Charles Demuth: Cross-Fertilization in the Arts." *Journal of Modern Literature* 6 (1977): 248–263.

Brooks, Van Wyck. "The Culture of Industrialism." *Seven Arts* (April 1917): 655–666.

———. "On Creating a Usable Past." *Dial* 64 (1918): 337–341.

Bürger, Peter. *Theory of the Avant-Garde*. Translated by Michael Shaw. Manchester: Manchester University Press, 1984.

Burke, Kenneth. "Subjective History." *New York Herald Tribune Books* 14 March 1926: 7.

Burrows, Jo, ed. *Reading Rorty: Critical Responses to Philosophy and the Mirror of Nature (And Beyond)*. Oxford: Blackwell, 1990.

Callan, Ron. *William Carlos Williams and Transcendentalism: Fitting the Crab in a Box*. London: Macmillan, 1992.

Cavell, Stanley. *The Senses of Walden*. New York: Viking, 1974.

———. *Pursuits of Happiness: The Hollywood Comedy of Remarriage*. Cambridge: Harvard University Press, 1981.

Chytry, Josef. *The Aesthetic State: A Quest in Modern German Thought*. Berkeley: University of California Press, 1989.

Clark, Bruce. "The Fall of Montezuma: Poetry and History in William Carlos Williams and D. H. Lawrence." *William Carlos Williams Review* 12 (Spring 1986): 1–12.

Clopton, Robert W., and Tsuin-chen On, eds. *John Dewey: Lectures in China, 1919–1920*. Honolulu: University Press of Hawaii, 1973.

Coleridge, Samuel Taylor. *Biographia Literaria*. London: Dent, 1917.

Connarroe, Joel. *William Carlos Williams's Paterson: Language and Landscape*. Philadelphia: University of Pennsylvania Press, 1970.

———. "You Can't Steal Credit: The Economic Motif in *Paterson*." *Journal of American Studies* 2 (1968): 105–115.

Conrad, Bryce. *Refiguring America: A Study of William Carlos Williams's In the American Grain*. Urbana and Chicago: University of Illinois Press, 1990.

Contact: Numbers 1–5, 1920–1924. New York: Kraus Reprint, 1967.

Cowley, Malcolm. *Exile's Return: A Literary Odyssey of the 1920's.* London: Bodley Head, 1934.

Cunningham, Frank. *Democratic Theory and Socialism.* Cambridge: Cambridge University Press, 1987.

Cushman, Stephen. *William Carlos Williams and the Meaning of Measure.* New Haven: Yale University Press, 1985.

Dembo, L. S. "'The Objectivist Poet': Four Interviews." *Contemporary Literature* 10 (Spring 1969): 155–219.

Derrida, Jacques. *Writing and Difference.* Translated by Alan Bass. London: Routledge 1990.

Dewey, John. "Americanism and Localism." *Dial* 68 (June 1920): 684–688.

———. *Characters and Events: Popular Essays in Social and Political Philosophy.* Volume I. Edited by Joseph Ratner. New York: Holt, 1929.

———. *The Early Works of John Dewey, 1882–1898.* 5 Volumes. Edited by Jo Ann Boydston. Carbondale: Southern Illinois University Press, 1969–1972.

———. *The Middle Works of John Dewey, 1899–1924.* 15 Volumes. Edited by Jo Ann Boydston. Carbondale: Southern Illinois University Press, 1976–1983.

———. *The Later Works of John Dewey, 1925–54.* 17 Volumes. Edited by Jo Ann Boydston. Carbondale: Southern Illinois University Press, 1981–1990.

Dijkstra, Bram. *The Hieroglyphics of a New Speech: Cubism, Stieglitz, and the Early Poetry of William Carlos Williams.* Princeton: Princeton University Press, 1969.

Douglas, C. H. *The Monopoly of Credit.* London: Chapman and Hall, 1931.

Doyle, Charles, ed. *William Carlos Williams: The Critical Heritage.* London: Routledge, 1980.

———. *William Carlos Williams and the American Poem.* London: Macmillan, 1982.

Duffey, Bernard. *A Poetry of Presence: The Writing of William Carlos Williams.* Madison: University of Wisconsin Press, 1986.

Eliot, T. S. *After Strange Gods: A Primer of Modern Heresy.* London: Faber, 1934.

———. *Christianity and Culture.* New York: Harcourt, 1968.

Emerson, Ralph Waldo. *Essays and Lectures.* New York: Library of America, 1982.

———. *The Portable Emerson.* New York: Viking, 1946.

Ewen, Stuart and Elizabeth. "Americanization and Consumption." *Telos* 37 (1978): 42–51.

Fisher-Wirth, Ann W. *William Carlos Williams and Autobiography: The Woods of his Own Nature.* University Park and London: Pennsylvania State University Press, 1989.

Flink, J. J. *Car Culture.* Cambridge: MIT Press, 1975.

Frail, David. "'The Regular Fourth of July Stuff': William Carlos Williams's Colonial Figures as Poets." *William Carlos Williams Review* 11. 2 (Fall 1980): 1–14.

———. *The Early Politics and Poetics of William Carlos Williams.* Ann Arbor: UMI Research Press, 1987.

Frank, Robert, and Henry Sayre, eds. *The Line in Postmodern Poetry.* Urbana and Chicago: University of Illinois Press, 1988.

Frank, Waldo. *Our America.* New York: Boni and Liveright, 1919.

———. *The Re-Discovery of America.* New York: Scribner's, 1929.

Fredman, Stephen. *Poet's Prose: The Crisis in American Verse.* Cambridge: Cambridge University Press, 1983.

Freire, Paulo. *Pedagogy of the Oppressed.* New York: Herder, 1972.

Friedman, Alan J., and Carol C. Donley. *Einstein as Myth and Muse.* Cambridge: Cambridge University Press, 1985.

Frye, Northrop. *Anatomy of Criticism: Four Essays.* Princeton: Princeton University Press, 1957.

———. *Fearful Symmetry: A Study of William Blake.* Boston: Beacon Press, 1947.

Gadamer, Hans-Georg. *Truth and Method.* Translated by Joel Weinsheimer and David G. Marshall. London: Sheed and Ward, 1989.

Gavin, W. J., ed. *Context over Foundation: Dewey and Marx.* Dordrecht, Holland: D. Reidel, 1988.

Gellner, Ernest. *Spectacles and Predicaments.* Cambridge: Cambridge University Press, 1979.

Gilbert, James Burkhart. *Writers and Partisans: A History of Literary Radicalism in America* . New York: John Wiley, 1968.

Goodman, Russell B. *American Philosophy and the Romantic Tradition.* Cambridge: Cambridge University Press, 1990.

Graff, Gerald. *Professing Literature: An Institutional History.* Chicago: University of Chicago Press, 1987.

Gunn, Giles. *The Culture of Criticism and the Criticism of Culture.* Oxford: Oxford University Press, 1987.

———. *Thinking Across the American Grain: Ideology, Intellect, and the New Pragmatism.* Chicago: University of Chicago Press, 1992.

Hallberg, Robert von. "The Politics of Description: W.C. Williams in the 'Thirties." ELH 45 (1978): 131–151.

Hartz, Louis. The Liberal Tradition in America. New York: Harcourt, 1955.

Hatlen, Burton, ed. *George Oppen: Man and Poet.* Orono, Maine: National Poetry Foundation, 1981.

Havelock, Eric A. *Preface to Plato.* Oxford: Blackwell, 1963.

Hegel, G. W. F. *Aesthetics: Lectures on Fine Art, Volume II.* Translated by T. M. Knox. Oxford: Oxford University Press, 1975.

Heller, Michael. *Conviction's Net of Branches: Essays on the Objectivist Poets and Poetry.* Carbondale: Southern Illinois University Press, 1985.

Hofstadter, Richard. *Anti-Intellectualism in American Life.* New York: Vintage, 1962.

Hyde, Lewis. *The Gift: Imagination and the Erotic Life of Property.* New York: Random House, 1983.

James, Henry. *The Question of Our Speech. The Lesson of Balzac. Two Lectures.* Boston: Houghton, 1905.

Jarrell, Randall. *Poetry and the Age.* London: Faber, 1973.

Kallen, Horace M. *Culture and Democracy in the United States: Studies in the Group Psychology of the American Peoples.* New York: Boni and Liveright, 1924.

Kateb, George. *Emerson and Self-Reliance* . Thousand Oaks, CA: Sage, 1995.

Kazin, Alfred. *On Native Grounds: An Interpretation of Modern American Prose Literature.* New York: Harcourt, 1942.

Kenner, Hugh. *The Pound Era.* London: Faber, 1972.

Keyserling, Count Herman. *America Set Free.* London: Cape, 1930.

Kronick, Joseph G. *American Poetics of History from Emerson to the Moderns.* Baton Rouge and London: Louisiana State University Press, 1984.

Kutzinski, Vera M. *Against the American Grain: Myth and History in William Carlos Williams, Jay Wright, and Nicolas Guillen.* Baltimore: Johns Hopkins University Press, 1987.

Lawrence, D. H. "American Heroes." *Nation* 14 April 1926: 413–414.

Lazerson, Marvin. *Origins of the Urban School.* Cambridge: Harvard University Press, 1971.

Lentricchia, Frank. *Criticism and Social Change.* Chicago: University of Chicago Press, 1983.

————. "Rorty's Cultural Conversation," *Raritan* 3 (Summer 1983): 136–141.

Leuchtenberg, William E. *The Perils of Prosperity 1914–1932.* Chicago: University of Chicago Press, 1958.

Levin, Jonathan. "The Esthetics of Pragmatism." *American Literary History* 6.4 (Winter 1994): 658–683.

Lloyd, Margaret Glynne. *William Carlos Williams's Paterson: A Critical Reappraisal.* Cranbury, NJ: Associated University Press, 1980.

Lukács, Georg. *The Theory of the Novel: A Historico-philosophical Essay on the Forms of Great Epic Literature* . Translated by Anna Bostock. London: Merlin, 1971.

McAlmon, Robert. *Being Geniuses Together, 1920–1930.* 1938. Reprinted and revised with supplementary chapters and afterword by Kay Boyle. London: Hogarth, 1984.

McDonald, Gail. *Learning to be Modern: Pound, Eliot, and the American University.* Oxford: Oxford University Press, 1993.

MacIntyre, Alistair. *Whose Justice: Which Rationality.* London: Duckworth, 1988.

Mailloux, Steven, ed. *Rhetoric, Sophistry, Pragmatism.* Cambridge: Cambridge University Press, 1995.

Makin, Peter. *Pound's Cantos.* London: George Allen, 1985.

Markos, Donald W. *Ideas and Things: The Poems of William Carlos Williams.* Cranbury, NJ: Associated University Press, 1994.

Mariani, Paul. *William Carlos Williams: The Poet and His Critics.* Chicago: American Library Association, 1975.

————. *William Carlos Williams: A New World Naked.* New York: McGraw Hill, 1981.

Martz, Louis. *The Poem of the Mind.* Oxford: Oxford University Press, 1966.

Marsh, Alec. *Money and Modernity: Pound, Williams, and the Spirit of Jefferson.* Tuscaloosa: University of Alabama Press, 1998.

Marx, Karl. *Selected Writings.* Edited by David McLellan. Oxford: Oxford University Press, 1977.

Mauss, Marcel. *The Gift: The Form and Reason for Exchange in Archaic Societies.* 1950. London: Routledge, 1990.

Mayhew, Katherine Camp, and Anna Camp Edwards. *The Dewey School.* New York: Atherton, 1966.

Mencken, H. L. *The American Language: An Inquiry into the Development of English in the United States.* 4th ed., plus two supplements, abridged, with annotations and new material by Raven I. McDavid Jnr. London: Routledge, 1963.

Michaels, Walter Benn. *Our America: Nativism, Modernism, and Pluralism.* Durham,: Duke University Press, 1995.

Miller, J. Hillis. "Williams' *Spring and All* and the Progress of Poetry." *Daedalus* 99 (1970): 415–429.

————. *Poets of Reality: Six Twentieth Century Writers.* Oxford: Oxford University Press, 1966.

Mills, C. Wright. *The Marxists.* New York: Dell, 1962.

————. *The Power Elite.* New York and Oxford: Oxford University Press, 1956.

————. *Sociology and Pragmatism: The Higher Learning in America.* 1942. New York: Oxford University Press, 1964.

Morson, Gary Saul, ed. *Bakhtin: Essays and Dialogues on His Work.* Chicago: University of Chicago Press, 1986.

Mottram, Eric. "'That Dark Instrument'—The American Automobile." *Talus* 3 (Spring 1988): 12–32.

Nelson, Cary. *Repression and Recovery: Modern American Poetry and the Politics of Cultural Memory, 1910–1945.* Madison: University of Wisconsin Press, 1989.

Nicholls, Peter. *Ezra Pound: Economics, Politics, and Writing.* London: Macmillan, 1984.

Nyland, Chris. "Scientific Management and Planning." *Capital and Class* 33 (1987):55–81.

Oakeshott, Michael. *Rationalism in Politics and Other Essays.* London: Methuen, 1962.

O'Gorman, Edmundo. *The Invention of America: An Enquiry into the Historical Nature of the New World and the Meaning of its History.* 1958. Westport, CT: Greenwood Press, 1972.

Oppen, George. *Collected Poems.* New York: New Directions, 1975.

———. "The Mind's Own Place." *Kulchur* 10 (1963): 7.

Oppen, Mary. *Meaning a Life: An Autobiography.* Santa Barbara: Black Sparrow, 1978.

Oppenheim, James. "Poetry—Our First National Art." *Dial* 68 (February 1920): 238–42.

Palattella, John. "Learning to be Contemporary Somewhere in the Middle of Modernism." *Contemporary Literature* 35.1 (Spring 1994): 182–194.

Pease, Donald E. *Visionary Compacts: American Renaissance Writings in Cultural Context.* Madison: University of Wisconsin Press, 1987.

Pitkin, Hanna Fenichel. "Rethinking Reification." *Theory and Society* 16 (1987): 263–293.

Poirier, Richard. *Poetry and Pragmatism.* London: Faber, 1992.

Pound, Ezra. *ABC of Reading.* London: Faber, 1951.

———. *The Literary Essays of Ezra Pound.* Edited by T. S. Eliot. London: Faber, 1954.

———. *The Selected Letters of Ezra Pound 1907–1941.* Edited by D. D. Paige. London: Faber, 1950.

———. *Selected Prose, 1901–1965.* Edited by William Cookson. London: Faber, 1973.

Quartermain, Peter. *Disjunctive Poetics: From Gertrude Stein and Louis Zukofsky to Susan Howe.* Cambridge: Cambridge University Press, 1992.

Rae, John B. *The Road and the Car in American Life.* Cambridge: MIT Press, 1971.

Rapp, Carl. *William Carlos Williams and Romantic Idealism.* Hanover, NH: University Press of New England, 1984.

Riddel, Joseph N. *The Inverted Bell: Modernism and the Counter-Poetics of William Carlos Williams.* Baton Rouge: Louisiana State University Press, 1974.

Rochberg-Halton, Eugene. *Meaning and Modernity: Social Theory in the Pragmatic Attitude.* Chicago: University of Chicago Press, 1986.

Rorty, Richard. *Consequences of Pragmatism: Essays 1972–1980.* Brighton: Harvester, 1982.

———. *Objectivity, Relativism, and Truth.* Cambridge: Cambridge University Press, 1992.

Ross, Edward A. *Principles of Sociology.* New York: Century, 1920.

Rotunda, Ronald D. *The Politics of Language: Liberalism as Word and Symbol.* Iowa City: University of Iowa Press, 1986.

Ruland, Richard. "Literary History and the Legacy of Pragmatism." *American Literary History* 6.2 (Summer 1994): 354–370.

Russell, Bertrand. *A History of Western Philosophy.* London: George Allen, 1946.

Sayre, Henry M. "Ready-Mades and Other Measures: The Poetics of Marcel Duchamp and William Carlos Williams." *Journal of Modern Literature* 8 (1980): 3–22.

———. "Avant-Garde Dispositions: Placing *Spring and All* in Context." *William Carlos Williams Review* 10 (Fall 1984): 13–24.

Schilpp, Paul Arthur, ed. *The Philosophy of John Dewey.* La Salle, Il: Open Court, 1939.

Schmidt, Peter. *William Carlos Williams, The Arts, and Literary Tradition.* Baton Rouge: Louisiana State University Press, 1988.

———. "Introduction to William Carlos Williams's 'Letter to an Australian Editor' (1946): Williams's Manifesto for Multiculturalism." *William Carlos Williams Review* 17.2 (Fall 1991): 4–7.

Scholes, Robert. *Textual Power: Literary Theory and the Teaching of English.* New Haven: Yale University Press, 1985.

Stanley, Sandra Kumamuto. *Louis Zukofsky and the Transformation of a Modern American Poetics.* Berkeley: University of California Press, 1994.

Steinman, Lisa M. "Once More With Feeling: Teaching *Spring and All.*" *William Carlos Williams Review* 10 (Fall 1984): 7–12.

———. *Made in America: Science, Technology, and American Modernist Poets.* New Haven: Yale University Press, 1987.

Stuhr, John J., ed. *Philosophy and the Reconstruction of Culture: Pragmatic Essays After John Dewey.* Albany: State University of New York Press, 1993.

Tapscott, Stephen. *William Carlos Williams and the Modernist Whitman.* New York: Columbia University Press, 1984.

Tashjian, Dickran. "History and Culture in 'The American Background.'" *William Carlos Williams Review* 11 (Spring 1985): 13–19.

Terrell, Carroll F., ed. *Louis Zukofsky: Man and Poet.* Orono, Maine: National Poetry Foundation, 1979.

———. *William Carlos Williams: Man and Poet.* Orono, Maine: National Poetry Foundation, 1983.

Thirlwell, James. "William Carlos Williams's *Paterson*: The Search for a Redeeming Language." *New Directions* 17 (1960): 252–310.

Thoreau, Henry David. *A Week on the Concord and Merrimack Rivers.* Princeton : Princeton University Press, 1989.

———. *Walden.* New York: Bantam, 1963.

———. *The Portable Thoreau..* Edited by Carol Bode. Harmondsworth, England: Penguin, 1947.

Tichi, Cecelia. *Shifting Gears: Technology, Literature, Culture in Modernist America.* Chapel Hill: University of North Carolina Press, 1987.

Tocqueville, Alexis De. *Democracy in America.* Translated by Henry Reeve. Oxford: Oxford University Press, 1946.

Trachtenberg, Alan, ed. *Critics of Culture: Literature and Society in the Early Twentieth Century.* New York: John Wiley, 1976.

Unger, Leonard, ed. *Seven Modern American Poets.* Minneapolis: University of Minnesota Press, 1967.

Wagner, Peter. *A Sociology of Modernity: Liberty and Discipline.* London: Routledge, 1994.

Walker, Jeffrey. *Bardic Ethos and the American Epic Poem: Whitman, Pound, Crane, Williams, Olson.* Baton Rouge: Louisiana State University Press, 1989.

Weaver, Mike. *William Carlos Williams: The American Background.* Cambridge: Cambridge University Press, 1971.

Welter, Rush. *Popular Education and Democratic Thought in America.* New York: Columbia University Press, 1962.

West,Cornel. *The American Evasion of Philosophy: A Genealogy of Pragmatism.* London: Macmillan, 1989.

Westbrook, Robert B. *John Dewey and American Democracy*. Ithaca and New York: Cornell University Press, 1991

"What is Americanism?: A Symposium on Marxism and the American Tradition." *Partisan Review* 3.2 (April 1936): 3–16.

Wheeler, Kathleen. *Romanticism, Pragmatism, Deconstruction*. Oxford: Blackwell, 1993.

Whitehead, Alfred North. *Science and the Modern World*. 1925. New York: Mentor, 1948.

Whitman, Walt. *Complete Poetry and Selected Prose and Letters*. Edited by Emory Holland. London: Nonesuch, 1971.

Williams, Raymond. *Culture and Society, 1780–1950*. London: Chatto, 1958.

Williams William Carlos. *A Recognizable Image: William Carlos Williams on Art and Artists*. Edited by Bram Dijkstra. New York: New Directions, 1978.

———. *The Autobiography of William Carlos Williams*. New York: New Directions, 1967.

———. *The Collected Poems of William Carlos Williams. Vol. 1: 1909–1939*. Edited by A. Walton Litz and Christopher MacGowan. New York: New Directions, 1986.

———. *The Collected Poems of William Carlos Williams. Vol. 2: 1939-1962*. Edited by Christopher MacGowan. New York: New Directions, 1988.

———. *The Embodiment of Knowledge* . Edited by Ron Loewinsohn. New York: New Directions, 1974.

———. "The Fatal Blunder." *Quarterly Review of Literature* 2 (1944): 125–126.

———. "Free Verse." *Princeton Encyclopedia of Poetry and Poetics*. Princeton: Princeton University Press, 1965; 288-290.

———. *Imaginations*. Edited by Webster Schott. New York: New Directions, 1970.

———. *In the American Grain*. New York: New Directions, 1956.

———. *I Wanted to Write a Poem*. Edited by Edith Heal. New York: New Directions, 1978.

———. "Letter to an Australian Editor." 1946. *William Carlos Williams Review* 17.2 (Fall 1991): 8–12.

———. *Paterson*. New York: New Directions, 1963.

———. *Selected Essays of William Carlos Williams*. New York: New Directions, 1969.

———. *Selected Letters of William Carlos Williams*. Edited by John C. Thirlwall. New York: New Directions, 1984.

———. *Something to Say: William Carlos Williams on Younger Poets*. Edited by James E. B. Breslin. New York: New Directions, 1985.

———. *A Voyage to Pagany*. New York: New Directions, 1970.

Wolfe, Cary. *The Limits of American Literary Ideology in Pound and Emerson*. Cambridge: Cambridge University Press, 1993.

Zukofsky, Louis. "Program: Objectivists' 1931." *Poetry* 37 (Feb. 1931): 268–284.

INDEX